SPORT INC.

SPORT INC.

Why money is the winner in the business of sport

ED WARNER

YELLOW JERSEY PRESS

LONDON

1 3 5 7 9 10 8 6 4 2

Yellow Jersey Press
20 Vauxhall Bridge Road,
London SW1V 2SA

Yellow Jersey Press is part of the Penguin Random House group of companies
whose addresses can be found at global.penguinrandomhouse.com

First published by Yellow Jersey Press in 2018

penguin.co.uk/vintage

A CIP catalogue record for this book is available from the British Library

ISBN 9781787290129

Typeset in 11.5/16 pt Baskerville MT Pro
by Integra Software Services Pvt. Ltd, Pondicherry

Printed and bound by Clays Ltd, St Ives Plc

Penguin Random House is committed to a sustainable future for
our business, our readers and our planet. This book is made
from Forest Stewardship Council® certified paper.

For W. J. Warner, Catford Tiger

ORDER OF PLAY

WARM-UP

The 'London 1948' room at the British Olympic Association's headquarters is dominated by a grainy, floor-to-ceiling photographic mural of the Olympic torch being held aloft by its final bearer before the ceremonial lighting of the flame to signal the opening of the Games. The athlete accorded this honour is a picture of purity, clad in pristine white vest and baggy shorts, not a logo in sight. Towering above the watching crowd is an enormous scoreboard, capital white letters spelling out Baron de Coubertin's famous edict: THE IMPORTANT THING IN THE OLYMPIC GAMES IS NOT WINNING BUT TAKING PART. THE ESSENTIAL THING IN LIFE IS NOT CONQUERING BUT FIGHTING WELL.

De Coubertin's gravestone commemorates him as the '*Rénovateur des Jeux Olympiques*'. The Games that the Frenchman restored in 1896 now bear little relation to his ideals though. The BOA may plot Team GB's quest for Olympic medals beneath this reminder of de Coubertin's sporting philosophy, but winning is its thing and money the driving force. This is nothing new. Just as the ancient Greeks awarded simply a crown of olive leaves to Olympic champions, so today medals are the only formal prize for success. The early victors were rewarded lavishly when they returned home from Olympia, however, foreshadowing the riches

1

earned by their modern counterparts. Even in the early years of the revived Games, successful athletes traded their prowess and reputations for financial gain, both on and off the track. The problem with ideals is that they don't pay the bills.

Atlanta 1996 is often cited as the nadir of the modern Olympics, commercial forces crushing what little remained of the movement's supposed spirit, but those forces haven't receded. If anything they've intensified, so that Atlanta might more accurately be remembered as having given birth to the current commercialised Games. The multinational corporate sponsors have, though, adapted their behaviour sufficiently for the public to be able to embrace the continued illusion of de Coubertin's Olympism, so allowing the Games to survive.

The early editions of the modern Olympics are social and economic curiosities, to be ranked alongside the distinction between gentlemen and players in cricket, the wage cap in football, and rugby union as an amateur sport in which players might find money tucked into the ends of their boots. Power has shifted away from the administrators of sports and the owners of teams to the sportsmen and -women who provide the action. Money has inevitably followed. This is not entirely a free-market economy, however. Restrictions and anomalies abound. And there is sufficient wealth in the system to attract and support a plethora of secondary and tertiary figures, from agents to consultants, advisers to sundry hangers-on. If top boxers fought solely for fun, they wouldn't attract the large entourages that they do.

The game may be the thing, but the ninety minutes on the pitch or ten seconds on the track represent a tiny fraction of the industry that supports the action. Estimates of the size of the global sports market vary wildly, partly due to definitional differences, but also to the difficulties of calculation common to all industries. One claim of a total equal to 1 per cent of the entire global economy is probably as good as any. That implies about $700 billion of sports industry revenues a year. Intuitively, this feels to me a little on the low side. But possibly that's because, like many fans, I spend far more than 1 per cent of my time thinking about sport.

This intuition is built on more than fandom, however. For just over a decade it seemed as though I spent only 1 per cent of my time *not* thinking about sport. I was chair of UK Athletics, the governing body in Britain for the largest Olympic sport. As a distinctly average club runner with a background as a City financier, I had replied to a job ad in the *Sunday Times* and found myself on the other side of the veil that screens fans from the workings of the sports that they follow. I went on to lead the successful bid to host the World Athletics Championships in London in 2017 and chaired its organising committee. Over the ten years I held the post I learned some things I wished, as a fan, I didn't have to know, but also gained an understanding of the influence that the public – largely unknowingly – exerts over sport.

Whatever the true scale of the sporting industry, money is its driving force. Ultimately, this finance comes from you, the sports fan. The choices you make about the sports you want to consume, and the manner in which you want to consume them, initiate the flows of money through their various brokers. The numbers involved, and the behaviours of those in control of the cash, may sometimes surprise, shock or repulse you. But they are a reflection of the power you, the fan, has in the sporting marketplace.

In *Sport Inc.* we will delve below the playing surface to reveal how money is pulling all the strings in today's sports market, meeting the individuals who bring the action onto our screens, plaster their logos on players' shirts, advise athletes on their commercial deals and direct the infrastructure of sport. We will also encounter a sportswoman banned for doping offences, an athlete cheated out of medals and the attendant financial rewards, and a professional gambler who blows the whistle on suspected match-fixing. Finally, we will take a glimpse into a technological future in which robots take over the sporting world. A future in which esports become part of Baron de Coubertin's Olympics.

1

FIFTY-SEVEN CHANNELS AND NOTHING ON

Gavin Patterson's office has all the hallmarks of the executive football nut. Signed boots and framed shirts bear witness to this Liverpool FC supporter's love of the game. But this is no ordinary chief executive, distracting himself from the humdrum of office life with reminders of sporting excitements away from work. He is the executive who has made the ultimate power play, concentrating his forces and going on the offensive, betting his company's future – and by extension his own career – on the allure of sport, and especially of football. As CEO of BT Group, Patterson is the architect of the most disruptive intervention in Britain's sports broadcast market since Sky bought the rights to the Premier League in 1992 and transformed its own fortunes in the process.

Botham's Ashes of 1981 were played out before a TV audience with only three channels to choose from, in the days before the snickometer, Hawk-Eye and the third umpire. Millions tuned in to watch. Root's Ashes of 2015, by contrast, largely passed the British TV viewing public by. The *Guardian* reported that the audience on Sky on the day that Joe Root took the catch that won the Ashes for England was a mere 467,000. And lest one thinks that the time travelled between 1981 and 2015 is too long for comparisons to be meaningful, it is reported that as recently as Flintoff's Ashes of 2005 the TV audience on free-to-air Channel 4 peaked at over eight million viewers.

The England cricket team first appeared on Sky TV's satellite service way back in 1990, when the upstart broadcaster's sports-led strategy was still in its infancy. A few years later Sky's founder, Rupert Murdoch, famously told shareholders of its parent company, News Corporation, that live sport was the 'battering ram' to get pay TV into people's homes. The power of Sky's purse has gradually put a financial block on terrestrial broadcasters, limiting them to highlights packages screened at a time when all but the most self-disciplined or technologically disinclined viewers must already know not only the score, but also the key incidents that occurred in that day's play. The threat to Sky's dominance in the UK is now coming, as with football and rugby union coverage, from Gavin Patterson at BT. By striking a deal with Cricket Australia, BT secured the rights to England's Ashes tour down under over the 2017/18 winter. One imagines that the agreement it struck had a little extra piquancy given the birthplace of Rupert Murdoch.

This relentless growth of the pay-to-view broadcasters may at first sight seem good news for the cricketing authorities. The England and Wales Cricket Board (ECB) had financial reserves of £36 million when it published its 2016/17 accounts. Two years previously, which covered a victorious home Test series against India and was a bumper period commercially, it made a profit of £28 million. A successful England team, performing in front of a pay-to-view audience, had reaped a handsome reward for the guardians of the sport. And yet who was watching any longer? Not just keeping an eye or ear out across the media for updates, but actually watching? In 2016/17 the ECB chose to make one-off payments of over £23 million to the first-class counties that comprise the backbone of professional cricket in

England and Wales in order to help them shore up their fragile balance sheets – a stark indication of the financial challenges that beset them.

Sport England, the quango charged with spending government funds and National Lottery income in order to increase the number of people taking part in sport, is a much-unloved organisation. Perhaps this is inevitable for a grant giver with finite resources to deploy. In part, though, this has reflected justifiable dissatisfaction among sports governing bodies at the quarterly survey of the population that Sport England used to help inform its decisions. Grumblings at the inadequacies of the survey led to an overhaul in its methodology and its name. The old Active People Survey has been replaced by the Active Lives Survey, a semi-annual summary of the population's physical activity based on about 200,000 online responses to invitations mailed to a cross-section of the nation's households. Data released in December 2016 under the old methodology reckoned 111,000 people aged fourteen to twenty-five were playing cricket on a regular basis. Four years earlier the estimated number had been 105,000. The first edition of the new Active Lives Survey, by the way, showed 365,000 adults of all ages regularly playing the game.

Cricket is by no means the only sport struggling to grow a static base of young players – indeed the likes of swimming and tennis have actually suffered sharp declines – but for all its riches the ECB must in its more introspective moments wonder whether its decisions about broadcast partners have condemned it to a niche existence. And as the current fourteen- to twenty-five-year-olds get older, if there are fewer cricket-savvy youngsters coming through to take their place, then that niche can only shrink. The ECB has announced that some of its new city-based T20 competition and a few England international T20 matches will be on free-to-air television in the form of the BBC, but this may prove a long road back into the national viewing psyche.

BT, the latest kid on the cricket square, is rarely hailed as a corporate success story. Widely criticised for its clunky customer service and the behaviour of its monopolistic landline supplier, Openreach, it labours under the burden of its state-owned origins a full three decades after it was privatised in the first wave of the Thatcher government's sales of the nation's utilities. Public perceptions, however, hide a somewhat different financial reality. Patterson was promoted to the CEO seat from within BT in 2013. Over the subsequent three years the company's profits jumped by 30 per cent, driving its shares far ahead of the overall UK stock market, before hitting an accounting scandal in its Italian operations in 2017 that put a dent in the leadership's reputation. Traditional business disciplines have been at play – restructurings, cost-cutting and acquisitions – but suffusing all of the management's strategy has been what Patterson himself describes in the company's annual report to its shareholders as the 'halo effect' of BT Sport.

Try telling BT that you are thinking of leaving their clutches and switching to another provider of its quad play of services – landline, broadband, TV and mobile – and like all its competitors it will likely offer you a deal to stay with it. After all, it's far cheaper to retain an existing customer than to win a new one. BT Sport is a key card in the company's hand. In 2017 BT raised the cost of BT Sport to existing customers from zero to £3.50 a month. Shrug your shoulders, however, say you've little interest in sport and are contemplating a switch to a different broadband provider and you may find a deal can be done. BT is willing to spend hundreds of millions of pounds on filling its sports channels with content only to give them away for next to nothing in the battle for quad-play customers. The halo may be priced like an afterthought, but it is nonetheless deemed to have substantial intrinsic value in the war for market share. And, crucially, the only way to watch BT Sport is to be a BT customer.

BT's innate advantage in this war is its established customer base. As the legacy provider of telephone services to British households it merely has to hold on to what it has got, sell those customers new products to bolt onto their basic phone line, and hollow costs out of its enormous inherited bureaucracy. Easier said than done, for sure, but covering the existing business with a glitzy coat of sporting paint is a relatively simple approach to the task in hand. In the context of a corporation with an annual income of £24 billion and operating costs of £20 billion, it also makes the £320 million a season BT is spending on the rights to screen forty-two Premier League football games seem much less of a gamble.

If, as BT claims, almost all of these matches achieve an audience of over one million viewers, then the rights fee paid to the Premier League equates to something under eight pounds per viewer per game. Indeed, the halo effect is much greater – the simple fact that I might have been able to watch a match has some intrinsic value to me as a customer, even if I didn't choose to tune into a particular game. BT has, of course, to factor in its production costs, from equipment expenses to Rio Ferdinand's contract as a pundit, but it can defray these through advertising revenues. And all along, its management can console themselves that the very existence of its sports TV platform is arresting the natural decay of its customer base inherited from a different era when it had the luxury of being a monopoly provider.

John Petter was the chief executive of BT's consumer division – Gavin Patterson's lieutenant with day-to-day responsibility for the company's sports broadcast strategy – before stepping down in 2017 to pursue his career outside the company. Although it was a relative newcomer to TV, he saw BT's entry into this market as being deep-rooted. 'The original purpose of telephone wires provided to people's homes in central London at the end of the nineteenth century was to relay sound from music halls into middle-class parlours, so there is a long history for telecoms and entertainment to be linked. There was long heritage and entitlement that we should be in this marketplace.' The trigger, however, was much more recent.

BT was an early partner in the London 2012 Olympics, supporting the organisers from the early days. 'We came in to prop up the bid and never thought that London would win, but of course it did win,' Petter remembers. 'We then had a sobering moment. If we failed to deliver the infrastructure, the whole world would see.' By capturing the public's imagination, the Games helped confirm BT's strategy. 'The Olympic experience really made us see and believe. While Sky had done an amazingly professional job in improving the standards of sports broadcasting, and especially football, sport had fallen out of the national conversation to some degree and that was more true of football than any other sport. Sky's games looked beautiful but many fewer people had them. So we thought there was an opportunity to recapture some of the spirit that you saw during the Olympics where everyone was talking about sport for the first time in a number of years. We thought there was a market in re-popularising football and being the challenger where we are used to being the incumbent.' The claim that football actually needed re-popularising might be the subject of many a pub debate, but BT had its strategy.

Being a challenger within a giant corporation has allowed BT to pursue its ambition of providing a very low-cost product – exclusively for BT customers – compared to its dominant competitor. In its first Premier League auction it secured the minimum number of matches available, less than it had hoped for. 'For the BT executive, we hadn't created a sports channel before. Had we known how difficult it is to do it, we might have hesitated more than we did. When we approached the problem initially we thought if we win the PL rights, job done. And in terms of where the cash outlay goes, that's largely true. But you've only got ninety minutes of live coverage a week. We then moved very quickly to buy lots of secondary rights. Plus, we bought ESPN as well, which gave us quite a big portfolio.' Financial analysts at bank Santander estimate that BT spends £775 million a year on sports content, offset by £150 million of advertising revenues and sales of its programming to pubs and third parties.

It took some time though for the company to be confident enough to charge for its product. 'What's happened to people who have tried to monetise the minority set of Premier League rights through a conventional model, the history has been pretty inglorious. You have Setanta, who went up in smoke. ESPN effectively gave up. We thought we had to do it differently.' BT's success in securing Champions League rights proved the tipping point in enabling it to bill customers for its sports channels. 'We felt we needed to have a second strong set of rights because to be the minority rights holder in the Premier League you are just one future auction from being taken out of business effectively if that's all you've got.'

Sky pays a higher rights fee per Premier League match it screens than BT, an average of £11 million for each of the 126 games a season it screens live – 46 per cent more, in part because it gets the prized Sunday afternoon broadcast window. And yet its viewing figures are not much greater than those for matches on BT, suggesting that ardent fans find their way to a screen regardless of the media platform a match is hosted on. Sky's challenge is very different to Gavin Patterson's. Three decades on from its noisy arrival on the broadcast stage, it now finds itself the incumbent player, targeted by a newcomer with a big budget. Finding new subscribers for its conventional TV packages increasingly hard to come by, the company now allows customers to pick and choose the sport they watch on a day-by-day basis. Paying £6.99 for a day of Sky Sports might seem like even more of a bargain if consumers realised that Sky was effectively paying a rights fee around 50 per cent higher than that for an average Premier League game. To Sky, however, every £6.99 is marginal additional revenue from consumers who have chosen to resist the temptation of a monthly contract and who might otherwise decide to wash the car, walk the dog, listen to games on BBC 5 Live radio, or rely on text updates from the match.

And text updates are increasingly what BBC Sport is reduced to; not only for football, but across the sporting spectrum. If you are tempted to counter with a list of sporting crown jewels that remain on the BBC – the Grand National, the football World Cup, the Olympics, Wimbledon tennis – then that is because that is just what government has deemed them to be: crown jewels.

The concept of sporting events with a national resonance that requires them to be broadcast to the British public dates back to the 1950s, the first list of such events being published in 1956. The arrival of Sky prompted revisions of the list to guarantee these broadcasts are free-to-air, so ensuring the widest possible audience can be reached. The current list is in two parts: those events that must be broadcast live free-to-air, and those that need only have delayed highlights made available this way. The first list consists of the Olympic Games, the football World Cup, Euro Championships, FA Cup Final and the Scottish final north of the border, the Grand National, the Derby, the finals matches at Wimbledon, the Rugby League Challenge Cup Final and the Rugby World Cup Final.

As is often the case, the list is as notable for its quirks and omissions as anything else. In years to come it may well serve as an insight into the sporting priorities of a bygone era. The Challenge Cup Final, but not the Six Nations? No Commonwealth Games, which is only on the B list requiring delayed highlights? More than anything, the apparently contentious choices at the margin reflect the negotiating power of the governing bodies controlling each event. As a sport with a narrow and largely regional fan base, the Rugby Football League is probably relieved that its annual domestic final remains protected on list A. The Rugby Football Union on the other hand must be delighted that it has full flexibility to play the TV rights market, given its sport's greater fanbase.

The BBC has most to gain from this state of affairs. The other terrestrial broadcasters have largely turned their backs on sport as too expensive for the audience figures it can command, too unreliable compared to the controllable environment of the talent show or game-show studio, and lacking in the resale opportunities that TV drama represents. The BBC, however, retains a strong sports heritage and an ethos matching its public service broadcast mandate that many believe live sports broadcasting fulfils – at least when it comes to 'stop the nation' events. And although broadcasters still have to pay a fee to screen events that are on the protected list, the enforced lack of competition from subscription channels must significantly reduce the costs for the free-to-air providers.

In 2009 an independent review panel set up by the government published a report into the future of free-to-air listed events. It was chaired by the genial sports journalist David Davies, once of the BBC and then for a dozen years a senior executive at the Football Association, so indubitably well qualified for the task at hand. The panel concluded that while there was still a rationale for protecting events that resonate with the general public, it advocated some tinkering with list A and believed that list B – the events that must have their highlights broadcast – had little value in the modern digital media world in which bite-size snippets can easily be made available via multiple outlets. In the few years since, the panel has been shown to have been correct, fragments of sport typically becoming available online soon after final whistles have been blown. Davies's report itself appears to have been left to gather dust though.

In the run-up to the London Games of 2012, a financially modest rights deal proved to have seismic consequences for the BBC. Determined to mark out the Paralympic Games as an event with its own special resonance, the London Organising Committee of the Games (LOCOG) sold the UK broadcast rights for the Paralympics to Channel 4 for a widely reported £10 million, thereby putting the two Games of that summer onto different terrestrial channels. The Beeb's sports executives were hopping mad, claiming that LOCOG had foregone their superior reach in favour of a modestly higher sum of money – certainly peanuts in the context of the multi-billion-pound Games – although one suspects the BBC negotiators can't have been blind to the consequences of their own naivety and parsimony.

Although the Paralympics is not on the government's protected list, its loss has been a bitter reputational blow for the state broadcaster. Channel 4, buoyed by the experience and audience reaction to its innovative programming in 2012, renewed its commitment for 2016 in Rio and again for 2020 in Tokyo, effectively pinching the BBC's inclusivity credentials from under its nose. Worse was to come for the Beeb when in 2015 it lost its grip on broadcast rights in the UK for the Olympics from 2022 to America's Discovery, which signed a deal across Europe with the International Olympic Committee. However, while the concept of the free-to-air list remains, Discovery has to ensure coverage in Britain that passes muster. The BBC is clearly the natural partner for it to meet its obligations, and the two broadcasters duly struck a sub-licensing deal through to 2024 that left the BBC with substantial but not comprehensive Olympics coverage. Maybe viewers won't notice much difference, but with the advance of technology and continued fragmentation of the broadcast market, the landscape in the next decade is likely to be radically different.

Certainly, the wall-to-wall, multi-platform Olympic coverage served up to the nation by the BBC in recent Games is already a thing of the past.

In 2015/16 the TV licence fee generated just over three quarters of the BBC's total £4.8 billion income. Meanwhile rights fees paid out by the Corporation to show sporting events were cited in the BBC's annual accounts as one area from which it would make savings to cope with the constraint of stagnant or falling licence income. This should come as no surprise as broadcasting sport does not have any financial upside for the BBC given its funding model. It can't sell its sports broadcasts worldwide as it can *Doctor Who* or the dramatisation of a John Le Carré novel; the sporting governing bodies own the rights to broadcast their events territory by territory. The most the BBC might hope for is a fee for providing the pictures that get screened overseas, but only if it is contracted to produce the images and has a clause to that effect in its contract. Increasingly that is not the case.

The inertia of the viewing public, who gravitate to the four major terrestrial channels in spite of the plethora of digital alternatives, stands the BBC's sports department in good stead when it analyses its costs. The Corporation may no longer be able to compete financially with the commercial heavyweights when it comes to bidding for broadcast rights, but the size of its audiences for the sport that it does show provides some protection in the perennial cost-cutting rounds it is subjected too. The BBC broadcast only 3 per cent of all the hours of sport televised in Britain in 2016, but that sliver of the total generated 44 per cent of the overall audience. Sky broadcast almost half of all sports hours shown that year for only half of the aggregate audience the BBC pulled in. Ninety-two per cent of the population watched at least fifteen minutes of sport on the BBC in 2016.

The net effect of high viewing figures and the broadcasting of events with relatively low rights fees (in part due to the governmental protection of the crown jewels events) is that broadcasting major sports costs the BBC up to around twenty-five pence for each hour watched by each viewer. Many big events cost less, and more run-of-the mill sport routinely tallies up at less than five pence per viewer hour. The contrast with Sky and BT Sport's rights costs per viewer for each of their Premier League games is stark indeed.

The IAAF World Athletics Championships in London in 2017 were shown to a British audience by the BBC, continuing its long-standing commitment to broadcasting the sport. The World Para Athletics Championships, held a month earlier in the same London Olympic Stadium, were by contrast on Channel 4, building on that broadcaster's relationship with Paralympic sport. Neither the BBC nor Channel 4 provided the principal footage for either event. That task fell to independent production companies Sunset+Vine and FilmNova.

The contracts to provide the host footage for syndication to global broadcasters for these twin world championships ran to millions of pounds, which was a burden falling on the organising committee's budget. We therefore had a clear incentive to drive down the cost without compromising the quality of the live feed for a worldwide audience, or in extremis breaching our contractual commitments to the IAAF and IPC. Whereas in the past we might have expected the BBC to be keen to bid for the work, if for no other reason than that it is well within its capabilities to deliver an excellent result, as it turned out it had no interest in doing so, and for understandable reasons. Why try and compete for a fixed-price contract on tight margins when you have a natural cost disadvantage compared to smaller, independent houses with much lower overheads?

The BBC has been, and remains, a valued broadcast partner for UK Athletics, screening its major events each year alongside highlights of the Diamond League global circuit and, to date, the

World and European Championships and the athletics pro-grammes within the Olympic and Commonwealth Games. While I was chair we rarely thought of switching to a satellite broad-caster, nervous that without our own equivalent of the continu-ous narrative of Test series, our experience of audience figures if we made the change might prove to be even worse than cricket's.

Live athletics on the BBC typically pulls in an audience of between 1 million and 2.5 million viewers, with considerable volatility as the event ebbs and flows. For example, Friday night at the Diamond League 2016 Anniversary Games in the Olympic Stadium attracted an average audience of 1.8 million with a peak of 2.4 million when Usain Bolt ran the 100 metres. The next afternoon's action generated a lower peak of 2 million, for Mo Farah's race, but still a healthy 10 per cent audience share across all channels.

Over the past decade these numbers have shown a gentle downward drift as viewing opportunities have proliferated across all media. If anything this reinforced our determination to re-main on terrestrial television. UK Athletics' Indoor Grand Prix in Glasgow at the start of 2016 had an audience peak almost double that of a live Arsenal FA Cup tie on BT Sport on the same afternoon. Doubtless BT were pleased with their viewing figures just as we were with ours, these being two organisations pursuing two very different agendas: one to sustain national interest, the other to protect a brand.

The decision to renew UKA's contract with the BBC in recent times was made easier by the continued existence of a rights fee for our events, even though pressure on that fee was downward in negotiations. The market for broadcast rights is increasingly polarised, with the growing dominance of the subscription broad-casters being to blame at both ends of the spectrum. At the top end fierce competition is driving the BBC out of the market, los-ing exclusivity for Formula 1 and Six Nations rugby in recent years, and live coverage of the golf Open, a B list protected event, to Sky. But at the bottom end satellite broadcasters have seemingly endless hours of broadcast time to fill between the centrepiece events that they have bet their ranches on, and little inclination to pay much to do so.

Viewing figures for club rugby on subscription television are very skinny, often numbered in the low tens of thousands, but if the broadcaster can avoid having to pay much of a fee for the right to show the games, then the total cost of getting them onto your screen can be very modest. The pay-off for the teams involved is increased visibility for their shirt sponsors and other commercial partners, probably at little cost in terms of reduced gate receipts from those choosing to watch from their sofas instead of attending in person. The risk for secondary and tertiary sports events is that there is a race to the bottom on rights fees. Indeed, the day may not be far away when paying to be broadcast becomes the norm, unless a sport wants its digital existence to depend solely on self-maintained streaming web channels. Mindful of the risks associated with niche broadcasting exposure, Premiership Rugby has agreed a deal with BT Sport and Channel 5 for five games a season to be simulcast on both platforms, so providing a free taste of club rugby for a national audience.

The BBC is already alive to this trend but finds itself constrained by its finances. The recent loss of high-profile events coupled with its lack of international syndication opportunities must surely drive it towards either abandoning the sports market entirely or focusing on a small cadre of specialist sports and events for which it pays little or no rights fees – and any crown jewels events for as long as this protected list continues to exist. Late in 2017 the BBC trumpeted a plan to 'reinvent free-to-air sports broadcasting' by streaming a thousand additional hours a year on its website, effectively competitions with narrow appeal. This might be seen as the BBC using minority sports and mass-participation events to fulfil its public service mandate while freeing up budget to speculate on non-sports programming with international resale potential. Such a confluence of forces can be seen in the BBC's broadcasting of the Great North Run each year, footage of which is provided by FilmNova – owned by the parent company of the race organiser – rather than the BBC itself. This achieves healthy viewing figures of a mass public event at a time that would typically otherwise have low audiences, early on a Sunday morning.

The bottom line for all broadcasters is that the event in front of viewers' eyes must be seen to matter to the participants. This is as true of the mass of runners in the London Marathon and the Great North Run as it is of professional sports. The search for a narrative may be as fashionable in this as in other corners of the media, but it is no less powerful for that. Rugby's Six Nations will always have more value than its autumn internationals until the day the nations combine to make a series competition of the latter. Football's Charity Shield will always be a whimsy, just as England's defeat to Iceland in Euro 2016 will linger in the memory for years longer than their 3–2 friendly win against Germany only three months earlier.

Building a narrative is now an integral part of the sports broadcast art, and not only because it fills screen hours before and after an event. The broadcasters are searching for an audience beyond the diehard fan, as he or she is guaranteed to tune in almost regardless of the wrapping that the sport comes in. Channel 4's Paralympic coverage began months ahead of time with athlete profile programming. Its live action was interspersed with comedy programmes, the *Last Leg* providing a left-field insight into the cast of sportsmen and -women who provided the Games action. The BBC uses its unrivalled website reach to prepare the way for live events on its main channels and their dissection afterwards. While this bolsters the investment the broadcasters have made in buying rights to show major events, again it crowds out screen time and funding for those sports or competitions that don't make the cut.

Average audience figures for major events far exceed the number of people playing the sport itself. Events with national resonance, such as those on the free-to-air list, traditionally attract interest well beyond regular followers of the sports concerned. Think, say, of the annual flurry of bets on the Grand National by people dusting off their online bookie account details for the first time since the previous year's race. Or the crowds lining the Thames to catch a fleeting glimpse of the Oxford and Cambridge Boat Race – how many of them will ever get any closer to a rowing eight? Although admittedly exceptional examples, they are reminders of the challenge that broadcasters face – of generating interest in their programming beyond committed fans.

One answer to this challenge is the broadcasters' use of talent, the pundits and commentators who over time become a comfort blanket for the casual follower who only tunes in for national sporting moments. The BBC's athletics talent roster comprises a clutch of past Olympians, world medallists and record holders, each already a household name before they made the transition to the microphone, their recognition often bolstered by appearances on popular BBC shows away from the athletics stadium. And yet their contribution to televised athletics can drive the most committed fans mad – not so much what they say as the quantity of airtime they are given, which crowds out the action itself, most notably the field events of jumping and throwing.

I've had numerous conversations with BBC sports executives down the years about their balance of live action versus analysis – 'chat' to the disgruntled. Their answer is that audience feedback is extremely positive about the punditry, the public finding engagement in the studio analysis, with the familiarity of former athletes a particular positive. The casual viewer, after all, makes up the bulk of the audience, which might well not be the case were the sport screened on a subscription channel.

It should be no wonder then that the BBC takes such a huge number of personnel to major sporting events, even though it does not itself generate the majority of the live action footage it screens. The Corporation took 455 people to Rio to cover 2016's Olympic Games. By contrast, Team GB numbered 366 athletes. The BBC counters charges of excess with its requirement to showcase British success, which cannot rely purely on footage provided by the host broadcaster, and by pointing to NBC's roster of more than 2,000 personnel to service the American audience. Having watched the Rio Olympics on both the BBC and NBC, it's fair to say that it was difficult to imagine quite what all the extra NBC staff contributed. Privately, however, the BBC would argue that the talent in front of the camera and all who support them make an Olympics for the watching British public as much as the action in the arena.

As the BBC gets squeezed further out of the live broadcast market, so its talent will disperse – witness Gary Lineker fronting both the BBC's *Match of the Day* football highlights programme and BT Sport's live Champions League coverage – or will have to be found other outlets for their public recognition. John Petter believes terrestrial sports coverage remains important, even for subscription services such as BT's. 'The importance of *Match of the Day* to Sky Sports is immense because it is the feeder for any-one who has an interest in the Premier League into Sky. We collaborated with free-to-air broadcasters to make the ecosystem bigger, to bring people in.' The return of the free-to-air prodigal son to English cricket will indeed take the form of a collaboration between terrestrial and subscription broadcasters.

The ultimate outlet for the BBC is its annual *Sports Personality of the Year* programme – or *SPOTY* as the Beeb would have us think of it these days. What once was a modest affair has now become the highlights package to end all highlights packages, a showcase for action footage increasingly provided by rival broadcasters to the BBC as its own rights diminish. And all hyped up as if it were itself a sporting event.

Andy Murray won *SPOTY* for a third time in 2016, a bumper year for British sport. The public votes on the night totalled 747,788. The BBC declines to release comparable figures for its *Strictly Come Dancing* show, but ITV's *X Factor* final was reported to have had 6.4 million votes cast only a week earlier, so one can imagine that the *Strictly* vote dwarfed that of *SPOTY* when the programmes were screened a day apart on the same channel. And therein lies the perennial challenge for sport: to make itself relevant to a national audience, to create a story that truly matters.

Football's Premier League in England has clearly built that narrative and successfully explained to the watching world why it does indeed matter. Leicester City winning the League in 2015/16 may be a once-in-a-generation event, but its extraordinariness helpfully highlighted just how competitive the Premiership is on a regular annual basis. Any team can beat any other, even if only a handful are likely to be in serious contention at the end of the nine-month season. In its latest TV rights negotiations, the Premier League, acting on behalf of its twenty member clubs, has secured £1.1 billion a year from international broadcasters for the right to screen matches.

Like many a football fan, I've found myself a long way from home just when my team is playing. One Saturday morning in Portland, Oregon on athletics duty I found a bar screening live Premier League matches over breakfast. I arrived in time for the second match of the day to find a bar full of Arsenal-shirted Americans watching the dying moments of a game which had kicked off at 4.45 a.m. local time. As they dispersed, West Ham and Chelsea fans arrived to watch their 7 a.m. kick-off while I sat in splendid isolation to mourn Crystal Palace's defeat at home to Leicester in front of the screen in the other half of the bar. NBC's six-year 2,280-game deal to screen the Premier League in the US was reported by the *New York Times* to be worth $1 billion. The average game NBC screens attracts an audience of around half a million viewers, so if the reports are correct, that's less than a dollar per viewer per game. Sounds like a bargain.

The key is to monetise those viewers – whether through advertising, subscriptions or both – and not to lose them to illegal streaming of matches or let them become happy to make do with snatches of highlights. Rapid shifts in viewing habits, especially among young fans most comfortable with new technologies, pose a challenge to the traditional TV rights model. The start of the 2016/17 Premier League season was notable for a fall in viewing figures for televised games just at a time when goals per game were on the up with attack-minded managers and leaky defences – so hardly a reaction to a decline in the quality of the product served up for the public. This could be an early sign of the threat of altered viewing habits. Ninety minutes seems an increasingly long time for today's youngsters to commit to a single activity. A mobile phone may once have been a distraction while sitting watching a televised sporting event; now a mobile device provides an alternative to doing just that, allowing sports consumption on the move. John Petter believes that 'all companies going forwards face the challenge of the new generation growing up with shorter attention spans and constrained willingness to pay. The key for sports is to find ways to make themselves interesting and relevant to the audiences coming through. BT is now showing some electronic gaming sports, exploring some new technologies as well. I think the next stage of this evolution is virtual reality.'

BT's willingness to price its sports product close to zero is pointing the way to a future collision between customers able to secure their kicks for free and sports reliant on broadcast revenues to make their sums work. A dollar per viewer per game may become a few cents per viewer per bite-sized highlight in tomorrow's world. As a fan, your consumption patterns are being monitored to determine over time not only how and when you are able to watch remotely, but the very nature and existence of sporting events themselves. And lest you forget, you can always still attend sport in person, which is as crucial to broadcasters as it is to the events' organisers, as we shall now see.

2

BUMS ON SEATS AND THE PRAWN SANDWICH BRIGADE

The European Athletics Team Championships in Leiria in Portugal in 2009 was hailed as a new dawn for the event, a revamped structure intended to haul it out of a trough of athlete and spectator ennui. An expanded Super League of twelve rather than eight countries, combined male and female teams, tweaks to the rules of competition: all the result of a lengthy project to explore ways to re-energise a weekend of athletics that looked likely to disappear off the radar screen for lack of interest. And the Estádio Dr. Magalhães Pessoa certainly delivered for a television audience.

At first glance it appeared as though the Portuguese public had embraced the event, the sun beating down on an exotic crowd dressed for the baking weather. Look twice, however, and you could see past the optical illusion wrought by a varied colour palette. Instead of competing in front of serried ranks of spectators, the athletes were surrounded by row upon row of empty seats of varying, largely pastel, hues. History doesn't relate what the broadcast rights holders thought, but they may just have fooled enough viewers into believing that they were watching what was a hot-ish ticket, or at the very least a mildly warm one.

Broadcasters hate empty seats in a stadium, for if there's one thing guaranteed to make the sofa-bound viewer reach for the remote control, it's the thought that what they are watching doesn't matter. If spectators can't be bothered to fill a stadium, then surely an event means nothing. Logic says that isn't necessarily true, but why would an event organiser or broadcaster want to run the risk of an audience at home drawing that conclusion?

The European Team Championships has struggled on under its revamped formula, under-loved and unsure of its place in the calendar, often unable to attract the best athletes. We hosted the event in the UK in 2013 at the Gateshead International Stadium. After a Herculean effort with the support of a number of local partners and agencies, we generated a more than decent crowd, although torrential rain on the second day prompted a number of no-shows. Lest you think the weather's just an excuse, the officials had to take the highly unusual step of moving the pole vault indoors for the athletes' own safety, so we're not talking a little drizzle. Three years earlier I'd presented an award to Steve Cram, local hero, in front of the Gateshead crowd at our Diamond League meeting. As we walked across the track into the infield, he swept his gaze across the half-empty stands and complained about UK Athletics' inability to sell tickets for the event. I bit my tongue, as there's a time and a place, but it was a reminder if ever I needed one that ticket sales are never easy, and certainly never as easy as a casual observer might assume.

The accountants Deloitte calculate a paid attendance of 70 million spectators at sporting events in the UK in 2016. Just under two thirds of this total, 45 million, was to watch football. The runner-up, horseracing, was a very distant second at 7 million, followed by rugby union and cricket. While the overall contrast between soccer and the rest is stark, in the absence of a major football tournament it is individual multi-day events in other sports that dominate the list of best-attended events. Just under half a million people went to the fortnight of tennis at the Wimbledon Championships; 327,000 attended the Formula 1 Grand Prix at Silverstone and almost as many the racing at Royal Ascot.

For the larger, more commercially successful sports, the blossoming of non-matchday income has significantly reduced the relevance of ticket and burger sales. Deloitte reckon that only 18 per cent of Premier League football clubs' revenues are generated from matchday sources. These are dwarfed by broadcasting income at 53 per cent of the total and sponsorship and commercial revenues making up the remaining 29 per cent. The latest TV rights deal is certain to tip the balance still further away from income from the paying spectator. The English game is not unique in this respect. Although matchday income has slightly greater proportional significance in Germany and Spain than in England, the contributions are even lower in France and Italy – both at 12 per cent.

But the greater the broadcast revenue flowing into top-flight football, the more important it is that every seat in the ground is full. Emptying seats when a leading club is losing at home and their fans are streaming for the exits can add to the spectacle – be sure that any commentator worth their salt will bring it to your attention – but vacant seats at the start of a game are strictly unacceptable. Television can demand antisocial kick-off times for travelling fans, but the sight of clumps of empty seats whatever the time or day still jars. And while a British viewer whose local knowledge encompasses Boxing Day rail challenges or late-night motorway distances might be forgiving, it would be unwise for those with a stake in the game to assume that an overseas audience will have such understanding. Deloitte calculate that there is a 96 per cent stadium utilisation rate in the Premier League, but methods of counting crowds are notoriously elastic – are non-attending season ticket holders counted in or out, for example?

– and even 4 per cent of seats unoccupied can catch the eye and leave the wrong impression.

English fans bemoan the price of tickets for top-flight football, but grounds are still close to being full for almost every game. The laws of supply and demand explain the climb in ticket prices, and still the major clubs have to operate long waiting lists for season tickets and work through planning authorities to expand their stadiums in inner-city residential locations with infrastructure that can barely cope with them as it is.

Recently there has been a successful campaign by supporters to win over the clubs to a cap on ticket prices for away fans. Perhaps their most persuasive argument was the vibrancy created by in-stadium rivalry between fans. Manchester United's Roy Keane was prescient with his complaint back in 2000 about the lack of atmosphere generated by wealthy supporters enjoying their prawn sandwiches: 'I don't think some of the people who come to Old Trafford can spell "football", never mind understand it.'

The prawn sandwich brigade, as the media coined the hospitality crowd at matches after Keane's comments, is nevertheless vital to football's economics. Not every bum on every seat has equal economic value; far from it. Higher ticket prices combined with premium hospitality can generate a profit margin many times greater than that from a season ticket holder in the cheap seats who chooses to eat and drink away from the ground on matchday.

Crystal Palace played its first ever FA Cup Final against Manchester United at the old Wembley Stadium in 1990. A ticket for the Olympic Gallery, a retro-fitted tier hanging underneath the stadium roof, cost £75 – the most expensive for the game. Twenty-six years later the club made its second Final appearance against the same opponents (third, if you count 1990's replay), this time at the new Wembley. A top-price general admission ticket was now £115. The Bank of England's inflation calculator shows the old Wembley's Olympic Gallery ticket would have cost just under £154 at the start of 2016. With little to choose between the capacity of the old and new Wembley stadiums, this might say something about the diminished cachet of the FA Cup and the relative dominance of the Premier League. But it is likely to say more about the growth of hospitality provision and premium ticketing at football grounds.

Around a sixth of the seats at the new home of the FA are in the Club Wembley tier of the ground or in corporate boxes. These are sold on multi-year licences with annual subscriptions running into thousands of pounds. The FA faces the headache of securing renewals of these lucrative licences as the original ones expire. You can be sure that they need the cheaper seats filled for this renewal process to be a success, for a premium ticket can only really have value if exclusivity is combined with scarcity. It would also help sales, of course, if the England men's football team lived up to its potential.

American sports fans appear to have little difficulty opening their wallets and paying hefty prices for tickets, and are prepared to cope with very fine pricing gradations according to the location of their seats. Take baseball's Boston Red Sox, for example. On Easter Sunday 2017 they played the Tampa Bay Rays at their iconic Fenway Park, styled by their marketing team as 'America's most loved ballpark'. There were thirteen different price points for tickets, ranging from $30 up to $190, and the Red Sox were entertaining the Rays four times over that weekend. Follow a sport in a much smaller venue, basketball, and you could end up paying multiples of these prices for a regular NBA match. And if you do get your hands on a ticket, as likely as not it will have been through an official reseller, where you will pay a premium on its original face value. Six months ahead of time, tickets for the Boston Celtics' last game of the season – a few days before the

Red Sox's Easter fixtures – were listed on their arena's official site at between $35 and $4,675.

Accountant PwC assesses that 15 per cent of the capacity at professional sports events in North America are premium seats and that these generate up to 40 per cent of a club's total seat-related revenues. It puts income from premium seating at $7.3 billion across the five major pro leagues and notes a trend in the industry towards these seats being located closer to the action on the field of play 'delivering immersive experiences to its highest end premium accounts'.

Location is everything for the American fan, not just being there, but being there in exactly the right place and being seen to be there to boot. Sit behind the catcher at a Major League Baseball match at just the 'right' elevation, and you could find yourself paying a multiple of the price of a ticket only a few blocks to the right or left, or a block higher or lower. You may have access to more expensive food, a different entrance and possibly a comfier seat, but you'll be watching the same contest as everyone else – albeit with a better view of the pitcher's action. For basketball, courtside is everything. When did you last see a politician or celebrity anywhere other than right up close to the action?

Sports ticket pricing came of age at the London Olympics in 2012. Two years out from the Games I took a call from Paul Williamson, LOCOG's director of ticketing, who wanted to talk me through his plan for athletics ticket pricing. I remember vividly his solicitude that I be sitting comfortably before hitting me with the news that the top-priced ticket for the athletics was to cost £725. A bargain, one might think, compared to the opening ceremony at £2,012, but a big ask for a sport that earlier that summer had failed to fill Gateshead for an international meet and provided an ex-athlete-turned-commentator with a stick to poke me with.

Williamson's argument was that I should be delighted that athletics was deemed worthy of being the most expensive ticket at the Games, the frivolity (not his words) of the opening and closing ceremonies aside, especially as the athletics venue was many times greater in size than for any other sport except football. If I could trust his market research, his modelling and his judgement then of course he was right – I should have been delighted. I confess that wasn't my first thought, nor indeed my second or third.

The hefty prices actually created little public stir. Tickets starting at £20 and a 'pay your age' scheme for youngsters drew much of the sting out of the announcement. And, anyway, what Williamson's research had shown him was that the public wanted to attend. This was the ultimate 'stop the nation' event. Maximising ticket revenue was essential for the organisers of the Olympic and Paralympic Games. In the event 97 per cent of available tickets were sold across both Games, raising £659 million towards the overall operating budget of £2.4 billion. The total cost of hosting the Games, once infrastructure costs were included, was far higher, a subject we will return to later when we ask why cities want to bear the expense of hosting major sporting events.

LOCOG proved very coy before and after the Games about revealing how many tickets were for sale at each price point for each competition. This was almost certainly because the supply of tickets at different price points is a dark art of the ticketing industry. When the £725 athletics tickets were revealed to the media, it was often reported that these were finish-line tickets, the prime location for an athletics meet and especially so if you want to see the climax of the blue-ribbon 100 metres. In reality, very few tickets were available on the finish line, in large part because the provision of media work-stations crowded that segment of the stadium; most top-priced tickets were in the middle of the home straight, as the athletes headed towards the finish. But for some sessions spectators with the highest-priced tickets found themselves on the opposite side of the stadium, and in the lower tier too, so likely to have a far better view of the finish-line action via the big screen than in the flesh.

Such was the demand for Games tickets that these spectators were probably simply grateful to get a seat at all, but they were victims – if that's not too harsh a description – of yield management by LOCOG's ticketing experts. Applicants for Games tickets indicated the price they wanted to pay for a ticket and whether they were prepared to pay more if they were not successful with their first choice. The organisers swept up all the data that the multitude of ticket applications contained and were then able to adjust the number of tickets available at each price point before running the public ballot. No one was forced to buy a ticket at a price they had said they weren't willing to pay, and no one received a ticket for a different part of an arena than they had been told they were applying for, as no such information was provided in advance, so in theory no one should have been unhappy. But the public had effectively determined the number of tickets available at each price. And overall ticket revenue was boosted accordingly.

What it did mean was that if in the ballot you managed to secure a lowest-priced ticket for one of the most popular events then you were very lucky indeed as the odds were even more heavily stacked against you than you might have imagined when you completed your application form. This approach to ticket sales works best when a balloted system is in operation. In turn, this relies on the expectation that there will be heavy demand for tickets, certainly that demand will exceed supply at some price points, and for a multi-day or multi-event competition ideally for at least some of the sessions overall.

Looking back now at the London experience, Williamson emphasises the importance of the statistics generated by people registering interest in the Games well in advance of 2012. 'Data doesn't lie,' he avers. By 2010 LOCOG had one million registrants, each having expressed some preferences as to the sport they might want to buy tickets for when the time came. This information dwarfed what was available from previous Games. 'There was no hinterland, no previous' in Williamson's eyes. Beijing provided LOCOG with no meaningful data; Athens was a small city with nothing in common with London; Sydney was from a pre-Internet age with applicants filling out paper forms.

What was not clear in the early stages of ticket planning was just how enthusiastic the public might become as the Games got closer. 'People don't know how passionate they are going to be further down the track.' So early work focused on relative pricing, using data from sign-ups to distinguish between sports. In the event, Williamson concedes they got some things wrong. For example, they underestimated the allure of handball, in large part because it had the cachet of being an event in the Olympic Park itself, a factor that only became apparent very close to the Games. In time, as the strength of public interest became clear, prices could be set, with the escalating costs of staging the Games making revenue maximisation a priority. The original budget for ticket revenue, Williamson states, was less than 60 per cent of the final sum achieved. Conscious that the public perceived that they owned the Olympics, even though it was a commercial enterprise, the organisers ensured that low prices at the bottom end took the sting out of criticism. The cheapest ticket for the opening ceremony was £20.12. Williamson saw this as akin to a public lottery: 'someone will win it'.

Impressed by Paul Williamson's success at LOCOG and his subsequent work for the 2014 Commonwealth Games and the 2015 Rugby World Cup, we engaged him to assist our own ticket experts for London 2017. For these twin championships ticket sales were absolutely crucial as, apart from funding from the

Greater London Authority, UK Sport and UK Athletics itself, ticket revenues were the only really major revenue-generating opportunity. Indeed, for the able-bodied event they made up around half of the revenues in our original budget.

The sale of tickets for the IAAF World Athletics Championships in London in 2017 was a textbook exercise. The strategies deployed by Williamson and others across a range of major events in the UK and overseas in the preceding years delivered the desired result. Their playbook had been refined over time. Now, the process began with market research based on the concept of constrained demand, conducted by a specialist consultancy. Respondents were asked a structured series of 'What if ...?' questions designed to assess the strength of their appetite for different events within the championships. This enabled early shaping of prices with the ambition of filling the seats available while maximising ticket revenue.

It worked. The stadium was full, matching the promise that all bidding cities make in the battle to host any event but which successive IAAF World Championship hosts had woefully failed to fulfil, and the budget for ticket revenues was comfortably exceeded. We knew we were going to be all right when we counted the applications for tickets in the initial ballot a year before the event. The public had applied for 200,000 tickets for the evening of the men's 100 metres final, widely expected to be Usain Bolt's last ever race over that distance, and at that stage we only had around 50,000 tickets for that session on offer. We were out of the starting blocks. Britain's 'big eventer' audience came out to watch. And the research and analysis meant that it wasn't just the blue-riband sessions such as the 100 metres final night that sold, but the 'shoulder' sessions too. In the end, we sold 705,000 tickets, earning a Guinness World Record for the best-attended IAAF World Athletics Championships, and by a considerable margin too.

The World Para Athletics Championships, however, were a very different story. One city, one stadium, one summer of world athletics, two championships. Only five years earlier the British public had embraced the Paralympics as no nation had previously, filling arenas for a joyous celebration of elite sporting achievement by athletes with disabilities. True, the success of the Olympics and some sense of missing out on them provided a welcome late impetus to Paralympic ticket sales, but the Para experience must surely have remained vivid in the collective memory only a few years after the closing ceremony. It was quite a surprise, therefore, to find that initial sales for 2017 were sluggish at best.

We posited a number of reasons for the differing sales for the two events as 2016 turned into 2017 and we built our contingency plans to fill the seats. Unlike in 2012, the Para event preceded the championships for able-bodied athletes, so we would have no follow-on sales impact from the sold-out IAAF Worlds – the constraint of the start of West Ham's football season precluded that, so the Para Worlds were being held in July and the IAAF event in August as stipulated by that governing body, leaving no opportunity to switch the two events around. There was no history of meaningful sales for any disability sports event anywhere in the world apart from the Paralympic Games themselves, and London 2012 aside these had often been thin. Indeed, the 100,000 tickets we sold during our first burst of marketing totalled more than every previous edition of the IPC's athletics championships combined.

What we didn't want to accept was that the Para Worlds should be deemed a second-tier event when it came to the quality of the sport served up by the athletes to the watching globe. London and Rio had both proved that would not be the case. But there was no doubt we were up against the twin headwinds of a far lower level of public recognition of Para sport, whatever engagement 2012 had created, and an understanding that 2017 Para tickets weren't as hot as IAAF ones, so potential buyers could afford to make a late purchase decision. And once such a perception takes hold, it is only possible to shake it off by selling tickets – something of a catch-22.

Ticket prices were not the issue. The demands placed upon a host city by the IPC are only a fraction of those imposed by the IAAF, and as a consequence the overall budget for the Para Worlds was far smaller. Tickets could therefore be correspondingly more affordable. This can, however, be a two-edged sword, reinforcing public perception that there is no jeopardy in waiting to buy. As the ParalympicsGB team returned in triumph from Rio we temporarily lowered prices for kids' tickets to three pounds and saw a jump in sales. Any lower and we wouldn't have been covering our marginal costs per ticket, but at least we were building a crowd.

Giving tickets away is the last refuge of the desperate event organiser and not to be recommended for a variety of reasons. We had tried it ourselves in the past, working with a sponsor who spent lavishly on what is known as fulfilment: in essence, committing resources to ensuring that recipients of free tickets not only genuinely intend to use them, but then do turn up on the day. Phone calls are made, emails sent, maybe even transport arranged to the venue. This is not a cheap exercise. If it was simply about generating revenue for the event organiser, the sponsor would have been better off just writing a bigger sponsorship cheque. And as a way of generating a crowd in a stadium it is clunky and inefficient. In reality, very many recipients of free tickets simply don't show up, whatever their original intentions. A free ticket is an option for your precious leisure time. If you are in possession of one, you have no compact with yourself not to waste it, and you are unlikely to feel any obligation to the organisation that gave it to you, however much they tried to make you think otherwise.

Over the years at UK Athletics we tried various methods of promoting disability athletics, our holy grail being that in time it would become an equal attraction in the eyes of the public. In 2013 it seemed as though we might have cracked it. Using the Olympic Stadium for the first time since the 2012 Games, we sold out two days of IAAF Diamond League athletics in ninety minutes and a one-day IPC Grand Prix Final for Paralympic athletes on the same weekend in a day and a half. However, a year later, with the Olympic Stadium unavailable due to redevelopment, we hosted the IPC Final on the same afternoon as our Diamond League meeting in Birmingham. Tickets gave spectators both events and they were marketed as a single afternoon of elite international athletics, but to our dismay most of the crowd melted away as the Diamond League ended and the IPC Final began. When we returned to the Olympic Stadium in 2014, the crowd for Sunday's IPC Final filled fewer than half of the seats. It was a sobering indicator of the half-life of the public's memory of London 2012.

The International Paralympic Committee faced the same challenge on a far greater scale in the weeks leading up to the Rio 2016 Games. Whether through incompetence, impecuniousness or a pragmatic decision to prioritise the Olympics over the Paralympics that followed, the Rio organising committee failed to shift more than a tiny fraction of the tickets for the Paralympics. The IPC took matters into its own hands, berating the organisers publicly and launching a campaign to create crowds. Its 'Fill the Seats' campaign garnered high-profile backing from the likes of Coldplay and Prince Harry and galvanised global support to raise money to fund tickets for local children and those with disabilities to attend the Paras.

In the event the $450,000 raised was modest given the publicity that it created, while the 15,000 people helped to attend the Games were a drop in the ocean compared to Rio's original plans for 3.3 million tickets for sale, later reduced to 2.5 million as the Games were scaled back under pressure of budgetary constraints amid Brazil's economic and political turmoil. And yet crowds at the Paralympics rivalled and often exceeded those for the Olympics, sport for sport. The genius of the Fill the Seats campaign was as much about the awareness it created as the money raised and tickets funded. The Brazilian public didn't know it wanted to attend the Paralympics until the Games broke through into its consciousness. There was no latent local demand, but demand – just in time – was created. Cheap prices compared to the Olympics and a repeat of London's blueprint of one Games following the other both doubtless helped, while those who attended would testify to the exceptional quality of much of the sport that they saw. But no one within or outside Brazil should assume there is a deep seam of spectating legacy for disability sport to mine in the coming years. The Paralympic movement still remains in comparative infancy and must scrap for airtime and a share of sports fans' wallets alongside many other sports worldwide.

By the time the curtain fell on the London 2017 World Para Athletics Championships we were able to look back on crowd numbers that confounded our fears of a year before. The late pick-up in sales materialised, the public having rightly deduced that there would be availability and that they could make a late decision. We hadn't relied on that surge taking place, however, and initiatives supported by the mayors of London and Newham to organise attendance at reduced prices for both schoolchildren across London and residents of the host borough helped swell crowds, as did ticket offers to sports clubs and other community groups. This wasn't simply an exercise in finding an audience, in many ways it was about creating one from a casual awareness of Paralympic sport. By the time the IPC flag was lowered at the end of the Championships, more than

300,000 had attended the event. A step forward, but with many more to be taken in the years ahead.

One problem many sports face is the size of the arenas needed to encompass them. The curve of the bends of a 400-metre outdoor athletics track can be adjusted, but the overall length of the track is sacrosanct. Consequently, it won't fit inside a conventional British football stadium, where the stands are tight up against the pitch. The organisers of Glasgow's Commonwealth Games decommissioned Hampden Park for a football season and built a raised platform to carry an athletics track – far cheaper than building a stadium from scratch, but a time-consuming and expensive solution for anything other than a major competition like the Commonwealths. If athletics was deconstructed and reassembled in the most efficient manner, the standard track would likely become 250 or $333\frac{1}{3}$ metres long, with a sprint straight down the middle or diagonally across. Throwing events would suffer, but smaller venues would become practical and financially viable. Crucially, crowds in the many tens of thousands would not be required to fill venues and so satisfy broadcaster demands.

Test cricket regulations require a playing area of at least 137 metres from boundary to boundary square of the pitch, precluding the sport being played in anything other than a specialist venue in England and Wales, although the Australians do manage to double up with Aussie Rules Football. This is an even bigger challenge than athletics as this most revered form of cricket takes five days to play. As the Test-playing nations have discovered, public interest in actually attending Test matches has recently dwindled. While English county cricket has for decades been played in front of minuscule crowds as Test crowds burgeoned, there now is a real possibility that all long-form first-class cricket in the UK, whether national or international, will be staged in front of sparsely populated stands.

The ECB's accounts make clear the importance of years in which Australia or India visit on tour. In these years the governing body makes a tidy profit, which in turn helps prop up the first-class counties' finances, but in other years the ECB's profits are slim. There can be no question that the Board and the Test-hosting counties work hard to promote attendances, but their efforts can't be helped by the sight of near-empty arenas on Sky TV when England are themselves on tour. Listen to the TV or radio commentators when England are overseas and it is clear that they are resigned to a future in which fan engagement with Test cricket is almost entirely remote. Most commentators are ex-players and struggle to disguise their dismay that they are now part of a sport that is increasingly played solely for television. The damage can be very real. As Durham County Cricket Club suffered financial collapse in 2016, much of the blame was ascribed to the costs of equipping its Chester-le-Street ground to host Test cricket matches for crowds that never came in sufficient numbers.

And yet, deep down, spectator interest can be conjured to the surface if circumstances are propitious. Clearly the Ashes series continue to show that. So too did the extraordinary climax to the 2016 County Championship season, Middlesex winning a three-way tussle for the title on the last afternoon in front of a raucous crowd that materialised as Yorkshire's wickets tumbled. Middlesex had last won the title twenty-three years before, and it felt as though some of the crowd hadn't been to a county game for that long. But they did that afternoon because they knew it mattered.

Boxing is a sport which excels in creating a sense of occasion, building on the genuine physical jeopardy involved. The O2 Arena in London can sell out for a major bout in minutes with ticket prices at the American end of the spectrum, football stadiums can be filled for the most hyped fights, and TV viewers can be tempted to stump up for pay-per-view experiences at prices that would get them through the actual turnstiles for many other sports.

Conservative sports administrators may recoil at the hyperbole and confected showboating that surrounds the promotion of boxing, but there can be no doubt that it works. It probably helps that there are natural constraints on the amount of boxing that can be promoted at the highest level – boxers can only fight so often. The boxing sanctioning bodies that have proliferated down the years have done their best to fragment their sport, but the public has resisted the confusion. They know who the true champions and contenders are, and it is the genuine match-ups that warrant the hype and fill the arenas. It helps too that a boxing contest is the ultimate scalable event, from a tiny local gym, through 800 or so seats in Bethnal Green's York Hall and 20,000 in the O2 Arena to 80,000 at Wembley Stadium. But the ring itself is only 6.1 metres square. With effective selection of a venue and promotion, the seats can always be full for TV.

There is much to learn from the red-in-tooth-and-claw promotion of boxing. A venue manager at the O2 once revealed to me how difficult they found it to host sporting events. I'd been talking to him about the possibility of fitting in a 200-metre indoor athletics track, but the size and shape of the O2 simply wouldn't allow it. AEG, the venue's operator, had found that sports ticket buyers were much more fickle – or perhaps simply fewer in number – than their bread-and-butter pop and rock concert audiences. Tickets for the 2009 World Artistic Gymnastics Championships had been a hard sell, even though this was an event that clearly mattered, while in its early years the WTA World Tour Finals were not much easier to shift, perhaps because the public even now isn't quite sure where this ranks in the list of important events in the tennis season. Boxing, however, was an exception, joined more recently by the NBA's regular season game transplanted to London, which carries with it an exclusivity for committed basketball fans based in the UK, whose experience of the NBA is otherwise confined to a screen. And hype is something American sports know all about, and are increasingly exporting along with their events.

Crowd behaviour is an endless source of interest for economists as they build and refine their financial models. Sporting bodies have a similar need to understand what creates a crowd and what will sustain it. As a fan, you may be just as comfortable in a sparsely populated arena as a packed one – maybe more so – but over time your attendance and the number of spectators around you will inevitably determine which sports are able to sustain their vibrancy and relevance, and even their very existence as commercial enterprises.

3

TWO WORLDS COLLIDE

'The wise heads that run the NFL have clearly not missed the fact that Londoners are going absolutely gangbusters for gridiron.' Never one to under-egg his pudding, in 2015 London Mayor Boris Johnson hailed Tottenham Hotspur's ten-year deal to host NFL games at its new stadium with characteristic alliterative hyperbole. He had a point, however. A year later the NFL had almost 40,000 season ticket holders for its four-game London series and sold the last 15,000 seats it put up for sale in fifteen minutes. White Hart Lane was to be the next step in a collaborative plan that dated back well over a decade. Patient socialism was winning the day.

Alistair Kirkwood presides over the NFL's expansion into the crowded British sports market. When we meet, his offices on a single floor in an anonymous block off Oxford Street are being crated up. Rows of helmets in the colours of the various NFL teams that have flown the Atlantic line a side table, awaiting packing. NFL UK has outgrown its home. Kirkwood, who has been with the NFL since 2000, is taking his business a half-mile down the road to a Leicester Square location that can house its expanded scale of operations and ambition.

'When we voted as an ownership group in 2006 to play regular season games internationally, there were two things going on.

One is a sense that we had to do something, not in a sense of achieving anything soon but certainly in the space of a generation. The second piece was that if we didn't put our absolute best product on, then the sports fan is now so knowledgeable that what we tried to do two or three decades ago, which is put friendly games on, would have no impact because the sports market is so competitive. There is so much great product out there.'

American football dominates the US landscape. Forty-five of the fifty most viewed television programmes in 2016 in America were NFL games – not just sports programmes, all programmes. Twenty-five million viewers watch regular Sunday-night matches. The sport is currently wrestling with a year-on-year decline in television audiences, but it is from a height that others can only look at with envy. Root around for the cause of its popularity and you can come up with a number of answers. One key reason might be scarcity. The regular season runs to only 256 matches over seventeen weeks, followed by a one-month eleven-game play-off series with the Super Bowl as its culmination. Contrast that with 2,430 Major League Baseball fixtures over six months with a play-off series appended. The much greater physical demands of football are a natural constraint on its season, but the rationing is also a very deliberate commercial ploy.

Controversial Cleveland Browns and then Baltimore Ravens owner, the late Art Modell, famously described his clique of NFL owners as 'thirty-two Republicans who vote socialist'. Whatever the truth of the owners' actual political and philosophical leanings, Alistair Kirkwood views the 'parity ethos' on which the League is founded as central to its approach to international expansion. The NFL is owned equally by each of its thirty-two franchise clubs. Votes on key matters require three quarters of them to be in favour if they are to pass. Over 80 per cent of all the major revenue streams the sport generates are shared evenly between the franchises. Local commercial rights extend only seventy-five miles from a club's home city, with everything else centrally negotiated for the benefit of all. Salary caps and salary floors encourage equal expenditure on players, this parity encouraged further by the structure of the draft system for recruitment of new talent. 'The ethos of the League is very much strength in numbers,' Kirkwood explains. 'You have a market such as Green Bay, which has a population of 100,000, that is not at a major financial disadvantage compared with a New York team, which has a market of ten to twelve million. We are conditioned over the last five decades to believe that no team dominating whether on or off the field will help the League as a whole.'

A study by management consultants A. T. Kearney endorses the commercial value of close competition in the NFL. It argues that the greater the number of close contests in a league, the more 'premium matches' with which to entice viewers and hence broadcasters. The consultant cites the sheer number of premium matches in the English Premier League as one explanation of the broadcast riches it enjoys. 'It is in the league's best interest to have as many high-performing clubs as possible – rather than one team dominating the pack – because that gives a lot more premium inventory to offer broadcasters. Thus one lever is optimising revenue sharing across clubs. In the United States this leads to high levels of parity in the NFL, which has had ten different teams in the past five Super Bowls.' Results in the past couple of years have altered this, but the past ten Super Bowls have nevertheless been contested by thirteen different teams. The equivalent for football's FA Cup in England is, coincidentally, thirteen too, emphasising the enduring openness of that venerable competition.

The 2006 vote of the NFL ownership group to go international was an early recognition that the sport might be at or near saturation point in its home market. Technology was changing and with it consumption patterns, opening up the prospect of overseas matches that didn't alienate the home audience. 'Every single sports fan, hard core sports fan, avid sports fan is conservative with a small "c",' Kirkwood believes. 'They don't like change, they harken back. The truth is that sports fans don't realise that they adapt and they move on. As sports administrators and business folk it is our job to be forward thinking and safeguard the future of the sport and understand and appreciate why sports fans will probably be reticent about change because all of it is built up from memories.'

London's attractions might be obvious in hindsight, but the city was not without its risks. The existing thirty-two franchises covered most major urban areas in the US, and the largest city without a team was a small fraction of the size of London. However, at the time over half of NFL players did not possess a passport, and transporting a match overseas was a massive logistical exercise. A roster of fifty-three players and around fifteen coaches per team plus all support personnel needed to be transported five to eight time zones eastwards to a venue with no experience of hosting the sport. Kirkwood remembers discussions about British three-pin plugs – as important as the need to ensure that Wembley's technology would support the quarterbacks' in-helmet communications systems.

The first regular season NFL game at Wembley in 2007 was very much a toe in the water. The Miami Dolphins hosted the New York Giants on a quagmire of a pitch, which made a lot of the headlines in the British press. Ahead of the game the NFL wasn't sure when it might be back, if at all; indeed Kirkwood says that was the case for each of the first five years of the London experiment. It was lucky that the Giants went on to win the Super Bowl that season – it was essential that teams did not feel they would be at a disadvantage if they played one game in a short season across the Atlantic. 'All sports people are superstitious and they follow trends. From having grudging willingness to come over we started to find people going, "Well if that worked for the

Giants, then why don't we think about going over as well." So that was a piece of luck.' In 2008 Kirwood avoided a sophomore slump, managing to bring over the San Diego Chargers as the designated away team, about the longest possible trip for a team in the League.

The designation of home and away team is anything but random. With each NFL franchise slated to have eight regular home games a season, negotiations between the League and the franchise owners are initiated each season with the search for a team prepared to give up a game in its home town in favour of an expat venue in London. The growth over the years in the number of London games to four each season creates a proportionately increased challenge in these negotiations, but also indicates that the owners have come to see the value of international exposure.

The NFL itself is the promoter of the London games: it owns the revenues, it buys the commercial rights, bears all the costs, transports the teams, provides them with training facilities. 'It means you have an equitable solution for thirty-two teams, because thirty-two teams are sharing the outcome of that.' The NFL compensates the designated home team by paying it the average profit the team generates from a normal home game. With an open books approach that goes with the League's parity ethos, this profitability is easy to observe. In effect, therefore, the NFL is paying for two games – one that never takes place back in America and another in London. And it is now doing this for four of the regular season games, so that the collective of NFL franchisees is picking up the bill for eight games in return for the revenues that the four London matches can generate. 'It's a loss leader,' says Kirkwood, but one that the NFL believes will prove justified over the long term.

The ultimate objective of the London expansion is as yet unclear; it may even be unknown to NFL insiders, who have been

at pains to grow gradually with minor experiments in timeta-
bling, venues and promotional activity each year. For four or five
years they had one game a year and doubters saying to Kirkwood, 'Yeah, but it's a circus coming into town.' Now they have
a returning team in the shape of the Jacksonville Jaguars, who
were first a designated home team in 2013 and have been back
every year since, and will appear in London through until at least
2020. The Jaguars come from a city with a population twice the
size of Miami, approaching 900,000 at the last count, but with a
low profile. Playing in London helps Jacksonville back home, promoting the city to a global audience. And in London a bespoke
fan base is gradually emerging. A London NFL game is a harle-
quinade of fans in jerseys from across the thirty-two franchises.
Alistair Kirkwood says it used to be a case of 'spot the Jags fan,
but now that's moved appreciably'.

    The Jaguars have been owned since early 2012 by Shahid
Khan. Just over a year later he bought Fulham Football Club, so
it is perhaps no coincidence that his NFL franchise is happy to
embrace London. Other franchise owners are also familiar with
the UK through their sporting and business connections. Stan
Kroenke, for example, controls both the Los Angeles Rams and
Arsenal FC; the Glazer family control both the Tampa Bay Buc-
caneers and Manchester United. Kirkwood acknowledges this
familiarity is helpful, but more important is the sheer size of the
London and overall UK sports rights market. 'In some markets
in order to justify the investment you possibly would have to be
the number one sport by the time you've finished. In this market
you could probably afford to be the number four or number five
sport and still be able to say that it was well worthwhile. So while
it's more competitive and more difficult, the actual size of the pie
justifies it.'

    Whether or not Tottenham Hotspur was ever serious in its at-
tempt to secure control of London's Olympic Stadium, it has now

thrown itself into a wholescale redevelopment of its existing White Hart Lane site. As with all such projects, the final financial cost appears likely to outstrip early expectations. One reason is that an American football capability is now embedded in the new stadium's design. That's not just a roll-in artificial pitch which would allow both brands of football to be played on the same weekend, but also back-of-house facilities including changing rooms that can encompass the sheer scale of gridiron.

The redeveloped White Hart Lane gives NFL UK greater flexibility in fitting its international games around British soccer and rugby fixture lists, but there is no guarantee yet that Tottenham will play host to a fully transplanted NFL franchise. Persuading eight teams to play one game a season in the UK is a long way from a single team establishing a competitive roster of players based in London and willing to fly repeatedly across the Atlantic to fulfil all of its away fixtures. Arranging passports for stars who may never have travelled abroad, let alone lived overseas, would be the least of the franchise owner's problems. As Kirkwood emphasises, the maintenance of playing parity remains a primary consideration. 'One of the reasons we go with patience is that we've actually been given incredibly valuable real estate. You can't drop the ball. You can't make a mistake with something that involves the competitiveness of the League. You can't get authenticity nor can you get credibility in a short span. If we get down to a franchise, our concern at the moment would be about the competitiveness of the team.'

For Tottenham's owners, an NFL franchise must surely be the ultimate ambition. Being paid for the use of its stadium a few times a year is likely to prove a slow means of recovering the costly bespoke elements of an arena designed to accommodate American football. A share of the profits of a permanent London franchise, or perhaps one with homes on either side of the Atlantic, would be a different and more attractive financial proposition altogether.

The NFL was actually beaten to the punch in establishing a transatlantic team franchise. In March 2017 Toronto Wolfpack played its inaugural league match in the third tier of English rugby league, the Kingstone Press League 1. The Canadian team ran out 76–0 winners away to the London Skolars at the New River Stadium, coincidentally on White Hart Lane, just over a mile and a half down the road from Tottenham Hotspur's stadium bearing the same name. The Skolars' arena offers seating for a little over a thousand fans, so just a modest stage for the commencement of this cross-continental sporting venture which has Super League status at the heart of its ambitions.

The RFL's chief executive at the time Nigel Wood, now head of the sport's international body, describes the arrival of the Wolfpack as 'a wonderful, typical rugby league story'. Its genesis was in the mind of 'an entrepreneurial character who stumbled into rugby league overseas somewhere and thought, *This is the most Canadian sport not being played in Canada*. With a financial prudence typical of the sport in Great Britain, Wood highlights that 'the League has said this has to be a fully underwritten initiative. They always have to be a net contributor. They don't have to necessarily make immediate money, but they can't look to take money out.'

The logistics of Toronto's participation in English rugby league might contain some lessons for the NFL, even though the scale of the sport is much more modest – the Wolfpack's own stadium, the Den, can hold only 9,000 spectators, and tickets for the inaugural season could be had for C$21 a game. The majority of the team's playing squad is British, augmented by a handful of Canadians and others signed during an intense player recruitment process around Jamaica and North America. Its fixture list is built around blocks of matches in Toronto alternating with blocks on the road in England. Visiting teams have all of their travel expenses paid by the Wolfpack's owners. It may come as no surprise that the team's principal sponsor is a Canadian airline operating flights from Toronto to Birmingham, Manchester and London Gatwick. In what is likely to be an expensive tilt at top rugby league status, every Canadian cent saved helps.

That the Rugby Football League has embraced an overseas team willing to cover the costs incurred by a physically remote existence speaks to the difficulties facing the sport in trying to break out of its northern English heartland. The challenges posed by the superior financial might of English rugby union and association football are considerable. The flow of players from the league to the union code is not one way, but it is heavily weighted in favour of union. And soccer continues to squeeze rugby league's natural fan base. A 3,430-mile jump westwards from the RFL's HQ in Yorkshire might seem a radical solution, but it is nothing if not ambitious.

Nigel Wood worries that the Wolfpack, chock full of ambition, might be too successful on the pitch too quickly. The Canadians were promoted to the second tier of the sport in England at the end of their inaugural season, having topped the third division. 'Sport is not edifying when it's a mismatch. It's just not right. And other clubs will resent that. So I think there's real expectations management needed. And again if it's too easy the Ontario public will come along and say, *This just isn't real sport is it?* So they are going to have to find that balance.' His excitement, however, is palpable. 'We are challenging ourselves in so many ways. And I know so many people are now looking at this. It could go there … What the RFL needs to make sure is that it is income generative and not just a fanciful vanity project.' Late in 2017 it was reported that plans were afoot, inspired by Toronto's success, for the creation of a New York team with ambitions to join the English game.

An overseas aspirant entrant to English football would of course find the doors of the Football Association, Football League and Premier League firmly shut. Celtic and Rangers have periodically mooted the possibility of switching their league commitments from Scotland to England, although Rangers' financial travails over recent years have undermined any claim it might hope to make to be able to compete at the highest level south of the border – at least for now. Whenever the suggestion has arisen it has gained negligible traction in England. Even if the truly global nature of football and the consequent existence of competitive local leagues could be cast aside in favour of blurred boundaries, the leading English clubs don't need either of Scotland's two biggest teams to enhance their product. And which team, in either of the top two English divisions, would be prepared to forfeit its position when the lure of Premier League riches is so great?

In the 2015/16 financial year, Celtic PLC – the football club's holding company – had revenues of £52 million, sharply lower than two and three years previously. In the 2016/17 season, Sunderland, the bottom club in the English top flight, enjoyed TV and commercial revenues directly from the Premier League of £93 million. Champions Chelsea received £151 million. Each year the media trumpets the Championship Play-Off Final, which determines the last remaining promotion place to the Premier League, as a game with a value of well over £100 million. This prize is potentially within the reach of all Championship clubs, each of which will make plans and harbour ambitions to win it. Owning an English club is the only way to get into the party.

One executive director of an English lower league club, who prefers to remain anonymous, described to me the dangers inherent in the Championship. 'This is a division that you either have to go up through very quickly – go straight up – or go straight down. You can survive one season or two at most before your players look around at the wages of the other teams and start asking you for a rise. Before you know it your wage bill is out of control and promotion is the only way to head off a crisis. Football is a business in which you can't afford to aim to stand still. If you plan to finish mid-table in the division you run too big a risk of just missing and getting relegated. So you have to keep spending to try and do better, just to be able to stay where you are.'

The British football system of promotion and relegation through a deep pyramid of leagues hasn't discouraged foreign buyers of clubs who might be more used to a franchise system with no danger of relegation. Periodically, American sports franchises switch location, often across a number of state boundaries. For twenty years Los Angeles went without an NFL franchise after the departure of the Rams to St Louis. In 2016 the Rams returned and were joined a year later by a second LA team, the Chargers, uprooted from San Diego and moved 120 miles up the California coast. The Chargers' move reversed their own departure from Los Angeles back in 1960, when the owners felt they couldn't compete in the same city as the Rams. Now, frustrated by the constraints of their stadium in San Diego, the current owners intend to share the new arena being built for the Rams. It may have taken almost six decades but the circle will have turned in full. One threat absent throughout was of relegation. Financial not sporting failure was the primary risk.

As the 2016/17 English football season concluded, fourteen of the twenty Premier League clubs were majority-owned by foreign investors, while almost half of the Championship clubs aspiring to compete in the top division had overseas owners. Of the serious contenders for entry to European competition for the next season, only Tottenham Hotspur might be thought to be under English ownership, by virtue of the largest shareholder in the Bahamas-registered company that controlled the club having been born in London. By then, though, he too was a Bahamian resident. Russia, Egypt, the UAE, Germany, Italy, Thailand and America all featured as the origins of the Premier League clubs' controlling shareholders. Some of these resemble absentee landlords, or at least have a very low media profile; others are happy to enjoy their share of the glory of success – witness Leicester's Thai owners' part in their club's title-winning celebrations.

The danger of relegation has clearly not prevented an invasion of foreign capital. This may be because of the stability of membership of the Premier League at its top end. Six teams have competed in every Premier League season since it began in 1992. Until 2016 this list numbered seven, but Aston Villa's relegation ended a run of competing in the highest division that stretched for twenty-nine years. Only weeks after Villa dropped out of the Premier League its American owner, Randy Lerner, sold control of the club to a Chinese businessman. Lerner had owned the club for just under a decade. It had previously been a publicly listed company on the London Stock Exchange, and his purchase in 2006 valued it at £63 million. He had also taken on the club's debts to the tune of £24 million.

Years of poor sporting performance followed by relegation were reflected in press reports that Lerner's eventual sale valued Aston Villa at little more than his purchase price in spite of the hefty inflation in football club values in recent years. It was also only a fraction of the rumoured asking price when he first sought a buyer a couple of years earlier. More significantly, Villa's accounts showed that it had failed to make money in every single year of his ownership, racking up total after-tax losses of £249 million. *Forbes* magazine trumpeted the $100,000-a-day cost of owning the club; the *Birmingham Mail* no doubt delighted fans of Villa's Birmingham City rivals with their £70,000-a-day report of the same analysis. Lerner had inherited the Cleveland Browns NFL franchise from his father in 2002 and sold it in 2012. Perhaps he found that neither the franchise nor the promotion/relegation sporting model suited his business portfolio.

A sports lawyer who has been involved in a number of purchases of English clubs, as well as many attempted transactions, reels off the prices at which various Premier League clubs might be available to buy today. Some are outlandish sums that would be contemplated by only the wealthiest gatherer of trophy assets, others are more realistic reflections of relegation risk or the constraints of current stadium capacity and quality. His message, however, is that no club is off the market. Even the apparently most secure owners can experience changed circumstances elsewhere that might necessitate a sale, or might have their heads turned by an offer at a bloated valuation. None, he suggests, is so wedded emotionally to their asset as to leave their financial sense at the turnstiles.

The low interest rates that have persisted since the collapse of Lehman Brothers in 2008 and the subsequent financial crisis have boosted the attraction of football clubs enjoying booming broadcast revenues. Now that the cost of borrowing in the United States has begun to move upwards once more, however, it may be that economic forces dampen enthusiasm for these as for any other investment asset. And if today's owners are indeed less likely to invest emotional capital in clubs than their predecessors in times past, then we should not be surprised if the seemingly relentless rise in valuations begins to stall. If the straws in the wind that suggest changing viewing habits also prove the harbinger of reduced broadcast revenues in future deals, then the attractions of football clubs as investments would diminish further. As yet, though, this is only speculation. Stock markets are said to climb walls of worry. Owning football clubs is no different. Reasons to worry are not necessarily reasons why prices must fall.

Vanity still appears a motivating factor behind many changes in ownership of football clubs. While this might be deemed not an issue for the authorities, pressure for the leagues to examine the finances behind new owners has led to increased scrutiny of business models, particularly by the Premier League. As well as examining whether owners are appropriate individuals, there is now some assessment of whether their financial plans stack up. Penalties exist for clubs who break the financial rules, and for those who go bust and renege on their commitments. Points deductions are a handicap assumed by any owner attempting to coax a phoenix from the ashes of administration. It is in no one's interests, however, for matters to get that far.

The FA and the leagues operate the Owners' and Directors' Test (formerly known as a Fit and Proper Person Test) to assess potential owners, conscious of the reputational issues at stake. Both were designed to weed out individuals with obvious conflicts of interest, such as stakes in or influence over more than one club, and those with tainted financial or criminal records. The English Football League describes the purpose of its test as 'to protect the image and integrity of The League and its competitions, the well-being of the Clubs, and the interests of all of the stakeholders in those Clubs'.

The application of such tests is no guarantee of their effectiveness in ensuring financial probity, let alone the existence of a credible business plan and consequent stability at a club. Controversy has often followed close on the heels of changes in club ownership. The same sports lawyer who believes all clubs have their price also claims that there are a small number of Championship clubs whose promotion, should it happen, would put the Premier League in a very difficult position as their owners would not – in his view – clear the higher regulatory hurdle that it sets, including the viability of financial plans.

Were the Premier League ever to bar a promoted club on the grounds of its ownership, we would be one big step closer to a franchise system taking hold in England. Rumours of the biggest clubs exploring a European league with fixed members, and of their unhappiness with the relatively egalitarian way in which TV monies are shared, suggest that a closed super league (whether domestic or European) is not entirely beyond the realms of possibility. If that were ever to occur then you can be sure that the gilded few's owners' wall of worry would disappear and today's asset values would balloon. Rather than a socialist quirk, the NFL model might yet become a blueprint.

4

THE ONLY TIME WE FEEL LIKE FOOTBALLERS

Football in the United Kingdom is a unionised profession. The Professional Footballers' Association was formed in 1907 and still describes its aims as 'to protect, improve and negotiate the conditions, rights and status of all professional players by collective bargaining agreements'. Its chief executive often attracts attention for the size of his salary, which is more akin to that of one of his members towards the top of the hierarchy of divisions than to a conventional union leader, but the PFA's activities are unashamedly traditional. This very much reflects where the footballing profession has come from and the perilous career of those not far below Premier League stardom.

When the PFA was formed, a maximum wage limited footballers' earning power. It wasn't until 1961 that Jimmy Hill, then PFA chairman, succeeded in having it abolished. At the time it was £20 a week – in today's money a little over £400 a week. The EFL estimates that footballers routinely earned more than the average worker before the Second World War, but that the limit imposed by the maximum wage gradually eroded the differential. The wage cap was achieving its desired effect of protecting the financial interests of the clubs' owners, but was doing so entirely at the expense of their employee players. It took the threat of strike action to secure Hill's victory, and then wages for the top players swiftly leaped. More than half a century on, the media still typically describes players' wages in weekly terms, even though incomes of millions of pounds a year for star players are more like the salaries of FTSE 100 executives than those of labouring men and women who might think in terms of a weekly pay packet. Wherever an individual player might come from, whatever his social background, it is clear that his profession has sprung from the working class with many of its accompanying employment rituals, practices and prejudices.

In the years since the abolition of the maximum wage, not only have rewards for the best players mushroomed, but freedom of movement has also increased. In 1995 the European Court of Justice ruled in favour of Jean-Marc Bosman in a case he brought against his club, RFC Liège, the Belgian FA and UEFA after a move he wanted to make to France at the end of his contract fell through because of Liège's demand for a transfer fee. Bosman's freedom of movement on completion of his contract was upheld, removing the ability of clubs to demand transfer fees on the sale of players at contract expiry. Where before footballers could be held in employment limbo even though their contract had expired (in the UK often waiting on a tribunal to opine on a disputed transfer fee), now they found their bargaining power significantly enhanced. A free agent commands no transfer fee, so can retain all of the benefits of signing and employing his services for himself (and of course his agent), and a player with pedigree and self-confidence can threaten to run his contract down as a means of securing a wage increase and contract extension when his existing deal has only a year or so left to run.

A footballer is, ultimately, a wasting asset for his employer – at least when viewed over the long term. Eventually he will become too old to play, or his career may end earlier than anticipated through injury or permanent loss of form. Companies write down the value of short-term assets in their books over a period of years intended to mirror their estimated lives. Computer equipment, for example, may have a third of its value charged to the company's accounts every year over its estimated three-year life. With the Bosman ruling, and the increased player power of recent years, the transfer fee paid by a club for a player – the equivalent of the cost of buying computer equipment – should for prudence be viewed as a cost to be spread over the length of a player's contract whereas once it was an entry price to a trading game that might routinely result in a profit.

A trading approach to owning and running a football club is far from being a thing of the past. There are still those known as selling clubs, perceived to have an eye to profitable player development, and maybe happy with a commensurate mid-ranking existence. Newcastle United's owner is widely reported to have instructed successive managers to buy only players in their mid-twenties or younger, with a view to their future marketability. However, top players now hold the trump cards, tilting the odds of success against those employers looking to profit from the transfer market. One consequence is that transfer fees now feature less in discussion of football transfer window activity, and player wages more – both in the reporting of actual transfers and in the frenzied speculation about the motivation behind possible deals. In many ways it is in the shared interest of footballers and their clubs that reward flows to players in wages rather than to their former employers in transfer fees. But then all clubs feature on both sides of the transfer market equation.

The annual accounts for Arsenal FC demonstrate a prudent approach to the financial treatment of player transfers. For the 2015/16 year, the club declared a £54 million deficit on what it terms 'player trading'. In aggregate the costs of acquiring Arsenal's playing staff, spread over the length of their contracts, resulted in a charge, termed 'amortisation of player registrations', of £59 million that year. Against that, the club generated only £2 million profit on the sale of a player registration – a sell-on fee for a former youth player who was transferred between two different clubs – and £3 million in fees for players loaned to other clubs. Arsenal's accounts trumpet a decline in profits on player sales and the steady rise in the cost of registrations as indicative of investment in its squad. This is not a selling club. It knows, however, that many of its supporters believe it is not a buying club either, whatever the accounts might say about record player investment. Arsenal ranks seventh in the annual Deloitte football money league of the world's wealthiest clubs. Just over a decade ago it was tenth. Pleasing accountants is one thing though; winning trophies something else entirely.

The maximum wage in football may have long disappeared, but mechanisms have been put in place that indirectly constrain salary bills. UEFA's 'financial fair play' regulations were introduced in 2010 with the intention of levelling the playing field, or at least tilting it towards an even surface. These rules also help save club owners from their own financial folly. Football is littered with the wrecks of aspirations, chairmen and their fellow investors overextending themselves in the pursuit of sporting glory and the fulfilment of childhood dreams. The growth in television and commercial revenues has simply raised the stakes in the game. However, financial fair play rules have introduced a safety valve that some deem a guarantee against failure, provided a club can remain in the highest echelon. The surge in investment interest in leading football clubs may have been triggered by the explosive growth in television income, but it has been assisted by the new regulatory protections.

The rules are still relatively new, their introduction controversial and their application problematic. They were updated in 2015, effectively softened, but have claimed a number of scalps in a short period of time. At the heart of financial fair play is a requirement that clubs get close to breaking even financially over a rolling three-year period, allowed to lose an aggregate of €5 million in each period. Certain expenditure is excluded from the calculation, including that on stadiums, training facilities, youth development and women's football. The calculation of losses includes activity in the transfer market. However, the loss limit increases to €30 million provided the incremental loss is covered by an injection of fresh funds from the owners or any related parties. Clubs also need to be able to demonstrate that they do not have outstanding bad debts to the footballing community.

In essence, UEFA wishes to ensure that its leading clubs live within their means. What the rules do not attempt to do, however, is force clubs with large debts to restructure their finances in order to reduce their borrowings. While the break-even stipulation prevents a build-up of debt, it does not ensure the reduction of existing obligations to less risky levels. Manchester United's debts, created consequent to the club's takeover by the Glazer family, have been a cause of fan concern ever since the change of ownership in 2005.

Many of the teething problems in the initial implementation of the rules, which in part prompted their 2015 revision, involved the definition of different spending activities by clubs – what was an allowable exclusion from the calculation and what wasn't – and what organisations constituted related parties, in particular sponsors whose association with clubs appeared deeper than usual. It may be, though, that the biggest problem was simply the novelty of the concept of financial prudence in football. In the highest-profile rule breaches, Manchester City and Paris Saint-Germain were sanctioned, receiving substantial fines and restrictions on the composition of their Champions League playing squads and on their transfer spending. Turkey's Galatasaray, a stalwart of European competition, received a one-year ban from

Europe in 2016 for failing to correct its overspending in spite of an earlier fine.

The English Premier League has its own financial rules for member clubs. They are less restrictive than UEFA's, focusing on restraint of wage growth and allowing much greater scope for fresh investment rather than attempting to enforce break-even. Any Premier League club with a wage bill above £67 million can only grow that bill by £7 million a year, unless it can generate compensatory income from net transfer activity, spectators or commercial deals. Television income is excluded. Clubs have some flexibility as to the base year for the calculation. Whichever route is chosen for what is termed 'short term cost control', the imperative is the same – to grow sustainable income to facilitate a more expensive playing squad.

The largest clubs have enjoyed substantial increases in commercial income in recent years and are unlikely to hit the limit on their wage bills; newly promoted clubs suddenly find themselves operating in a transformed financial environment, with the challenge of how to deploy their new riches effectively. It is the middle-ranking clubs, established in the Premier League but neither entirely certain of staying there nor confident that an investment to push for Europe will ever bear fruit, who are most likely to feel the constraint of the cost control regulations in their player dealings. They may also be in greater need of permission to lose money provided it is covered by the injection of new funds. The Premier League sets a limit on these losses of £35 million a year, against UEFA's €30 million (£24 million) over three years. By contrast, the English Football League allows losses of up to £39 million over three years for Championship clubs, with more generous transition arrangements for those recently relegated from the Premier League.

As long as the Champions League and Premier League continue to command a global audience, their governing bodies can afford to focus on protecting clubs from their own monetary folly. However, any challenge to their dominance might create new tensions around financial fair play. Foreign incursions into the established football market are not new. China's current aspirations in many ways mirror those of America's Major League Soccer, which started in 1996 and has periodically been a remunerative hunting ground for the world's leading players and their agents. The difference is that the MLS has usually been regarded as a pre-retirement billet for star names such as David Beckham and Thierry Henry, who can add lustre to a young roster of domestic players; whereas teams in the Chinese Super League are luring players still in their prime for sums far in excess of those available in the European game. Brazil's Oscar left Chelsea for Shanghai SIPG at the tender age of twenty-five. There are restrictions on the number of overseas players in the CSL, and in the middle of 2017 a substantial financial levy was imposed on the transfer of overseas stars to help fund the development of young Chinese players. This took a lot of the heat out of the market. Nevertheless, if the inflation China has helped stoke at the top end of the salary market cascades down, then major European clubs may suddenly find that the limits in their leagues' financial regulations begin to cause a serious headache.

Viewed from an English or even European perspective, it would be easy to feel affronted by the Chinese challenge to Premier League hegemony, but this would be to ignore the impact that the EPL and Champions League have themselves had on other football markets, soaking up talent and broadcasting dollars. And although Major League Soccer has never really materialised as a global threat, this does not mean that newcomers cannot change a sporting landscape.

Cricket has been in a seemingly perpetual state of self-analysis and attempted transformation in the forty years since Kerry Packer's brash challenge to the established order. World Series Cricket, spawned by Packer's Australian television interests, signed many of the game's leading players and introduced a series of innovative features, from coloured clothing to day/night matches. The value of the players themselves became readily apparent, enabling them to break free of the mindset of indenture to their club or county and their country. Packer correctly identified that international caps might have massive emotional value, but there was a price at which players would forgo them.

While World Series Cricket was a blatantly commercial enter-prise, it paved the way for the rebel cricket tours of South Africa that breached the anti-apartheid sanctions imposed on that coun-try. Cricketers showed themselves willing to work outside the sport's traditional governance structure. Only four years after the advent of WSC, a team of established English stars toured South Africa, stirring controversy and triggering bans from the official England side. Teams followed made up of players, in turn, from Sri Lanka, the West Indies and Australia. Derided as mercenar-ies, the tension surrounding the rebels reached a climax in 1990 when the final tour by English players was cut short after Nelson Mandela's release from prison.

One legacy (albeit at some distance) of these twin challenges to the establishment has been the central contracting of interna-tional cricketers, and with it greater rewards for them. Although the sums involved might seem paltry by comparison with those earned by top footballers, they represent many multiples of the income of first-class cricketers below international level.

In England first-class cricket survives financially because of Test matches, and Test cricketers have become increasingly con-scious of their contribution to the maths of the system. The in-troduction of central contracts at the start of the millennium created two tiers of first-class cricketers. Those centrally con-tracted have their play controlled by the ECB. While they still have a county affiliation, they are only able to play for their county side with the permission of the ECB and if it suits the interests of the England team. In return, they receive a £700,000 salary (with a 25 per cent premium for the captain) plus appearance fees on top. Anyone from outside the contracted list who is picked for England still receives his appearance fee, with his county compensated for his time playing for the national side and hence unavailable for county selection. Under this system, an England cricketer making regular Test, one-day international and T20 matches might expect to earn around £900,000 a year for his efforts.

Contrast this with the incomes of those toiling away on the English county cricket circuit. The trade union for cricketers, the Professional Cricketers' Association, has agreed recommended minimum salaries with the ECB. These are age-related and for 2016 ranged from £16,870 for an eighteen-year-old to £23,899 for a twenty-four-year-old. It is probably safe to assume that most first-class cricketers' incomes are not vastly greater than these recommended minimums, and as the floor is not legally binding some cricketers take home less, especially those who do not play many games in a season. The ECB imposes both a salary cap and a salary floor on the first-class counties. The minimum for an entire county's playing staff is only £750,000, so just above the base salary for a single centrally contracted England player. In early 2015 the maximum was reduced to just under £2 million as the ECB sought to shore up the finances of the tottering county system.

Australian cricket has its own central contracting system, which proved the subject of a noisy and protracted dispute between the players' union and the governing body, Cricket Australia, in 2017. Mutual brinkmanship meant existing contracts expired without new ones being agreed. The biggest bone of contention was Cricket Australia's desire to scrap a long-standing revenue-sharing agreement with the players. For a while it was feared that scheduled international matches – including the approaching Ashes series against England – might be cancelled; for a few weeks 230 cricketers were redundant, and an A team tour to South Africa was scrapped, before the pay wrangle was finally resolved.

Freedom of labour movement is at its most obvious when it comes to the brash newcomers to the cricket party, the T20 leagues in India and Australia – the IPL and the Big Bash. Much of the excitement surrounding the IPL is engendered by the player auction that precedes the action each year. The auction system is complicated, intended to ensure a mixture of local and international talent, and designed to protect the interests of the owners of the team franchises. Media interest focuses on the auction of the star players, with reserve prices set and the consequent risk of embarrassment for big names that have misread possible demand for their services. The so-called marquee players can command hundreds of thousands of pounds for their contribution to a seven-week tournament. The 2017 auction saw England's Ben Stokes bought by Rising Pune Supergiants for a record sum for an overseas player – 14.5 crore, or £1.7 million.

Even with the strong growth in their central contract salaries, it is easy to understand why the desire of English players to be involved in the IPL has been a long-running source of tension between the ECB and its player employees. The English governing body has also coveted the commercial riches that the various T20 franchise leagues have generated around the world. In response the ECB is creating its own new league from 2019, based on city franchises rather than its member counties. The counties have had their objections assuaged by the promise of money. It will be interesting to see where the real spoils accrue in time, whether to players, franchise owners or the ECB and its counties. And whether yet more demands on the bodies of the leading players and the stardust they generate are sustainable.

The major American sports do not have the problem of overseas rivals muscling in on their territory. The domestic baseball season may culminate in the World Series but, with the exception of the Toronto Blue Jays, the contestant teams are drawn exclusively from within the United States. American football's Super Bowl may draw a global audience, but its four games in London represent the only meaningful spread of the sport outside its homeland. Basketball and ice hockey have greater international reach, but the American leagues dwarf all others around the world. The challenge for these US sports is to ensure they are constantly competitive, that there is sporting jeopardy to attract audiences. This challenge is made stiffer by the power of market forces.

English football's competitiveness is maintained by its long chain of divisions. Premier League television riches are only guaranteed for as long as your club remains in that top tier. There can be no resting on laurels, although promoted clubs very occasionally decline to play the investment game and gamble on improving their financial situation by maintaining an underpowered playing squad. Hull City's recent forays into the Premier League, for example, have been marked by underinvestment, and consequently by unhappy managers and fans.

Without the danger of relegation, American sports have taken a twin approach to levelling the playing field. They have put in place financial restrictions intended to prevent the biggest franchises acquiring all the best players, and they proactively intervene to give weaker teams priority in the acquisition of new talent.

The NFL operates both a minimum and maximum salary cap, not dissimilar to that of the ECB but on a totally different scale. For the 2016 season, each of the thirty-two teams had a core limit on salaries of $155 million, augmented by any underspend in previous years carried forward. In addition, over a four-year period in aggregate they were obliged to have spent at least 89 per cent of their salary cap limit on salaries. The team with the highest adjusted cap for that season was the Jacksonville Jaguars with a $190 million limit, having significantly underspent in prior years. The team has had a high loss percentage in recent times. The two facts are unlikely to be entirely coincidental.

NFL teams source new talent each year through a highly engineered draft system. Not for them British soccer's network of talent scouts signing up pre-teen prospects who are then processed by the top clubs' academies. Instead, American football, alongside other US sports, relies on the college system to bring talent to its attention. The draft is then structured as a highly refined version of playground team selection, with franchises selecting rookie players in an order determined by how badly each team performed in the previous season. Worst performer gets first pick in each of the seven rounds of the draft, all the way down to the reigning Super Bowl winner who gets last choice. Positions in the selection queue can be traded, but the basic principle is to help those who need help the most. The rookies' individual salaries are then determined by the point in the draft process that they are picked – the sooner they are picked, the more they are paid.

Drafted players become indentured servants of their team, although most rookies who come out of the draft with a contract are probably not concerned that they have been subject to such a restrictive process. Their union, the NFL Players Association, maintains their interests via collective bargaining with the NFL. A player's free-market opportunity comes further down the line should he be successful. After three contracted years a player becomes á restricted free agent, giving him the option to move franchises but with his existing club able to bid him back by matching any rival employment offer. After four contracted years, he becomes an unrestricted free agent and is able to capitalise fully on his value. For the employer, the aggregate salary cap creates a boundary for negotiations with individual players.

The National Basketball Association and Major League Baseball both operate similar systems of salary cap and draft, although both are softer at the margins than the NFL process. Each effectively taxes teams that spend above the stipulated limit on salaries rather than imposing a hard ceiling. Tax rates increase in line with the degree of overspend. This allows a wealthy franchise to spend extra money in search of better sporting performances, as long as it is prepared to pay an escalating marginal tax on top of every additional dollar it invests in its roster of players.

Six MLB teams paid a record total of $74 million in these so-called luxury taxes for the 2016 season. Taxes are used by the MLB for a variety of purposes, from the development of the game to boosting players' retirement funds and direct recycling to teams spending below the soft ceiling. The LA Dodgers and New York Yankees paid the lion's share between them in 2016, at a marginal tax rate of 50 per cent on their salary overspend. The Yankees have paid tax for fourteen years in a row. Given the sponsorship and broadcast riches accruing to the sport, it seems that the tax is increasingly viewed as a necessary cost of pursuing success in the baseball business.

It is hard to imagine European sports adopting the American draft system, however much they have embraced salary caps. Premiership Rugby begins its online description of its own salary cap by lauding 'commercially successful sports around the world' that have caps; American's NFL and NHL are the first two such sports it then cites. However, its cap system is crafted to fit the non-American system of talent identification via scouting and youth development through a club system, and subsequent player registrations subject to transfers for fees. The Premiership allows two players per club to be rewarded outside its £6.5 million overall cap, so that stars from both at home and overseas can be retained, and makes adjustments to reward home-grown talent, to allow for injuries and to compensate for players called up for international duty.

Those international rugby players add considerably to their club incomes when turning out for their countries. Late in 2016, for example, it was reported that the Rugby Players' Association had reached agreement with the RFU on a new four-year deal for England players that contained a match fee of over £20,000 a game plus bonuses. The RFU's indisputable riches – it had income of £407 million in 2015/16 and finished the year with reserves of £193 million – have long proved an incentive for England's players in their periodic financial negotiations with the governing body. Collective bargaining by unions remains central to the employer–employee dynamic here, as in cricket and in the major US sports.

Rugby league in Great Britain does not enjoy the revenues of the union version of the code. However, it prides itself on a greater degree of financial stability at professional club level, with a salary cap at the heart of its strategy. Nigel Wood was RFL Chief Executive for a decade and was a party to the evolution of the cap. 'The sport was a market leader before other sports thought of it. It is still a fundamental part of our league equalisation strategy. It started off as an anti-insolvency measure to stop people spending more than they have. But there are now more effective ways of dealing with anti-insolvency, like making sure the statutory payments to the Crown are managed very quickly. So now it is a much more sophisticated intervention to promote good practice on behalf of clubs.'

Conscious of the continued vulnerability of rugby league to an exodus of talent to union, the Super League's teams agreed to raise its salary cap in 2017. The vote, apparently, was a tight one, clubs torn between the constraints of the cap and awareness of its benefits. The cap of £1.825 million per club will be increased by increments to £2.1 million for the 2020 season. The various exemptions to the cap were also eased, including the addition of a second marquee player as well as a dispensation for players returning to rugby league from other sports. Nigel Wood is conscious of the risk to the clubs' hard-won stability. 'It's all very well moving the cap, but look at the aggregated losses of all the franchise owners. We've substantially eradicated loss-making businesses. The modus operandi for rugby league has been to build secure businesses without benefactors having to put millions of pounds in every year. We've got average losses down to about £80,000. You've got to manage your economy, your ecosystem. You can't manage it for protecting the benefit of the odd player.'

The contract between a player in a team sport and his club remains an oddity in the world of employment. Most of us wouldn't think of ourselves as saleable commodities to be traded between employers. Similarly, we are highly unlikely to be offered multi-year employment contracts with few enforceable sanctions relating to the quality of our performances at work. In a short and sometimes perilous career the protections offered by lengthy contracts have considerable value, however much their constraints might rankle for an unhappy player.

Sportspeople in individual sports have no such protections. The golfer must make the cut on a Friday evening to earn any prize money from a tournament, and there are no appearance fees on offer. Lose in the first round of qualifying for the Wimbledon Championships at tennis and you'll take a princely £4,375 of the £31.6 million prize pot. Make it through to the first round proper, though, and you are guaranteed at least £35,000. The financial pyramid in tennis is very steep, the vast majority of professionals toiling to make a living on the international circuit, responsible for their own expenses and their earning power constantly in jeopardy from injury or illness, to say nothing of their form and the luck of the draw. Only one man and one woman each take home the £2.2 million first prize at Wimbledon.

The governing body for international tennis, the ITF, has responded to concerns about the sheer number of people trying to make a living on its professional circuit. In 2017 it announced the results of a study that revealed 14,000 players competing in professional tennis events, around half of them winning absolutely no prize money at all. It said that its review had 'established that there are too many players trying to compete on the professional circuit; too few players are breaking even; and the age of these players is increasing'. Its solution was to alter the sport's competition structure, including the introduction of a new entry-level ITF Transition Tour, its objective to 'radically reduce the number of professional players competing for ATP and WTA ranking points'. It claimed that 'extensive modelling work has led to a recommended professional player group of no more than 750 men and 750 women players'.

The ITF hopes that its changes constitute a reality check for those dreaming of making a living from their ability with a racket, but it will be hard to stop people dreaming when the rewards for the sport's icons are so great and so visible. Online platform Opendorse estimated Roger Federer's sponsor endorsements to have a value to him of $58 million in 2015, the highest of any sportsperson globally. Novak Djokovic was seventh with $31 million of endorsement income and Maria Sharapova twelfth with $23 million.

At least golfers and tennis players have a highly structured and busy circuit of events to play in, sustained by sponsor interest and the desire of broadcasters to fill their schedules with sports they have committed to for the major events. Where these circuits are less well developed or supported or non-existent, a sportsperson's living is even more perilous. One young sprinter described the annual Diamond League meeting in the London Stadium as the only time he and his fellow athletes get to feel like Premier League footballers. There may be fourteen meetings on the Diamond League circuit, but not every athletics discipline is represented at every one, and there is a limit to how many athletes can compete in each event. You can't fit nine hurdlers on an eight-lane track. Most athletes have to rely on their race agents and meeting promoters to secure them a place in a starting line-up, sometimes for a modest appearance fee but very often for no more than expenses and the chance to take a tilt at winning some prize money. The problem the athletes face is that, aside from the star names, there is often very little between the physical capabilities and personal bests of many contenders. Sharp elbows, consequently, can be an asset off the track as well as on it.

Athletics is not a unionised profession, nor is boxing, which given its inherent dangers might be considered fertile ground for collective action to protect participants' interests. As it is, individuals depend on the various governing bodies to provide systems that protect them, while relying on managers and promoters to arrange evenly matched contests for them that create fair opportunities to progress their careers. The risks in such a structure are obvious, and not just the financial ones.

Individual sports have flirted occasionally with the adoption of team structures or models. In part this is a reaction to increased public interest when they do successfully find a team dynamic that works. The Davis Cup in tennis and Ryder Cup in golf have the power to expand public interest beyond normal levels of awareness. The Olympics and Paralympics meld individuals into a national team that unlocks sponsor cash. Cycling's tours and road races use a team dynamic to deliver an individual victor.

The problem can be the individuality of the stars concerned. Schooled to win for themselves, a team dynamic may prove alien. Often too, individual commercial interests hold sway. Watch any

Diamond League athletics meeting and you will see swathes of athletes wearing identical kit – whatever the current year's colourway is from their Nike, Adidas or Asics kit sponsor. Countless attempts to ensure athletes are kitted in differing colours to ease identification, or even to wear their country's international kit at an invitational meet, have foundered on the manufacturers' determination to promote this year's fashion to the watching public.

Collective bargaining and all the financial protections that flow from it is a very long way away in individual sports. So too, whatever the feeling when performing in front of a packed stadium, is the wealth of a Premier League footballer. However glamorously a sports event may be presented, the rewards for those on the field of play are often far lower than you, the watching fan, might presume. The money available from consumers of sport is, after all, finite, and this constraint is felt acutely by the vast majority of those trying to make a living by playing whatever game their talents and natural attributes have suited them to.

5

TWENTY QUID A COFFEE

The agent stood alongside me at the hotel reception desk, a sheaf of passports in his hand. Reluctant to catch my eye, although we knew each other pretty well. Meanwhile one of his star clients was entertaining the hotel staff, being pushed around the lobby on a luggage trolley by one of his entourage. Being able to dodge the check-in admin was all part of the full service offering, but for the agent a long way shy of the glamour of organising the client's sponsorship deals and managing his media profile. Little wonder he appeared keen to get the menial task completed without being spotted.

Agents' working lives are typically played out in the shadows, allowing ample room for inflation of the mythology surrounding their trade. Occasionally incidents break through into the public arena that seem to confirm the myths. Olympic champion fleeced of £48,000 by his agent, who has a gambling habit and is jailed for eighteen months for the crime. FIFA looking into the details of a world record player transfer that is said to have earned an agent tens of millions of pounds. US agent receives suspended prison sentence after pleading guilty to giving college American footballers illegal financial inducements to sign with him on turning professional. Like the vast majority of professions, however, the truth for most is much more prosaic. Agency is a crowded business in which for most the pickings are slim and a hard grind the norm.

The Football Association website lists almost 1,700 registered intermediaries, those individuals recognised as being able to act as agents for players in England. The number of professional footballers in the country is unclear but unlikely to be more than two or three times the number of intermediaries. Many agents on the register act across a range of countries, reflecting the truly international nature of the sport and its supporting industry, but even so the ratio of players to agents indicates that for most of the latter the spoils must be small to non-existent.

In 2015 the previous licensing system for agents was replaced by the list of registered intermediaries, each individual required merely to pay a small registration fee and to be deemed of good character and reputation. This change was at FIFA's instigation. The global governing body had been struggling to control the agency industry and decided to devolve responsibility to the national football associations, along with reducing the requirements necessary to be recognised as an agent. The larger established agencies in the UK, members of the Association of Football Agents, explored legal action against FIFA's deregulation, fearing damage to their businesses from the lowering of entry standards; meanwhile the number of registered intermediaries mushroomed.

Deregulation went hand in hand with an increase in transparency, so that the new regime was not entirely lighter touch. FIFA now requires national associations to publish the total fees paid by clubs to agents, as well as the names of agents involved on both sides of every transaction involving a player. The first set of data unveiled in England by the Football Association highlighted the concentration of power and money, both at the highest level of the game and within a small number of the most influential agencies. In addition all of the fees paid to intermediaries in player transactions must be routed through the FA's central clearing house. This at least gives the governing body the opportunity to observe the market maelstrom, if not to exert much control over it.

In the four months October 2015 to January 2016, which included the less busy of that season's two transfer windows, English clubs paid £54 million in fees to intermediaries through the FA clearing house. This sum included the fees paid by clubs on behalf of their players, as usually these are deducted from footballers' wages by their employers, as well as any fees picked up directly by the clubs as part of the deals with players. Eighty-six per cent of the total was accounted for by the Premier League clubs. Manchester United alone spent £10 million. Liverpool's payments of almost £7 million were only just below those of all twenty-four Championship clubs combined. League Two clubs parted with only £163,334, six of them paying nothing at all to agents.

In the subsequent twelve months to January 2017, covering two transfer windows, agents' fees swelled to £221 million, 79 per cent relating to Premier League transfers. Manchester City this time topped the table, closely followed by Chelsea and Manchester United. New managers had arrived at each of these clubs during the period in question.

Agents' overall income from English football greatly exceeds their fees. It is bolstered by the commercial endorsements they arrange on behalf of the most bankable players, away from any image rights deals they might secure with their clients' clubs. They also represent managers, who themselves have lucrative contracts and are prone to frequent job changes – most often not at their own instigation. The largest agency businesses also advise corporate clients and their brands on sponsorship of clubs and players. Most significantly, however, the fees agents earn for advising clubs directly on player transfers and contract negotiations are not routed through the FA and don't need to be declared to the governing body.

The regulations governing the relationship between players, clubs and agents allow considerable latitude for negotiation and bespoke contractual arrangements. While the FA publishes guidelines on the maximum percentages that agents should earn from transactions, these are not mandatory. If, as appears the case, the test of an intermediary's good character is basically not having a criminal record, then there is little practical barrier to almost anyone entering this world of big numbers. Legal training might be useful, but agents are not tested on their understanding of the regulations and their ethical import.

Three is the magic number in the regulations governing intermediaries. The recommended limit on agent fees paid by a player is 3 per cent of his basic gross income. This measure excludes any performance bonuses but can include signing-on and loyalty fees. Similarly, there is a recommended limit equivalent to 3 per cent of player income for clubs' payments to intermediaries. The regulations also advise that an agent's share of a transfer fee be limited to 3 per cent. The key, however, is that 3 per cent is merely a guideline, not a ceiling.

The executive director we met earlier discussing the perils of the Championship tells me fans should put little store in the published figures. He has worked for a number of teams up and down the league ladder, and has seen numerous deals that have bent or circumvented the regulations. One of the simplest dodges is for an agent to invoice a club for general scouting services when actually their work relates to a specific transaction. Nothing goes through the central clearing house and the club then looks smart in its dealings with agents in the published data. The player involved also avoids tax on the agent's fee, which might otherwise be deemed to be a benefit he has received.

More insidious is the influence of agents on managers and owners, which distorts the transfer system. After years in the game this director says nothing any longer surprises him. When I ask about new owners who try to resist the tricks of the agency trade he is unequivocal. 'Football is a small club. Often owners coming in from the outside are used to competing against three or four rivals in the industry they have made their money in. They then think they can replicate their success in an industry with dozens of competitors, but they can't. Everyone has a chance to compete in football and they have to go with the system rather than think they can break it.' With so much money sloshing around the game, and the margin between success and failure so fine, temptation can find its way to any door. This director has found it easy to push temptation aside, but others will not have had the same scruples. 'If I found a million pounds on the street and kept it, I wouldn't feel good about myself. So why would I want to take a bung of ten thousand quid from an agent to help get a deal done on the wrong terms for my employer?' He knows, though, that such offers do get made.

In the UK an intermediary is forbidden from owning an economic interest in a player's future transfer value. This legislates against players effectively being owned by agents and hawked around clubs. But while this abuse of the system may be outlawed in Britain, agents are allowed to represent both player and club in a transaction – so called dual representation – which might be considered just as great a threat to the integrity of the transfer market. A footballer has to give prior consent for his intermediary to do this, and the relevant declaration form that must be lodged with the FA requires the player to confirm whether he has or has not taken legal advice, either independently or from his union, the PFA. While the relevant boxes for the player to tick are in bold near the bottom of the form, it is not obligatory for him to seek counsel before granting consent for his adviser to advise his employer at the same time. It is hard to envisage dual representation being appropriate in most walks of life, so it is difficult to fathom why it should be acceptable in football. However much a player may be paid, whether he's a novice or a superstar, this approach leaves him vulnerable at what might be a critical juncture in his career.

In reality, the 3 per cent guideline is often massively exceeded. Also, dual representation appears the norm in the highest-profile transfers rather than the exception, so further multiplying agents' rewards. Unless the governing bodies decide in future to publish the details of each transaction, we can only guess at the sums changing hands in a particular deal. This further step towards transparency is unlikely ever to be taken, though, given commercial sensitivities. Meanwhile, the only winners from the system of dual representation and uncapped fees would appear to be the agents themselves.

The FA's first published list of all transactions involving intermediaries covered April 2015 to January 2016. Leicester City would be crowned Premier League champions only four months later. The club featured in nineteen transactions on the FA's list. Not all were player transfers; some were contract renegotiations with existing playing staff such as Jamie Vardy. A transaction involving Vardy is logged at the end of the transfer window, coinciding with press reports of a new contract for Leicester's star striker as the club entered the run-in of its triumphant season. Of the nineteen transactions, one featured a player going abroad on loan, two showed no intermediary being involved on behalf of the player. The other sixteen listed the same intermediary as acting for both player and club in each transaction. In reality, the player–agent relationship determines the structure of clubs' own agency relationships and the flow of fees in deals. In effect, clubs' use of agents is entirely driven by the expediencies necessary to get their transfer business done.

It may be that Premier League chairmen resent paying agents, in the same way that home sellers can choke on estate agents' fees, but if they do then the numbers suggest that they have swallowed any qualms along with their pride. Refusal to meet a fee demand could see an agent steer a transfer target to a different employer, while fans are only likely to judge clubs negatively on their position in the FA's table of fees paid if their team underperforms. Succeed, and agents' fees can be dismissed as a necessary cost of doing business.

The bond between agent and footballer can be strong and can start young. So young that the regulations seek to intervene. Players are not allowed to be signed to an intermediary before 1 January in the year of their sixteenth birthday, and until they are eighteen any representation contract with an intermediary must be countersigned by a parent or guardian. All players are protected by a time limit of two years on their representation contracts with agents. However, two years is a very long time at such a formative age for a footballer. With clubs themselves identifying talent at a very young age and lavishing support on developing players at well appointed academies, it is little wonder that it is difficult to keep agents at bay. Remember too that players can break into senior professional teams while still minors. Clubs and agents are engaged in the same numbers game, filtering large pools of aspirant players in search of the very few that can make it through to the top of the professional game.

While a few agents have allowed themselves to become part of the media narrative around football transfers, most prefer to operate out of the public gaze. One – 'The real agents aren't seen'– tells me that he enjoys doing the school run in his tracksuit without advertising his profession to fellow parents and being inundated with requests for tickets and insights into the football world. Effectively a sole trader, he's on the list of FA intermediaries and has plied his trade for the best part of two decades. As a promising young player he was offered terms at a leading club but took a realistic view of his likely prospects and headed for university instead. Now he has a strong track record, particularly involving transfers of players from Europe into the UK. He has worked with, and for, a number of the largest clubs in England and on the continent.

Our agent is happy, if anonymously, to expose what he describes as the 'Wild West' of the football market. The 3 per cent fee guideline, he argues, is rendered irrelevant by clubs' desperation for success. 'Are you thirsty, Ed? You *are* thirsty? Well, that cup of coffee will cost you twenty quid.' Nice though the coffee was, I'd have needed to be very parched to have handed over that much to the barista. Preying on clubs who are up against transfer deadline day and in competition for talent, however, agents can name whatever fee they like, and frequently do. Some hawk client players around clubs, some hawk players who are not yet their clients and may never be, and others trade on strong club relationships to go looking for players to fill known gaps in squads.

What is clear is that club owners with scruples about fee rates and the people they are dealing with are destined to lose. 'If an agent just out of Wandsworth Prison has the next Wayne Rooney on his books, everyone is going to take his call.' One can only hope the FA's good character test might kick in at some point. It may be that a club never knows the final destination of the fees that it pays on a transaction. Registered agents can have side deals with other parties. Once a club has paid an intermediary's invoice, it has discharged its formal duties, although it may be vulnerable to forces and relationships beyond its field of vision. Managers and directors of football have favourite agents for all sorts of reasons, not all of them straightforward.

Players, our agent tells us, don't care what their transfer fee is; it's just a number and doesn't go to them. 'Most footballers want to know just two things: what is my wage, and am I in the team?'

Insecurity on either count creates opportunity for an agent. Poaching of talent is rife. Indeed, our agent tells his clients that if they are not wanted by other intermediaries then something is going wrong with their career. He views the players on his books unsentimentally, having shed any emotion years ago. He's no longer interested in their dressing-room woes or whether they think their manager doesn't like them, unless these point to the possibility of a future transfer. 'Everyone in football is effectively self-employed, on a consultancy contract with no guarantee of renewal.' The executive director echoes this view. He cites a leading manager describing players as 'slabs of meat'. 'And he was right. You have to take the personality out of it. Bob Paisley was right all those years ago: can they play forty-two league games?'

Managers' security of tenure is the flimsiest of all. 'The most important clause in a manager's contract is the sack clause,' our agent says. 'In what other profession would you go home to your wife when you get a new job and the first thing she asks you is how much you'll get if you're fired?' This insecurity, as well as pressure on managers' time, spells opportunity for agents. 'A top manager may have a hundred agents calling him. But he may only really trust half a dozen. How many games can Rafa Benítez watch in a weekend? He must then work with agents who he can trust to bring him players that really meet his needs.'

The ban on agents acting for minors is easily circumvented. Contracts are drawn up and put in the drawer until the day the player comes of age. If the agent is also acting on behalf of the club, then he can take a fee in advance of a contract signature. Agents hanging around academy matches are not doing it for love of the game. 'And if you take a youngster from Leeds to Man United, you can forget ever being allowed near the Leeds training ground again.' 'Is the Dad in on the deal?' is a frequent question. If he is, it can either cement or scupper a transaction, depending on how the father is treated. Would our anonymous agent en-

courage his son into the game? Only if he was a nailed-on certainty to succeed. 'Otherwise he could be earning £75K to
£100K a year in the lower divisions until, at thirty-four, he's
earning zero. And then what would he do?'

In the transient world of football employment a player with a
lengthy career may end up having far fewer agents than clubs.
While this may not always reflect any loyalty of player to agent,
it can indicate a dependency that is established at a young age,
nurtured by the agent and hard for the player to shake off. This
dynamic is not unique to football. Athletics is a sport of fragile
careers. Individuals pursue their profession without the fallback
of employment, and so are bereft of contractual protection and
the practical and emotional benefits that a corporate structure
can provide. In Britain, National Lottery funding via the governing body can replicate some of these supports, but as it is re-
viewed annually its precariousness is obvious. Athletes' loyalties
to agents and sponsors, especially their kit suppliers, can be far
stronger than to any other entities in the sport.

The unique bond between agent and athlete was brought
home to me at a recent IAAF World Championships when a British medal winner chose to have her agent as her chaperone in
doping control immediately after her event. Anti-doping proto-
cols permit an athlete to have a witness with them when they
provide a sample for the doping control officers, so as to be sure
that due process is followed. This chaperone will usually be a
member of the team management or coaching staff; as frequent
observers of drugs tests they are more likely to spot an administrative error than outsiders. Here, though, was an athlete whose
first thought in her moment of triumph was to stick close to her
agent. It's unlikely their conversation extended much beyond the
shared excitement of the moment, but the commercial implications of success were doubtless high up the agenda in the following days and weeks.

Seasoned athletics hands will tell you there's not the money in the sport that there once was, and not enough of it to go round. That's probably more a reflection of the comparison with football than an objective analysis of the numbers. Certainly, the competition bandwagon rolls on around the globe, and the lobbies of athlete hotels at Diamond League meetings and major championships are heavily populated with agents making a living from the sport. The football comparison is stark for many sports, not just track and field. In rugby, George Ford's 2017 transfer from Bath to his former club Leicester Tigers was reported by the media as a £500,000 transaction, breaking the record for a transfer between English clubs. Peanuts by football's standards, where the first £1 million transfer took place almost four decades ago. Half a million pounds doesn't buy you much of a footballer these days, but it can land you a stellar fly half it would seem. Agents' opportunities to make money are scaled accordingly. Ford's annual salary at Leicester, by the way, was reported to be £450,000, another indication of the gulf between rugby and football at the highest level.

Just as there are superstar athletes in a sport of modest rewards for the majority, so there is a small coterie of highly successful agencies and agents. Ricky Simms' Pace Sports Management, domiciled in Monaco, is generally regarded as leading the field in athletics, with Usain Bolt and Mo Farah among its list of clients. It cites its services as 'competition planning and management, contract negotiations and servicing, marketing and promotion, merchandising and brand building, social media optimisation, coaching, financial, legal, medical, travel, visa and accommodation management'. All of which helps explain just how tight the relationship between athlete and agent can become.

Ricky Simms and Pace do not feature on either the *Forbes* 2016 list of the fifty most powerful sports agents or the magazine's list of the forty most valuable sports agencies. Nor indeed do any specialist athletics agents, although a small number of multi-sport agencies on the list do service track and field. This may be in part a function of *Forbes*' methodology of tracking the estimated fees from player transactions, which is necessarily inexact given the private nature of the deals concerned, and possibly also its focus on US sports. Nevertheless, the preponderance of the big American team sports alongside soccer on its lists is no surprise. *Forbes* bases its calculations on the maximum commission allowed by sports' governing bodies in the absence of specific data, and features baseball, basketball and American football most often. It crowns baseball agent Scott Boras the world's most powerful agent with $132 million of commissions generated from contracts with a value of $2.2 billion. Soccer's Jorge Mendes, with Cristiano Ronaldo on his books, comes a rather distant but still decent second with estimated fees of $73 million. If you could generate commissions of $10 million you would scrape onto the bottom of the top fifty, which doesn't seem a great deal given the riches in major team sports, suggesting many agents fly under *Forbes*' radar.

Although the numbers are big in American sport, US controls over agents are sometimes more restrictive than FIFA's. The NFL Players Association imposes a 3 per cent limit on the fees that agents can earn on player transactions – a ceiling rather than a recommendation as in soccer. Late in 2016, much to the chagrin of agents, the fee percentage embedded in the sport's template contract, its standard representation agreement, was reduced from three to one and a half. Although the 3 per cent upper limit remained, agents now had to persuade clients to move up from the standard 1.5 per cent, adding an extra dimension to their negotiations to maximise their take from footballers.

The NFLPA's change to its fee guidance was felt more acutely lower down the scale of player experience. Agents often fund young players looking to break into the professional game, in essence speculating on emerging talent in the hope of acquiring a client with a future in the sport. An agent will hope his commitment to picking up early expenses will be rewarded by future commissions as a footballer makes his way up the ranks. By halving the likely take from rookie clients, the NFLPA skewed the financial odds more heavily against those agents scraping a living at the bottom of the talent ladder. The change in default commission came on top of existing restrictions on agents' freedom to negotiate non-standard contract clauses for rookie players, constraining their ability to demonstrate the value of their negotiating prowess to prospective clients. One specialist law firm has already noted a developing trend of rookie footballers choosing not to use an agent when signing their first contract.

American football may have placed restrictions on agents' rewards, as has basketball, but in the Land of the Free other leading team sports have taken the opposite approach. Ice hockey's NHL has no cap on agents' fees. The Major League Baseball Players Association, the union established for baseball's top stars in 1966, takes a free-market approach both to players' salary negotiations with their employer clubs and to fee arrangements with agents. In 2015 the MLBPA declared the average Major Leaguer's salary as just below $3.4 million. The Association has now negotiated a minimum wage in its collective bargaining with the clubs. For 2018 that minimum is $545,000. The agreed minimum for Minor Leaguers is $88,000.

Baseball players are free to agree whatever fees they wish with their agents, with the proviso that an agent cannot take a fee that would result in a player's salary dropping below the minimum. Fees in reality are believed to be typically around 4 per cent, therefore higher than American football's limit but equal to the ceiling set by basketball's NBA. The level at which fees have settled in baseball suggests that American football is attempting to create a ceiling that is artificially lower than would pertain if the market was freed up.

Player unions are powerful bodies across all the major US team sports, as evidenced by occasional strikes and lockouts that have remained fresh in the memory for years after. The 1994–5 baseball strike decimated two seasons of the sport. Through successive collective bargaining rounds the MLBPA has demonstrated the strength of solidarity. The combination of a minimum wage and salary freedom can be considered a double triumph when compared to restrictions elsewhere. For agents the unrestricted market has obvious appeal. It is unlikely to be a coincidence that the agent topping the *Forbes* power list is a baseball specialist.

If today's sporting superstars are akin to corporations, with their activities on the playing surface spawning a range of commercial enterprises intended to monetise their fame, then the agents that serve them act increasingly like these corporations' chief executive officers. The very best CEOs have a fine attention to detail – an essential attribute when servicing a demanding client. Just occasionally that might mean the agent/CEO having to operate below their pay grade, tweaking a tweet on a social media feed managed on a star's behalf, or having to check them into a hotel rather than delegating the task to a junior member of staff. This interplay between agent and client is a subtle one, and it is often difficult to discern where power truly lies. As a fan it is for you to decide whether your sympathies lie with either party or neither. My own experience is that, as in most walks of life, it is impossible to generalise, with all that humanity has to offer on display on both sides.

6

MR ONE PER CENT AND THE KING OF SHAVES

Usain Bolt won the 100 metres at the Rio Olympics by eight thousandths of a second, reeling in his rivals in customary fashion after his usual comparatively slow start. As he crossed the finish his nearest competitor was a metre behind him and Bolt gave every appearance of easing off rather than bursting over the line. No need for the photo-finish judges to be called into action as they had been at the previous year's World Championships in Beijing. A metre ahead over 100 metres. The world's greatest sprinter had confirmed once again that he was 1 per cent better than the best of the rest. In a sport which is all about directly measurable ability, 1 per cent is all that it takes to have a financial worth many multiples of those trailing in your wake. It did no harm to Usain Bolt's earnings that he also has charisma in abundance to back up his athletic prowess.

Athletes time their training each year so as to peak at the major championships of the summer. Although the Olympics do not offer prize money to medallists, and winning the World Championships secures a reward of only $60,000, the commercial benefits of gold medal status are such that everything is geared to one competition a year. Competing too frequently can jeopardise an athlete's chances of success at the major event, and so the leading players typically enter just a handful of meetings ahead of a championships to hone their preparations. Over the course of a season Usain Bolt may have raced only half a dozen times, plus a full load of heats and finals at the prime event of the summer. Lesser athletes might compete slightly more frequently, but all need to maximise their competition earnings from a roster of appearances that is necessarily slim – certainly by comparison with those in team sports, who can play weekly or more often through a long season.

The Diamond League is the premier series for international-standard athletes. Prize money ranges from $1,000 for an athlete finishing eighth in an event up to $10,000 for the winner. A $50,000 first-place prize is on offer in each event in the season's two finals, which have a total prize pot of $3.2 million. While for second-string athletes these prizes are significant, for the leading stars they are merely the icing on the cake. Appearance fees are what really matter, the top athletes trading on their status as major championship medallists to help the meeting organisers shift tickets and secure sponsor dollars.

The owners of Diamond League meetings are mostly private enterprises, although the two British meetings are organised by the national governing body, UK Athletics. Each meeting commits to spending at least $1.5 million on prize money, signing up athletes to compete and funding their travel and hotel accommodation. Around half of this total is likely to be devoted to athlete appearance fees. Every year the League rates the quality of each meeting on a variety of criteria, including the standard of the athletics itself as measured by the number of world-leading marks posted by competitors. Fines are handed down where meetings fall short of required standards. The promoters therefore have a double imperative to spend their appearance fee budgets in full and wisely; both to boost crowd numbers, and to remain in favour with the League, which has a periodic opportunity to replace meetings with new host cities.

The crowd-pulling status of Usain Bolt has been peerless, and was reflected in the appearance fees he commanded before his retirement at the end of 2017. Every Diamond League meeting contains either a 100 or 200 metres, and had a lane available for him to run in should he so desire. And other meetings outside this elite series presented similar opportunities to showcase his talent and for him to fine-tune for major championships. As Bolt's legend grew, so did his appearance fee. The sums are confidential, but the media has speculated that it was in the region of $300,000 or thereabouts for a mainstream meeting. It may have been more for any novelty event that was clearly reliant on the stardust he could sprinkle. By international footballer standards, where such a sum might be earned weekly, or by comparison with global boxing champions or Formula 1 drivers, such sums are far from extraordinary. However, they dwarfed the fees earned by his competitor track and field athletes.

A single Diamond League meeting typically requires around 170 or 180 athletes. At the two British meetings UK Athletics would pay appearance fees to just under half of this cohort, the remainder of the athletes competing solely for the available prize money. The average appearance fee was around $10,000, although this masks a wide disparity between the bulk of athletes paid between $1,500 and $5,000 and the handful of ticket-shifting stars who earn considerably more. A big name international athlete with genuine public recognition might be paid as much as $60,000. British stars can do better than that, but only in the UK market. As soon as they compete abroad they are just one of many international athletes, reliant on having a reputation that cuts through to the local public consciousness.

In a year in which Bolt ran the 100 metres at our London Diamond League meeting, we could assemble the remainder of the field for perhaps $15,000 or just a little more. So his 1 per cent performance advantage on the track translated into an appearance fee many times that of all his competitors combined. By contrast, we might spend around $150,000 assembling a women's 100 metres field in which three or four world-class athletes went head to head with real uncertainty as to the outcome. None would be paid anything like Bolt's fee, but each was better rewarded than all the other male sprinters.

I never had Chancellor George Osborne pegged as an athletics fan, but he was instrumental in enabling us to sign Usain Bolt to appear at our events. I'd only spotted Osborne a couple of times at the Olympic Stadium during London 2012, once in the hospitality hurly-burly out of sight of the track, but not in the seats watching the action, and once when he was roundly booed by the crowd when presenting medals at the Paralympic athletics. At that moment of public opprobrium I was in the stands next to Sports Minister Hugh Robertson, who made little attempt to contain his amusement at his government colleague's discomfort. Only a few months later, however, the chancellor announced a tax exemption for our 2013 Anniversary Games without which Bolt would have continued to avoid competing in the UK, just as he had done since 2009 – Olympics aside. Sports fan or not, Osborne put his Paralympics experience behind him and bowed to financial wisdom in the name of Olympic legacy.

British tax law has been an impediment to the nation hosting international events throughout the twenty-first century. A landmark case back in 2006 saw Her Majesty's Revenue and Customs prevail over tennis star Andre Agassi. In essence, the law lords ruled that HMRC was entitled to a share of Agassi's income from his sponsors such as Nike and Head by virtue of him playing tournaments in the UK, even though the money was paid to a company in his name domiciled outside Britain. The taxman's argument was that sports stars enjoy commercial in-

come because of their success in competition, and that consequently tax should be paid on a proportion of their total income
equal to the contribution playing in the UK makes to their success. If being a tennis star rests in part on playing in Britain, then
the commercial income that stardom generates is subject to the
British tax regime.

Major sporting events deduct basic tax from a player's appearance fees and prize money before paying them the balance. Provided the player is domiciled in a country that has a relevant
double tax treaty with the UK, he or she is able to offset this tax
deducted against any liability to the taxman back home. In effect,
they won't be taxed twice on the fees and prizes earned in Britain.
For the top stars, though, commercial income from sponsors
swamps the money generated by prizes and appearance fees. As
a result, the tax claimed by HMRC from commercial sources can
be greater than the income a player earns directly by playing in
the UK. A number of stars have shied away from British events
as a result, among them golf's Sergio Garcia – from the PGA at
Wentworth – and tennis's Rafa Nadal – from Queen's Club –
judging that the UK tax bill they would trigger would be greater
than their possible earnings from the events concerned, even if
they won them. In 2011 the press reported Nadal explaining his
decision not to play at Queen's: 'The truth is, in the UK you have
a big regime for tax, it's not about the money for playing. They
take from the sponsors, from Babolat, from Nike and from my
watches. This is very difficult. I am playing in the UK and losing
money.'

The big stars nevertheless do show up for the Wimbledon
Championships and golf's Open Championship, even though
neither event has a tax exemption. Top overseas players recognise
that their global commercial value hinges on success at these
major tournaments. While the short-term tax implications of
participation might be severe, the long-term financial equation

makes it imperative for them to compete. The cachet of winning a major is not just reputational, but monetary too. And the financial opportunity it creates can endure well beyond a player's career and deep into their retirement.

The British authorities' application of the tax regime has shifted over time. Initially, international sportspeople had their commercial income taxed according to the number of days they spent in the UK. However, this then shifted to a much more onerous calculation based on the proportion of their annual competition days they undertook in Britain. So, a sprinter who raced ten times in a year would be obliged to have 20 per cent of her commercial income subject to UK tax if she raced in both the Birmingham and London Diamond League meetings. This would apply even if she spent only a few days in Britain over the course of the tax year. HMRC's calculations have been softened a little in recent years, now taking into account all training days worldwide. But still the tax barrier remains.

Considering the complexity of the law and the record-keeping burden it creates for sportspeople, one must assume that it's a costly system for HMRC to police. In 2010 a clutch of organisations across affected sports, including tennis, golf and athletics, commissioned a report which concluded that tax raised under these arrangements probably totalled around £7 million a year. Even if this was a wild underestimate (and remember that the report was undertaken for lobbying purposes) it seems unlikely that the sum raised can justify the consequences for the British sporting industry – or possibly even HMRC's costs of administration.

Some major events only take place in the UK because the government grants a tax exemption for competitors. Such an exemption is a strict requirement of all bidders for the Olympics and Paralympics, the Commonwealth Games, football's Champions League Final and the IAAF World Athletics Champion-

ships, for example. It has become routine for British bidding committees to ask for and secure tax waivers for such events from the
government. It is also possible to seek a one-off waiver for other
lesser events, but the sporting industry has become frustrated at
the inefficiency of this ad hoc system.

George Osborne granted tax exemptions for the London Anniversary Games in 2013, 2015 and 2016, as well as for the Diamond League meeting held in Glasgow shortly before the 2014
Commonwealth Games. Each one entailed specific legislation. In
shepherding the 2016 measure through Parliament, the financial
secretary to the Treasury cited 'an exceptional opportunity to
prolong the legacy of the 2012 Olympic and Paralympic Games'
as the government's justification. In truth, it was all about enabling UK Athletics to persuade Usain Bolt to run in London
rather than elsewhere on the international circuit, so boosting
ticket sales and creating a necessary buzz in the run-up to the
2017 World Championships. Loosely defined, this could be
deemed a 2012 Games legacy. A full stadium would provide justification for the controversial decision taken to retain the athletics track in the Olympic Stadium. None of the parties to that
decision wanted to see a half-empty stadium. And the Bolt effect
was demonstrable, ticket sales jumping on the announcement
that he was going to run. As he wouldn't have competed in London without the tax exemption, HMRC didn't actually forgo any
tax from him. Indeed it will have enjoyed the VAT on all spending
relating to increased attendance at the meeting, including on
tickets themselves. It is little wonder that a range of sports hosting
such events in the UK that are just below major status rail against
the system.

Most athletes on the circuit would be delighted to have the
problem of juggling their competition schedule to minimise their
tax liability while maximising their income. In those years during
which UK Athletics did not have a tax exemption for interna-

tional athletes, we did not lose any competitors we wanted to engage apart from Usain Bolt, which simply highlighted the Jamaican's unique earning power in the sport. The majority of athletes plying their trade around the world live with considerable financial uncertainty. This includes all those Brits without the economic scaffolding of National Lottery funding.

James Ellington is a British sprinter who has regularly represented his country in recent years and in particular is a stalwart member of the relay squad. A late developer in athletics, and not training full time, he was outside the system of Lottery support from the funding agency UK Sport as the London Olympics approached. Running 200-metre times that placed him on the fringes of the British team as an individual athlete, he became financially reliant on whatever income he could accumulate on the athletics circuit and from sponsors. He earned fifty pounds a session coaching at a south London youth scheme and remembers, 'I was training two to three days a week, which at the time I thought was full time, which is crazy because I didn't really have any other clue. I was thinking, *I need to make money without putting as much effort in as it's tiring.*' Frustrated at being one of the have-nots in the system, he turned to eBay in an attempt to find a commercial backer.

'I sat down with some young quirky PR guys, throwing some ideas around the room, and they said, "What about eBay?" So they went off brainstorming and they put me on eBay, sent out a massive press release to two hundred media outlets, did a photo call down at Crystal Palace. Seven or eight photographers turned up. I was there looking poverty-stricken in my white vests and my white shorts, freezing my arse off. It was like three degrees. It was horrible, I was shaking for two hours. The things you do for money!'

James Ellington's eBay auction gathered widespread publicity and a highest bid that exceeded his reserve of £30,000. The winning bid turned out to be malicious, but his campaign did flush out a sponsor in the form of the King of Shaves. 'I was on *BBC Breakfast*, on the red sofa, and the King of Shaves – Will King – messaged me on Twitter and said, "If nobody does sponsor you get hold of me and I'll sponsor you. I want to do the deal."' It's not clear whether the shaving company supported the sprinter in spite of, or because of, his beard.

Ellington explains his eBay reserve price as being a full-time wage of £15,000 plus the same amount to cover the cost of his training and competing. As well as highlighting the vagaries of the commercial market for the mass of athletes, this also gives a useful insight into the cost of pursuing the sport in search of prize money and medals. The auction did, however, have an unantici-pated consequence.

'Then I felt the pressure. I'm going to have to win the trials now because I've been on TV and I'm telling everyone, "If I can train full time I'll be number one in the country and win the tri-als." And at the time you had the likes of Marlon Devonish and Christian Malcolm and they're probably sitting there thinking, *Shut up! Who are you? Some young boy. Who are you talking?* At the trials I had thirteen members of my family there, I had the flippin' world watching, I had King of Shaves with his money on me, thinking you've got to win and go to the Olympics. I went through the heat and I ran 21.2 seconds and I saw Danny Talbot and all those guys, Christian, run 20.6 and I'm thinking, *Oh my God!* And that's one race, as I'm walking out for the final, where I wish I could rewind to two months before and prepare for it again. I'm never scared but I was shaking. I thought, *I have to win this. This isn't a joke any more.* Having seen my heat everyone in the media thought I was going to flop, and I literally had to run for my life. That's the most pressured race I've had in my life. Forget the Olympics and all of that. And I won it and it was the best feeling ever. 20.56. Bad conditions as well.'

King of Shaves doubled its commitment to Ellington, even though he ran poorly at London 2012. 'He really set me up. I could put a bit of money away and I thought, *Cool, a bit of breathing space.* I've never grown up with money, so I know how to value money. I've never splurged.' That autumn he was granted Lottery money as a member of the relay squad. 'Lottery funding's been my main income. It's a massive help for athletes. There's a few lucky individuals who don't need the Lottery as they've got massive kit deals. There's a divide in the sport. The tough thing is that it's all about medals really. The divide is so drastic.'

Ellington may have put himself up for public sale, but he's proud not to have undersold himself commercially, even though he has missed out on opportunities. 'I've never had sponsors. I've always said athletes at international level don't know their worth. There's so many brands out there that throw athletes kit all the time and they get away with it because athletes get excited. But they're not paying you any money. When you're a kid that's all right because you're living with your parents and you don't have to feed yourself. But when you're an adult and you're having to pay your bills and survive, it's an insult. I'd think, *Hang on, I'm making every team, I'm on TV regularly, which is a big thing for brands, and if it wasn't for athletes putting the brands around, they wouldn't be out there.* There are loads of athletes out there running around in kit and they're not being paid. I've always painted my spikes over. I don't want to piss the brands off, but I'm not wearing their stuff for free. It doesn't have to be a lot. Just give me some incentive to step out there and feel proud. Otherwise I think I'm getting extorted. Kit's not going to pay my bills.'

It would be good to report that James Ellington's sporting story had a happy ending, but as yet that remains unclear. He won gold medals at two European Championships, and a switch in focus from the 200 to the 100 metres saw his personal best drop to a sliver over ten seconds in 2016 – still a few metres behind Usain Bolt though. At warm weather training in Tenerife at the start of 2017 he was riding pillion behind fellow athlete Nigel Levine when a car travelling towards them on the wrong side of the road ploughed into their motorbike. Ellington's injuries were substantial, leaving him facing a lengthy recovery process.

This athlete knew how vital the safety net of medical support provided by the National Lottery was, having been well acquainted with the harsh financial climate outside the system. When we meet, Ellington is a few months into rehab and confident of his recovery. One eye, however, is on his post-athletics career. Sprintfit is a business he is developing with a partner to coach professionals in other sports how to run effectively. 'As soon as I'm making way more money from Sprintfit than I am from athletics – which wouldn't be hard – then I'll just fade it out.'

In putting himself up for an eBay auction, James Ellington was effectively selling the right to have him endorse a product and to use his image in the process. Trading of endorsements and image rights is central to the economics of modern sport, causing headaches for team owners and governing bodies, and also for the taxman. At the heart of this trade is the recognition that a sportsperson's value is partly related directly to their efforts on the field of play, and partly to the halo effect their reputation can create for companies and brands.

Footballers' arrangements with their clubs now typically split into two contracts. The first is a conventional contract of employment. The second is a contract between the club and a company set up on behalf of the player to own and manage his image rights. These rights are not simply for photographs of the footballer, but also cover a wide range of identifiers. They might include his nickname, initials and autograph – in effect any unique way in which the player can be identified and that identification used in association with a commercial enterprise.

The principal benefit to the player of this arrangement is that while his employment contract is taxed at the top personal income tax rate, his commercial income is subject to corporation tax, which is levied at a far lower rate – currently 19 per cent in the UK, so less than half the highest personal rate. When money is eventually paid out of the image rights company to the player, he will be subject to income tax on what he receives. However, canny management of the flows of cash can ensure that tax is minimised. For example, a foreign player can wait to draw on the image rights funds sitting in his company until after he has left the UK. Not surprisingly, many image rights companies are domiciled overseas, potentially benefitting from lower tax rates or more lenient regimes. A British player might delay receipt of commercial income until he has retired, effectively treating the payments as a pension. He will still be liable to tax, but he may have few or no other sources of income at this stage and so should end up paying a lower total tax bill over the years.

The differential between the tax rates for personal and corporate income clearly opens up the possibility of tax evasion if a disproportionate amount of a player's total income from his club is deemed to relate to his image rights. In response to abuses of the system, HMRC has set a pair of limits in an attempt to minimise tax leakage. First, a maximum of 20 per cent of a footballer's total remuneration from his club can be deemed to relate to image rights. Second, clubs can only spend a total of 15 per cent of their commercial revenue on image rights arrangements with their playing staff. Such constraints are likely to prove advantageous to some players but restrictive for others. A second-string player with no material value beyond his contribution on the pitch may effectively bank a windfall in the form of an artificially low tax bill. Conversely, a star whose value extends far beyond his output in matches might have a deemed commercial value much greater than his total club remuneration, and hence be missing out on a higher tax break if the limit did not apply. Individuals can argue the case for a bespoke arrangement with the taxman, although it is hard to secure exemptions.

There can be no doubt that the image rights industry irks HMRC. Late in 2016 its then head of enforcement, Jennie Granger, told the House of Commons Public Accounts Committee that forty-three footballers, twelve British clubs and eight agents were then under investigation by a specialist team looking at the question of image rights across the sports and entertainment industries. She claimed the team's work had pulled in £158 million from the football industry in the previous two years. The subject was topical at the time. Earlier in the year it had been reported that José Mourinho's arrival at Manchester United as manager had been held up because his image rights remained the property of his previous employer, Chelsea, rather than the manager himself, and were the subject of difficult negotiations between all the parties.

It may be that the scope for exploiting image rights to manage tax bills is reducing. The spring budget in 2017 promised 'guidelines for employers who make payments of image rights to their employees to improve the clarity of the existing rules'. Tax lawyers and tax accountants will doubtless be at the ready. If any of their clients questioned the seriousness of HMRC's intent to ensure tax compliance within football, the dawn raids on Newcastle United and West Ham United seven weeks after the budget will have left them in no doubt. The Revenue, supported by the French authorities, announced that the raids and accompanying arrests related to 'a suspected £5m income tax and national insurance fraud'.

It is not just in the UK that image rights attract the interest of the tax authorities. Lionel Messi and his father were convicted of tax fraud in 2016 in Spain in a case relating to his image rights. A year later the same authorities also accused Cristiano Ronaldo of using an offshore company to avoid declaring income, including from image rights. By late 2017 the case had yet to be heard.

It is unusual for a player, or manager, to cede ownership of his image rights to his employer. Instead, clubs typically enter into licensing deals that enable them to exploit the individual's endorsement value in support of their overall commercial strategy. Conflicts can arise where the individual has existing associations with major brands in the same area as their club's sponsors. This was reported to be another devil in the detail of Mourinho's contractual negotiations with Manchester United, the two having different watch and car endorsements for example. Certainly, marrying the interests of club and player is a perennial challenge in team sports. This is multiplied when it comes to the management of national teams.

In the aftermath of London 2012, at UK Athletics we found ourselves in need of new sponsors, having relied on them heavily for financial support for both our televised athletics meetings and the British team over many years. Along with most of Britain's Olympic and Paralympic sports we discovered that the prospect of the next Games being held in Rio de Janeiro was significantly less attractive to British companies than London. Many sponsors folded their tents or reduced their financial commitments. As a consequence, the market was crowded with sellers of sporting rights; buyers clearly had the whip hand.

From a long list of possible commercial partners, our marketing team gradually whittled down the prospects to a few that appeared to represent strong contenders. One was Santander UK, which had reputational issues around customer service to address and for whom sports sponsorship appeared a possible route to an enhanced reputation and greater public recognition. Through many rounds of meetings, we allowed ourselves to become privately enthusiastic about our chances of securing a deal to back the British athletics team.

The trail went cold, however. Shortly after, Santander unveiled its new wall-to-wall advertising campaign featuring Rory McIlroy, Jenson Button and 'our own' Jessica Ennis-Hill. With hindsight, the bank may not have gone with the best racing driver, but they certainly secured the best golfer and athlete that the British Isles had to offer. Of course, we had no idea what financial commitment Santander made to the three stars, but in all likelihood the bank got all of the benefits it was seeking from an association with athletics for less than the cost of sponsoring the entire British team through the governing body. A smart strategy.

The key is that Jessica Ennis-Hill, quite rightly, was never 'our own', however often she competed for Britain and whatever support UK Athletics and UK Sport may have provided during her career. The use of individual sportspeople to promote teams, both domestic and national, is financially critical to the funding of those teams though. This becomes a key element in contractual arrangements between team and individual. In receiving National Lottery funding, athletes have to commit to a number of days of promotional activity in support of the Lottery. This aside, however, their commercial appearances are all by negotiation. At the domestic level in team sports, clubs can tie players into promotional commitments from the outset of their employment. It is a different matter at international level. Sports such as cricket with its central contracts can replicate the arrangements typical of domestic teams, but when a footballer is called up to represent his country, the overriding interests of both his day-to-day club employer and any personal sponsors can place powerful restrictions on his national team's commercial activity.

Kit manufacturers are among the most powerful players in the three-way tussle between club, country and individual. The restrictions on athletes and players when it comes to representing their club or country are codified in team-member agreements and employment contracts, and they are expected to conform to strict dress codes when on duty. For a British Olympian, this is broadly defined as 'from plane to plane'. From the moment the athlete steps onto the plane to fly off to a Games until the moment he or she disembarks back at Heathrow a few weeks later he or she is expected to wear Team GB's training, leisure and competition wear provided by official kit supplier Adidas at all times. The one material exception is competition footwear – ostensibly to allow athletes to make the best choice for their performances – so shoes become the ambush marketing opportunity for Adidas' rivals. The same is true of all major nations' Olympic teams, and also of team sports, including football, rugby and cricket. We've yet to see footballers dangling their boots around their necks as they leave the pitch, but this familiar sight in athletics is not because athletes find running spikes uncomfortable on their laps of honour; it is because the individual may be paid to ensure the three stripes of Adidas on their feet detract from the Nike swoosh on their team shirt, or vice versa.

The kit battle in athletics is waged primarily between Nike and Adidas, although Puma dress the high-profile Jamaican team and Asics have signed up a handful of nations. Puma have an individual deal with Usain Bolt as well as with his national federation. This means Jamaica has avoided the frustrations of dealing with its key athlete that bedevil so many national teams. The British athletics team was kitted out by Adidas until 2013, which made it relatively easy to agree promotional activity with Adidas-sponsored athletes such as Christine Ohuruogu and Jessica Ennis, but torturous to work with Nike-sponsored athletes – at least when we wanted them to appear in British vests. That year we changed our kit sponsor to Nike and the difficulties reversed. With clothing companies paying athletes substantial sums for instant public association with their marques, it is no wonder that they resist the use of imagery of them sporting rivals' products. Petty as it may seem, it can even be a struggle to persuade an athlete to agree to attend a press conference in their British kit the day after they have won a medal, their agent dancing to another sponsor's tune and arranging a rival conference in its own branded clothing.

Kit deals form a significant part of sportspeople's income, and not only the top stars. The manufacturers have talent-scouting teams with budgets to sign up youngsters across all the major sports in the hope of establishing relationships that will endure with those athletes who become successful. In the early days these may simply involve the provision of kit and a modest sum of cash, but they can scale up quickly to tens of thousands of pounds for those deemed to have the right mix of potential and personality. And those who become stars often find themselves with the same kit sponsor throughout their career and beyond it into a retirement of media punditry or sports politics. These relationships can run very deep.

One of Seb Coe's early missteps as newly elected president of the IAAF was resisting calls for him to relinquish his relationship with Nike on the grounds of a potential conflict of interest. Under a barrage of criticism, he eventually conceded, but having run in Nike kit for almost all his career and become contracted to the company in retirement, it would be no surprise if he reactivates the relationship when his presidency draws to a close. Even now Coe can occasionally be seen at events wearing the Nike swoosh, although previously Adidas and now Asics are the IAAF's official kit sponsor. At an athletics meeting in Australia in early 2017 his decision to use sticky tape to cover the New Balance logo on the England shirt he was wearing while watching his country compete met with tweets of derision. His Nike shorts and sneakers below the shirt remained unadulterated.

It's inconceivable that members of Team GB or the England football team could one day compete in non-identical uniforms, whatever the pressures exerted by athletes and players on the back of their personal kit sponsorships. Or is it? Britain's triumphant Davis Cup team of 2015 did not all play with the logo of the official supplier to British Tennis, Nike, on their chests. Nor that of team sponsor, insurer Aegon. Look back at photos of their victory celebration and you will see team captain Leon Smith in full regalia, but Andy Murray's tracksuit carrying only the Union flag and the rest of the team shorn of Nike but happy to promote Aegon. Murray's commitment to Davis Cup tennis was instrumental in Britain's rise to the top, but he was an Under Armour player with his own roster of sponsors including financial services giant Standard Life, a direct competitor of Aegon. Finding a commercial accommodation was doubtless one important element in the governing body securing his commitment to the team.

One American athlete, middle-distance runner Nick Symmonds, railed against the restrictive uniform requirements of USA Track & Field, his Nike-sponsored governing body, ahead of the 2013 World Championships in Beijing. Symmonds, a Brooks rather than a Nike athlete, had won a silver medal at the previous Championships and qualified for the US team for China at the American trials. His refusal to sign the USATF team-member agreement cost him his place on the plane. As a principled stance, whatever the legal rights and wrongs of his argument, this takes some beating. Symmonds was injured ahead of the Rio 2016 Olympics and retired a few months after. This left his lone stand against what he perceived to be the tyranny of the kit companies and the bodies they sponsor as the final high-profile event in his competitive career. We are unlikely to have heard the last of Symmonds, however, nor of the issues he raised about the rights of individuals and the apportioning of the spoils in international sport.

When you enter a shop in search of a new pair of trainers or pull on the replica football shirt of your favourite team plastered with its sponsor logos, you become part of the mighty power

struggle between the brands who have chosen sport as their battleground. The stars, the teams they play for and the owners of
the events they compete in are acutely aware of their role – and
their financial value – in this contest for consumer awareness and
approbation. You may believe you are impervious to brand managers' stratagems, but they believe otherwise, and their decisions
are critical to the flow of money through the sporting economy,
and in sorting the financial haves from the have-nots.

7

TOXICITY OUT OF THE WATER

When Americans look back on Rio 2016, their abiding memory might be Simone Biles' four gold medals. The nineteen-year-old stood only four feet eight inches tall, but she had the personality of a giant and a backstory that combined with her gymnastic prowess to capture the heart of her nation. Just as likely, though, they will remember Ryan Lochte's downfall. The swimmer's claim that he had been robbed at gunpoint when in fact he had caused criminal damage at a gas station while inebriated received blanket coverage across the globe. By the time he was back in the US and appearing in apologetic mode on NBC, his spiky green hair had become a demure brown to match the disgraced sportsman's contrite demeanour. Already, however, all four of Lochte's sponsors were deciding to sever their ties with him.

Ryan Lochte's Olympics had not brought him his hoped-for success in the pool. A single gold relay medal was a modest addition to his eleven medals from previous Games, and was overshadowed by the five golds of compatriot Michael Phelps. A chemical reaction between his silver hair dye and the chlorine in the Rio pool – the apparent cause of his green-tinged coif – vied with his sporting underperformance as the narrative of Lochte's summer before his tall tale of armed robbery spiralled out of control. The immediate aftermath of his exposure bore all the hallmarks of a PR scramble designed to limit the damage to his value as a commercial asset. Although the first reaction of sponsors was to reach for the termination clauses in their contracts, his handlers would have been aiming to prepare the ground for his eventual rehabilitation.

Others had gone before – witness the storm around the breakdown of Tiger Woods' marriage – and others would come after. Indeed, Maria Sharapova's success earlier in 2016 in holding on to Evian and Head as sponsors showed that there is no such thing as a guaranteed lost cause. While some companies dropped the Russian tennis star from their rosters when she was banned for a doping offence, the water company decided to stick with her, and racket manufacturer Head went so far as to describe her ban as a 'flawed decision'. Nike had a change of heart and reversed an initial separation. By the time she returned to competition at the Porsche Grand Prix in Stuttgart in April 2017, her PR handlers could congratulate themselves on an effective rearguard action, ensuring her coterie of partners was undiminished. Porsche itself was on the list.

Nike has form in sticking with athletes mired in controversy. It dropped Lance Armstrong in 2012 when evidence of his doping offences cited by the anti-doping agency USADA became impossible to ignore. However, the sportswear manufacturer re-signed sprinter Justin Gatlin when he returned to athletics after serving the second of his doping bans. This apparent lack of consistency suggests there are gradations of offence in the eyes of sponsors. Similarly, Sharapova's case demonstrates that different companies can reach opposite conclusions about the threat to their reputations posed by sportspeople who topple from their pedestals. Those inclined to leniency, or loyalty, are likely in large part to be making a judgement about the willingness of the public to embrace a repentant sinner and to engage with a tale of redemption, and the value to their brands of being associated with a successful recovery. Sharapova may also have benefitted from the media and fans of tennis having less doping fatigue than watchers of, say, cycling or athletics.

While for some companies a squeaky clean image is essential, for most a little light controversy – on and off the field of play – may be no bad thing. The imputed value of media coverage for a brand is at the heart of nearly all sponsorship decisions. A commercial property needs to be in the news to be seen, and ideally not just at game time. Confected puff pieces from PR companies can fill empty newspaper column inches and website space, but it is the unscripted stories that tend to take on a life of their own, multiplying coverage and with it brand imagery and recognition. Chelsea FC's media exposure went sharply up when the club fell out spectacularly with manager José Mourinho early in the 2015/16 season, even though in the comparable period a year earlier it had been in the process of putting together a winning run on the pitch that would lead to the Premier League title. This surge in media interest came just after the club had agreed a new partnership deal with a Thai company that had identified football as the platform from which to launch its product into the British market, so providing a wholly unexpected demonstration of the reach of the Chelsea brand that was central to the sponsor's plans.

Carabao is one of the leading energy drinks brands in its manufacturer's home market of Thailand, where it takes its name from local rock star Aed Carabao and his eponymous group. The singer is a founding partner in the drinks business, whose shares are listed on the Bangkok Stock Exchange. The Carabao logo of a buffalo skull atop a red sun motif is ingrained in the consciousness of local consumers, but at the start of the 2016/17 football season was completely unknown in Britain. Carabao's international CEO at the time, Peter Gutierrez, had plotted a route to

British consumers' psyches that focused on football, and began with a bold financial commitment to the power of the Chelsea FC brand. 'Remember, 750 new soft drinks have tried to launch in the UK in the last three years alone. Most of them have failed. So there's a lot of buyer fatigue around, people calling up for a meeting to discuss new products. Getting customer attention is a real challenge.' Gutierrez's solution was to get his distinctive buffalo logo onto Chelsea's training kit in a multi-million-pound sponsorship deal, ensuring a continuous association with the west London club and its global fan base. The deal was announced in November 2015, less than a month before Mourinho was sacked.

'Our sponsorship of Chelsea FC's training wear came from our insight that football support has changed. Global fans, especially in newer Asian markets, today follow a portfolio of global teams – Bayern, Man U, Liverpool, Real Madrid, PSG, Barcelona, Chelsea. So Chelsea have huge support, not just from "Chelsea till I die" diehards but from a growing community of multi-club followers. The other phenomenon that I love to focus on is the nature of that following. It is 24/7 and the followers want to know what is going on, in real time. That means they are online news-hunting, and when they find what they are looking for – the players, the staff of Chelsea FC are wearing Carabao training wear, because that's what they live in all week, even on match day until the moment the tracksuit comes off for the start of the match. I predict, in part as a result of Carabao's partnership with Chelsea, that training-wear deals are one of the next big nuggets of value to be unlocked within football – and indeed other sports – for the big clubs and brands who enjoy global followings.'

Gutierrez likens the drama of top-flight football to the 1980s TV soap *Dallas*. 'There are good things happening in one episode and then catastrophes the next. From a domestic point of view, you can't go wrong. Everyone wants to know what's happening at Chelsea.' And the persona of the club's current manager only helps. 'The other thing that is serendipitous is that Antonio Conte is right on-brand.' Whether swinging from the roof of the dugout or diving into the crowd, the Italian manager is undeniably good box office. In Asia Chelsea's profile is 'phenomenal', Gutierrez observes. 'It's as if they are like the Asian economy. They are both the new kids on the block. There's an unspoken kinship there somewhere subconsciously. So the sponsorship deal immediately has a value in Asian markets.' It's not just in west London that fans want to know how the players are training, what they've had for breakfast and who's fallen out with whom.

The sheer scale of public interest in football leaves room for a new entrant, even though the blur of advertising images that envelops the sport highlights the challenge of creating awareness. Carabao UK's former head reels off the statistics from the company's market research: 22.7 million fans in the UK, 7.5 million of them energy drinkers, broadly spread geographically. The growth of the women's game is especially appealing, as women often make the buying decision in the drinks market, especially once a brand is established. Gutierrez cites 7.5 million female football fans in the UK, the interest in the UEFA Women's Euro 2017 tournament and inspirational role models in the Chelsea Ladies FC team as integral to the sponsorship decision he took. 'I think investments of the type we made represent great value as long as they are used as an opportunity not only to do the obvious things like using the first team to billboard a brand logo in the case of Chelsea, but to mine the full possibilities that lie, some of them undiscovered, others ignored, in partners. Football is on a marketing journey of its own trying to pick its way out of a macho male corner into a more enlightened and much bigger world, which is exactly what Carabao is trying to do with energy drinks, so the two are on very similar missions. Both football and energy drinks need to transform their appeal. Football is well on the way and both want this same thing.'

Three months into its inaugural sponsorship season with Chelsea, and with its logo also on the shirts of Reading FC, Carabao moved to embrace the other ninety league clubs in England when the Football League announced the company as the latest title sponsor of the EFL Cup. The EFL had gambled on having an unbranded competition for a season while it sought a replacement for the departed Capital One credit card company. Carabao was duly unveiled as the latest sponsor of a competition that has numbered the Milk Marketing Board, football pools company Littlewoods, electrical retailer Rumbelows, Coca-Cola and a couple of beer brands as its partners over the past four decades. The League did not reveal details of the deal, although the BBC reported it as being valued at £18 million over three years. Unsurprisingly, the accompanying press release pointed to the promise of greater awareness in Asia for the newly named Carabao Cup.

Peter Gutierrez saw the EFL's cup competition as a means of addressing fully the third of the population that consider themselves football fans. 'Doing it with one club is difficult. Doing it with all ninety-two clubs is a wonderful opportunity. That's why we went down the EFL route. There are a few great things about it. One is that it's the first big final of the season. Another is that the early matches gave us a chance to engage with the wider community before the big boys got engaged. There are some great backstories about all the star players such as Wayne Rooney being blooded in the League Cup. And then there comes a point when the top clubs are in it to win it. Big matches can and do happen. This year you had a Manchester derby and Liverpool versus Tottenham in the last sixteen. Think about that in terms of both domestic and global appeal. The other thing is the League Cup is littered with stories of giant-killing. Oxford have won it. QPR have won it.'

Judgement as to the success of Carabao's twin assault on the football market (or triple including Reading FC) will depend on sales of its energy drinks in the years to come. In the meantime, Gutierrez says it will likely rely on conventional measures of 'media value' generated by eyeballs on the red buffalo, 'a brand with zero awareness, going from zero to something, spending a lot of money on a property'. He describes Carabao as a company 'going for it. When I was there we did make clear-sighted calculations, but were allergic to talking ourselves out of great opportunities.'

Even before the result of the Chelsea and EFL ventures is known, Carabao is looking to replicate its football route to market in other territories. A six-year shirt sponsorship of Rio de Janiero's Flamengo was announced at the end of 2016 with a value reported in the media of R$190 million (£49 million). The country is football crazy and unlikely to fall out of love with the sport any time soon, while Flamengo is the nation's best-supported team in spite of its lack of success in recent years. Eight years on from the club's last Série A title, its new sponsor is clearly investing heavily in the hope that Flamengo can join the list of global football brands collected by today's polygamous multi-club followers, while helping Carabao to crack the crowded Brazilian drinks market in which its product is entirely unknown.

It has been calculated that 80 per cent of Fortune 500 companies in the United States invest in sport. And yet one specialist report describes sports sponsorship as 'arguably the riskiest weapon in the marketers' armoury', citing the possibility of backlashes from fans and the fragile popularity of sports and their stars. There is a sense too that company sponsorship can still be the personal plaything of business leaders excited by the opportunity of indulging their own passions at the expense of their shareholders. Consultants IEG estimate that the global sponsorship market in 2015 totalled $57.5 billion, just over a third of it in the United States. Of the latter, 70 per cent was devoted to sport as opposed to the arts, entertainment and other causes. That's a lot of scope for sporting self-indulgence from the leaders of the world's corporations.

There can be no doubt that this appetite for sport in board-rooms is a godsend for an industry which relies heavily on spon-sor dollars to balance its books. Consultants A. T. Kearney cal-culate that in 2013 35 per cent of the estimated $76 billion revenues from sporting events worldwide came from sponsorship. The sale of broadcast rights accounted for a similar proportion, and ticket sales only 27 per cent. UK Athletics has worked with a few different sports marketing agencies over recent years in its search for commercial partners for its events. One, the Sports Consultancy, was founded by Angus Buchanan, a lawyer and former professional yachtsman who was the youngest crew mem-ber in a record-breaking non-stop circumnavigation of the globe back in 1994. Over the past couple of decades he has seen what he describes as the 'clichéd chairman's whim' diminish in impor-tance in commercial decisions, but not entirely disappear.

'A chairman would sponsor a sport on the basis of personal preference – and some instinct, you'd assume, that the fit was good for the brand, that the sponsorship was good for the busi-ness – but then let the marketing department make an *ex post facto* justification of the decision. But I still feel that, more often than not, there's some level of preference working at C-suite level – chief executives and chief financial officers – and above around sport.' Buchanan cites Virgin Money's decision to replace Flora as title sponsor of the London Marathon as just such a modern hybrid of preference, instinct and analysis. 'The kernel of that idea was something that Richard Branson really identified as an opportunity. And I'm absolutely certain that you could characterise it as a chairman's whim. But instilled in all of that was a fair sense of what was absolutely right for the brand and the business, and when analysed it works extremely well for the company.' The challenge for the marketer, then, is to seek out marriages between sports and businesses that, as he portrays it, 'work well for left brain and right brain'.

That said, measurement of the impact of sports sponsorship is critical and has become more sophisticated over time. Traditionally, companies have used yardsticks created by the advertising industry and its media buyers. Consultants calculate 'equivalent media value' created by sponsorship programmes. In essence, this equates the financial impact a sponsor achieves to the visibility it would get from money spent on conventional advertising, whether on TV, billboards, in print media or online. The number of eyeballs that see a sponsor's logo is central to the analysis, refined to reflect the demographic of those who are watching. The challenge for sports is that this fails to take account of the wider benefits of sponsorship that they are attempting to sell to potential partners, whether hospitality for key clients, staff engagement or community benefits. Angus Buchanan believes that 'sport falls into a trap of justifying itself by the advertising industry's, by the media buyers industry's, set of rules. Sponsorship is much better value than an ad campaign because you can do so much more with it.'

Management consultants McKinsey, in their search for new business, have claimed that swathes of companies fail to assess the impact of their sports sponsorship effectively. 'Considering the huge amounts involved, you would imagine sponsors of athletes and events have clear answers when asked about their return on investment [ROI]. You would be wrong. Industry research reveals that about one third to one half of US companies don't have a system in place to measure sponsorship ROI comprehensively.' As well as failure to measure, McKinsey also highlight research suggesting that many companies fail to spend sufficient sums on top of their core sponsorship contracts in order to make the most of their support for a sport or team. This 'activation' spending is a vital part of any sponsorship arrangement and might involve, for example, direct promotions to customers or an ostentatious presence for a brand at sports events.

Dairy company Müller went to great lengths to publicise their sponsorship of London 2017, from promotions on their packs of yogurts, through an athletics-themed television ad campaign fronted by Nicole Scherzinger, to kids' activities at the event itself. They almost certainly achieved higher public awareness for their association with the championships than the IAAF's own global sponsors, who made less apparent effort to shout about their involvement. Similarly, Lloyds' Local Heroes activation programme probably ensured the bank had greater consumer impact within the UK than any other sponsor of London 2012.

McKinsey cite activation spending that typically ranges from as little as $0.50 for every $1 spent on buying core sponsorship rights up to $1.60. Just placing a logo on something isn't enough, you have to spend more to 'own' it. As these figures show, this activation spending will often dwarf the basic terms of the sponsorship deal, and typically little or none of this additional outlay will flow to the rights holder – the sport or team itself.

Getting the nuances of activation activity right is vitally important to the perceived success of a sponsorship. As consumers have become more discerning, or cynical, in their attitude to big business, so in Angus Buchanan's eyes this importance has increased. 'People are becoming a little bit blind to the brand just slapped on the shirt. It's important that it's there, but it only works if it is supported really well by engaging digital campaigns to show that it is really adding value to sports, spectators and fans. It's less a passive slap your brand on the property, smack its arse and let it charge off into the distance; you have to be much more engaged with the audience by using content to support what you were doing traditionally via perimeter signage or shirt sponsorship. Your contribution as a brand to a sport must be genuine. People cry bullshit very quickly these days if they think it looks less than authentic, or if they think you are simply riding their interest in the sport. There has to be an authentic engagement and it has to go beyond simple signage. It must run deeper than that.' On the plus side, he sees evidence in America in particular of fans increasingly exercising consumer choices in favour of those brands that they view as supporting the teams they follow.

The rapid shift in advertising spend across all industries from traditional media to digital platforms creates challenges for sports and their sponsors steeped in old methodologies for reaching consumers based around logo visibility on shirts and at events. Even the sight of rugby players coated in the paint from sponsor logos on the middle of the pitch may in time become a thing of the past. The logos could just as easily be digitally applied for television audiences, and spare those in the ground the sight of strangely shaped logos designed to appear normal to those viewing through the TV cameras' wide-angle lenses.

The principal digital challenge is the proliferation of noise online and on mobile. The opportunity is to cut through this and interact with consumers – if a company can find them – who exactly match the profile of those deemed most likely to buy their products. Sponsorship in the modern age can strike a target audience more surgically, which means that conventional metrics of impact, such as equivalent media value, are of greatly diminished worth. Angus Buchanan worries that the marketing industry is struggling with the crossover from the old to the new world. 'Digital gives you real levels of engagement, but the numbers are smaller than you would otherwise be claiming through broadcast, so effectively it's a much narrower form of very direct and very personal communication of the sports audience with the brand. But the industry is still measuring that by the cost per thousand that you would otherwise be paying to get that exposure. There still doesn't seem to be a very elegant measure of the value of the sponsorship.'

Digital drives conventional media too, so blurring the measures. Carabao celebrated April Fool's Day with the online launch of a new small can of its energy drink, which it called Kantebao in honour of Chelsea's diminutive midfielder N'Golo Kanté. 'Half the size, twice the energy,' its spoof ad claimed. On a day crowded with sporting leg-pulls, the online campaign made the conventional media's round-up of the best of that year's 1 April crop.

The 2017 edition of Deloitte's annual analysis of its football money league, *Planet Football*, lists the total Twitter, Facebook and Instagram likes and followers of the top twenty clubs in the world, alongside their total revenues, average attendances and playing performances. FC Barcelona tops the table of digital acolytes, although it is second on the income list behind Manchester United. The Catalan club had revenues of £464 million in 2016 and 159 million followers across the three platforms. Many of these fans will be double-counted, but its 96 million Facebook likes is a strong indication of the club's global reach. The population of Spain by contrast is 46 million, its Catalonia region 7.5 million and the city of Barcelona itself only 1.6 million. The wonder is that the club is not able to drive much higher revenues from such a huge base of people worldwide interested in following its fortunes, who are engaged with the digital world and therefore capable of entering into a financial transaction without setting foot in Barcelona's Camp Nou stadium.

The figures for other clubs are less stark, and the total number of digital supporters falls sharply as you scan down the Deloitte money league. Chelsea, eighth in the table, have 63 million digital followers; Inter Milan, in nineteenth place, attract a mere 9 million. Nevertheless, for the largest football clubs, their ratio of financial income to followers suggests that they may currently only be scratching the surface of potential sponsor income in the online age. A comparison with the NFL, although very crude, underlines the point. Trackalytics lists the Dallas Cowboys as the NFL franchise with the most Facebook likes at just under 9 million, so less than a tenth of FC Barcelona's. In 2016 the Cowboys had revenues of $700 million and *Forbes* estimated the franchise to have a value of $4.2 billion. Even the Jacksonville Jaguars, bottom of the Facebook list with only 600,000 likes, had revenues of $344 million. A wide variety of factors are at play, in particular the peculiarities of the NFL's structure, but the Americans are clearly much more proficient at mining fans' interest in their sport.

Just as holders of sporting assets may be failing to capitalise fully on their value, however great the sums involved in individual transactions might seem, so many corporations struggle to convert their association with sport into a meaningful uplift in their recognition and respect among consumers. One consultancy specialising in insight analytics, Alva, has produced an assessment of the impact of Rio 2016 sponsorship programmes. It measured changes brands enjoyed as a result of the Olympics using three criteria: visibility, likeability and advocacy. These are intended to work inwards to the heart of the value of sponsorship for a company: creating awareness, overcoming a general passivity or neutrality towards a brand and then generating very positive endorsement of it.

Alva's study concluded that the International Olympic Committee's eleven global Olympic partners enjoyed a 34 per cent increase in visibility during Rio, but only a 2 per cent improvement in their likeability. Perhaps surprisingly, McDonald's enjoyed a 10 per cent boost on this measure but Coca-Cola a 7 per cent fall. The consultancy cites online excitement generated by athletes queuing for the burger restaurant in the Olympic Village, contrasted with health concerns over the drinks giant's association with the Games. This just goes to show the fine line between creating positive and negative vibes. Moving on to the third measure, Alva observed, 'When we ran our analysis of which global Olympic partners had generated the greatest level of brand advocacy, the stark finding was . . . that none of them had.' Overall, it awarded a gold medal to Samsung, silver to McDonald's and bronze to Procter & Gamble, but warned the corporate world that sports sponsorship was unlikely to boost advocacy, and that increased visibility would not necessarily translate into likeability. In the summer of 2017, ten months after the Rio Games, McDonald's shocked the marketing world by terminating its IOC sponsorship contract three years early, so ending an Olympic relationship stretching back over four decades.

Sports, companies and agencies alike can regularly be heard bemoaning the toughness of the commercial market. In part this is simply business as usual in any industry. Growth in sponsorship continued unabated through the global financial crisis, when it might have been expected to be one of the first items of discretionary corporate expenditure to be cut. The fallout from the collapse of British bank RBS certainly included reports of its new management trying to terminate a slew of sports sponsorship arrangements that had been signed off by its ousted leaders. This, though, appears not to have been a typical business reaction, so testifying to the strength of commitment to sport as a way to consumers' affections.

Surveying the resilience of spending on sport, Angus Buchanan describes sponsorship as 'acyclical'. The challenges, and hence the grumbles about toughness from those within the industry, lie in the proliferation of sporting properties vying for corporate supporters and the fragmentation of the media. Overall spending on sports sponsorship may continue to rise, but competition for sponsor dollars appears to be outstripping the available cash. New sports are emerging, notably esports; others are becoming wiser and more aggressive in their approach to sponsors; and some of the larger sports such as cricket are developing novel formats of the game that create different propositions to take to market. Football's strong growth – an acyclical dream for its owners – makes the market even more crowded for other participants. At the same time, sponsors must confront the modern digital age, even if they are unsure as yet exactly how to reach their target audience. It may be in future that they will be able to do that more precisely and at far lower cost. But for now their uncertainty is likely to necessitate even greater activation spending than before on top of their base sponsorship costs, if only to make sure that potential customers don't slip through the online cracks.

Your decision about which football, rugby or cricket team to support, or which sport to follow, may well be a seismic one for you personally, involving a major emotional commitment that could last a lifetime. By contrast, your decision about which yogurt or energy drink to consume before you leave home to watch a game, or which beer to buy if you stop off at a bar en route, may be the product of barely a moment's thought or simply an instinctual reaction to those options you happen to be presented with. Be sure though that your choices are being monitored and, as far as possible, assessed in relation to your sporting allegiances. The stronger the correlation, the healthier the financial prospects of those sporting loves that you have committed your heart to.

8

RELEASE THOSE BIG MONEY BALLS

David Pond, CEO of GB Wheelchair Rugby, waited by the phone on 9 December 2016 for a scheduled early-morning call from the chief executive of UK Sport, Liz Nicholl. At the same time, UK Athletics' CEO, Niels de Vos, sat waiting to hear from Nicholl's director of performance, Chelsea Warr. Both were about to hear the outcome of their submissions for elite sports funding through to the Tokyo 2020 Games. Only one was to hear what he wanted.

De Vos relayed the good news for athletics to me within minutes of taking the call from Warr. It may have been wisdom after the event, but he said he knew we would be all right when he was told that Warr rather than Nicholl would be talking to him. With hindsight, Pond concedes, 'I was slightly suspicious it was Liz making that call.' Wheelchair rugby was denied Lottery funding for its elite team and supporting programmes. It was only right that the top woman should have taken it upon herself to break the news. Suddenly British 'murder ball' was cast into the Games wilderness, victim of the overall success of Team GB and Para-lympicsGB in Rio. 'I have to be honest, it was a massive shock for me,' Pond recalls. 'Although Liz said – and I wrote the words down very carefully – that we had medal potential, she said that their money just wouldn't stretch far enough for us.' British sport had simply been too triumphant in Rio.

Sporting success has many fathers, and it is too simplistic to explain Britain's rise up the Games medal tables solely by the growth in financial investment channelled through UK Sport. Nevertheless, this rise in funding is routinely credited as being the most significant factor in transforming an Olympic team that won one gold medal in Atlanta 1996 to the country that came second in the Rio table with 27 golds. The birth of the National Lottery in 1994 was followed shortly thereafter by the formation of UK Sport in 1997 and its authorisation as a distributor of Lottery funds. Rio's success prompted retrospective credit being given to former prime minister and renowned sports fan John Major for his original foresight in facilitating these developments.

London's triumph in 2005 in winning the right to host the 2012 Games enabled UK Sport to lobby successfully for a jump in overall funding to mint British medals at a home Olympics and Paralympics. In his budget of spring 2006 Chancellor Gordon Brown announced a total additional £300 million exchequer investment in elite sport to supplement UK Sport's Lottery income. The Beijing Games bore the first fruit of this, and success at London 2012 gave UK Sport the ammunition to lobby for sustained funding, with the ambition of Britain being the first nation to move on from a home Games to win more medals at the next Olympics and Paralympics. In the four years to March 2017 UK Sport invested £387 million of its overall £543 million income into what it terms World Class Performance, across the Winter and Summer Games, but crucially not into every British sport entering a team into those Games.

Only a few weeks into my job as UKA's chairman in 2007 I distanced us from the medal targets being bruited in the months after the chancellor's investment increase. 'I refuse to be hanged on that target' did not endear me to those who had fought so hard to persuade the Treasury. Understandably so. At one seminar shortly after my comments UK Sport's director of policy and communications at the time, Tim Hollingsworth, cornered me to complain that I was jeopardising all that they had worked for.

With targets, of course, come sanctions, whether to individuals' jobs, athletes' personal funding, or organisations' overall income. The bluntness of the medal target stick was brought home most frustratingly to me after the London 2012 Olympics. Our head coach, Charles van Commenee, the most plain-speaking of sporting leaders, had told the media on the way back from our team's Portuguese training camp ahead of the Games that if athletics didn't hit the top of its six- to eight-medal target range, as set by UK Sport, then he would feel obliged to resign. In the event, notwithstanding Super Saturday and his team winning four gold medals for the first time since 1964, van Commenee felt honour-bound to follow through on his promise as the team's six-medal total, while in the range, was not at the top of it. There was doubtless a complex set of factors at play in his decision, but we were left without an excellent head coach after hitting our target, and all because Charles had set one of his own.

Whatever UK Sport may have thought of van Commenee's choice, his clarity of decision-making would have chimed with its own approach. A number of governing bodies received funding ahead of London 2012 because their teams gained entry to the Games solely by virtue of being from the home nation. UK Sport was quick to chop them from funding post-London if they hadn't succeeded. The highest-profile casualty at the end of 2012, certainly the one that received the most publicity, was GB Basketball. This was a governing body created specifically to deliver teams for London. Britain's only previous Olympic basketball appearance was in the last London Olympics, in 1948. This time its men's team won a single match, its women none. Not enough to point the way to success in Rio, and so UK Sport money disappeared, and with it almost certainly any realistic hope of future global success. An appeal saw this funding reinstated, only for it to be withdrawn again a year later. Basketball may be a sport with a huge young inner-city following, but for UK Sport that is for Sport England and the other home countries' sports councils to nurture. Unless elite success can be grown out of this grassroots base, to the point at which its international achievements demand recognition, UK Sport will deploy its resources elsewhere.

Decisions at the margins are always likely to be the most contentious, and conversations with UK Sport directors suggest that basketball was never close to being on the right side of the funding line after the home Games. The furore around these funding decisions – fast becoming a tradition – died down pretty quickly. This was not the case four years later in the aftermath of the Rio Games.

Again, UK Sport presented a case to government that must have proved compelling. Crimped by a slowdown in National Lottery sales, Chairman Rod Carr was nevertheless able to announce funding for sports' World Class Programmes that was in aggregate only 3 per cent lower for the four-year Tokyo cycle than for the years leading up to Rio. And he had a few million pounds up his sleeve to make adjustments over the coming years, meaning that the overall Tokyo investment would equal that for Rio. The ambition this time was 'to deliver more medals and medallists, across the Olympic and Paralympic Games, to inspire the nation'. As if to prove we had learned a lesson from my public objections of a decade earlier, or perhaps simply out of relief that cycling was the only major sport to suffer a material funding cut, UK Athletics provided a supportive quote from our CEO to adorn the UK Sport press release.

Four sports joined David Pond at GB Wheelchair Rugby in receiving the worst of news that morning: archery, badminton, fencing and weightlifting. What was different this time was that a sport that had won a medal in Rio – badminton – had suffered the swing of the funder's axe. This wasn't what any sport had been led to expect. Nor did others see the blade coming. Pond had no inkling that his sport would be dropped from the list. In the difficult days and weeks that followed he looked back on all his dialogue with UK Sport and, even with the benefit of hind-sight, he could not spot any clues. The wheelchair rugby team had finished fifth in Rio, in line with its funding level for those Games. It had been deemed what is termed a Podium Potential sport, and therefore required to demonstrate that it was on the way to winning a medal at a future Paralympics. As it was, Great Britain, the reigning European champions, were only seconds away from a victory in Rio that would have put them into the top four and playing for a medal. 'But for the bounce of a ball we'd have been in the semi-finals,' Pond argues. Little wonder that he was floored by his call from Liz Nicholl.

UK Sport funding for elite sports is geared entirely towards success at the Olympic and Paralympic Games. All other compe-titions are regarded merely as stepping stones towards the major quadrennial event, and as indicators of possible outcomes at those Games. Many of Britain's Olympic and Paralympic sports governing bodies are now almost wholly dependent on Lottery funding. As a consequence, other global and regional interna-tional competitions have lost a lot of their importance, often to the chagrin of many within the sports concerned. Cycling is per-haps the prime example. Arguably Britain's most successful Olympic sport in recent times, British Cycling's focus on its riders peaking at just the right moment every four years means that the UCI Track World Championships has become little more than a development or training event for the British team.

At UK Athletics just under 40 per cent of the organisation's income flows from UK Sport in support of its World Class Pro-gramme. The wealthiest Olympic sports are ineligible for UK

Sport funding by virtue of their financial strength. Tennis pays its own way, as does rugby, and so too would football if it could overcome its local political differences to re-enter teams for future Games. Of the funded sports, most have far greater reliance on Lottery income than athletics, having fewer commercial opportunities in the form of sponsorship or the staging of events that can turn a profit from spectator and television income. It is little wonder then that they have to play to UK Sport's rules.

GB Wheelchair Rugby's submission to UK Sport for Tokyo, David Pond states, was for around £750,000 for each of the four years. In addition, UK Sport would provide Athlete Performance Awards (APAs) totalling £180,000 a year. In the Rio cycle UK Sport funding made up almost the entirety of GBWR's income, aside from some sponsorship from BT. Once the initial shock of hearing UK Sport's decision had subsided, one of Pond's first actions was to place his small staff on notice of redundancy at the end of the coming March when the Rio funding cycle expired. 'That left me with no performance staff at all, except that the head coach came back and said, "Look, I will do this as a volunteer, because I believe in this so much."'

Rugby's dozen wheelchair athletes hopeful of continued support received similar notifications. For some, very severely disabled and with consequently narrow employment prospects, Pond's fear was that a life on benefits beckoned. 'Some of our athletes will be on basic disability benefit, so between £400 and £600 a month, having been on £15,000 a year. And they've lost all support around them. So we're trying to match them up with local gyms, local sponsors. And that's tough. For some of our spinal injury guys it takes them two hours in the morning just to get into their wheelchair. These are people who have amazing day-to-day challenges. I find it unsavoury. It's just an ugly decision. It's an unnecessary decision. Because it's such a small amount of money really.'

UK Sport's funding for elite sport splits into three parts. Governing bodies receive central funding so that they can operate their World Class Programmes. Some of this defrays the organisations' central overheads, but the vast majority pays for everything from key staff – coaches, sports scientists and medics – and training facilities to the cost of delivering teams to major competitions. In addition, UK Sport supports other key organisations that are part of the Games conveyor belt, most notably the English Institute for Sport, which provides medical and sport-science services to most of the sports, and both the British Olympic Association and the British Paralympic Organisation, which each bear the cost of kitting out, transporting and managing the GB teams at the Games.

The remainder of UK Sport's funding goes on the APAs that support individual athletes' living costs, effectively enabling them to pursue a full-time sporting existence. Some 1,100 sportsmen and women are supported in this way, their annual APAs dependent on their past success, an assessment of their future potential and the sport they are in. At most, these awards were £28,000 per annum in 2017. Provided individuals organise their affairs sensibly, APAs do not incur a tax liability as the tax authorities deem them to be direct grants that are not given for professional or employment services rendered. Maximum awards for those on the lowest tier of assessment are £15,000. All of the awards are means tested. Any income an athlete has over £65,000 a year results in a pound-for-pound reduction in their APA.

UK Sport estimates that the value to each athlete of all of the services provided by a World Class Programme, which they might have to otherwise forgo or fund by other means, ranges from £23,000 to £60,000 a year. Add these to an APA and, assuming an unfunded athlete would indeed have to spend tens of thousands of pounds on pursuing a sporting career, it can be seen that being granted access to a World Class Programme is a transfor-

mative opportunity. In practice, only the most financially fortu-
nate athletes can afford to replicate the range of services provided by governing bodies in the UK Sport system. Most on the
edge of funding but not quite in the fold have to take a very different approach to their sport, working full or part time, seeking
private sponsorship or benefactors, and often taking a less than
ideal approach to injury management and medical treatment.

In return for an APA, athletes have to make certain commitments as to their behaviour, so as to uphold the integrity and
reputation of the system. APAs are funded entirely from the National Lottery, and in return athletes have to commit to a set
number of appearances on its behalf every year. It is no coincidence that GB track and field athletes often thank the Lottery in
trackside interviews immediately after their events – the UK Athletics media team schools them to remember the source of their
support. Having passively resisted UK Sport's requirement to
carry the National Lottery logo on our team kit, we were keen to
ensure we delivered a balancing positive for Camelot, the Lottery
company.

For the most senior athletes, those with commercial opportunities generating income far in excess of the £65,000 means test
threshold, the UK Sport system can feel too restrictive at the
margins. Very occasionally, one of the British stars will decline to
enter into a contract to receive World Class Programme support.
For top sportspeople, though, the ancillary benefits of the system
are substantial, whatever notional value might be attached by
UK Sport. And even if a top athlete resolutely declines to sign,
they will continue to be supported by UK Athletics as if they had
entered into a formal contract. It is in no one's interest for them
not to receive whatever support they require to perform at their
best, system or no system.

Such refusals are very much the exception, however. And yet
sometimes up-and-coming athletes, usually at the behest of high-

ly protective or over-interested parents, will hold out against signing up to the system. Early in my tenure at UK Athletics we en-
listed the help of one of our stars, even though commercial
concerns were holding up finalisation of her own contract, to try
and persuade a young female distance runner of the folly of
spurning Lottery funding. Not because of the hard cash involved,
but because of the support services on offer. We had heard that
the youngster, still at school, was sleeping in a special tent at home
to replicate the benefits of living at altitude. If that was true, presumably money wasn't an issue for her family in the pursuit of her
career, and living outside the system can be a motivational spur,
but for the vast majority being part of it is the sensible choice.
Why else would the largesse of UK Sport, and by extension the
British government, be so envied around the world?

Every year the governing bodies review the list of sportsmen
and -women on Lottery funding. Individual performance plans
are updated for achievements and progress in the year past and
objectives reassessed for the remainder of the funding cycle.
Names are added to the list and others removed. Invariably, controversy ensues. Just as UK Sport cannot support every sport, so
each discipline has only a finite number of available slots that it
has negotiated with the funding agency. Often the most difficult
decisions involve athletes who have sustained injuries. These have
been suffered in the year just gone, or an athlete might be on the
comeback trail from an earlier injury. In these instances the objective data of performances in competition has to be overlaid by
the subjective judgement of medics and coaches. With only a
binary outcome possible, to fund or not to fund, these are very
much forks in the road for the athletes concerned.

The existence of a system that supports 1,300 sportspeople
nationwide and has been in existence now for as long as many of
these athletes have been alive is bound to create some feeling of
entitlement. This is especially true for those who have tasted the

benefits of National Lottery support and are suddenly faced with its removal. For some, such a loss provides an incentive to prove the bureaucrats wrong, to force their way back into the national team and a return to the funding cocoon. Such ambitions are rarely fulfilled, but it is impossible to tell whether this demonstrates the efficiency of the selection system, or whether the removal of funding directly determines the outcome.

Although an APA is often likened to an employment contract, in spite of HMRC's verdict otherwise, the inability of an athlete whose APA is terminated to find alternative 'employment' highlights a key difference between the sportsperson's existence and that of someone in regular work. No one likes losing their job, but most of us have the opportunity to seek a related or even identical berth elsewhere. Sprinters may turn to bobsleigh, disabled athletes can often excel in a different Para sport, but these are the exceptions that prove the sports rule. Thousands of hours of practice in a single sporting discipline do not prepare you for many, if any, immediate alternatives. Just watch the struggles of numerous recently retired athletes, especially those without gold medals, to break into the media, motivational speaking or celebrity circuits. Without the protections that normally accrue to those in employment, including contractual notice periods and any benefits that come with length of tenure, athletes are especially vulnerable when their Lottery funding is halted.

Athletics is one of the very few sports that accepts unfunded British athletes on its team. UK Athletics has relatively prescriptive selection policies – typically, the first two athletes past the finishing post in the official national trials, provided they meet the international championships' entry standard, with a third place available as a selectors' pick. Consequently, it is open to any athlete, funded or unfunded, to perform their way onto the team. By contrast, team sports rely on the alchemy of selectors looking at dynamics between athletes, and even British Cycling eschews pure performances in timed events in favour of its own analysis of medal potential. This is another consequence of a system which downplays all events apart from the four-yearly Olympics and Paralympics.

This does not insulate UK Athletics from selection controversies; if anything it heightens them. Critics complain that the selectors favour funded athletes when it comes to their discretionary picks, even going so far as to claim that the head coach and his or her team want to avoid the embarrassment of a medal being won by an athlete from outside the UK Sport system. In turn, UK Sport has been known to criticise UK Athletics privately for taking large teams to major events, believing that if the majority of selected athletes are unlikely to win a medal this dilutes the chances of those who might reach the podium as the less likely medallists soak up the precious time of the coaching team and support staff.

Therein lies the conundrum for the governing body: whether to toe the UK Sport line and pick a narrow team of possible medallists (either at the current Games or preparatory to success at a future one), or to open selection to the largest possible team, recognising that winning the right to wear a British vest will be the pinnacle of many athletes' careers and an achievement worthy of celebration in and of itself. In practice the 60 per cent of UK Athletics' income generated away from UK Sport funding gave us the freedom to pursue our own selection agenda, something denied to sports almost entirely reliant on public funding. That did not immunise us from complaints from within our sport whenever we left athletes at home that could have been selected, but that will always be the case unless the UK adopts the entirely trials-based system deployed in the United States. And athletic talent in Britain is not so plentiful that this could ever be a sensible route to maximising medal success – with or without a Lottery funding system.

To UK Sport every Olympic medal has equal value, gold for gold, silver for silver and bronze for bronze. Ditto Paralympic medals. The disparity between the two Games is stark, however. The Olympic investment for the four years to Tokyo totals £265 million, the Paralympic sum a mere £71 million. And yet the British Paralympic Association took a team of 264 to the Rio Paralympics, against 366 by the BOA to the Olympics. So Para sports provided 42 per cent of the combined British team for Rio, but will receive only 21 per cent of the UK Sport funding for Tokyo.

Many sports deliver Games representatives from integrated performance programmes, Para athletes training alongside their able-bodied counterparts in shared venues, often with shared coaches, medical and other support staff. It is possible that the headline funding figures do not take full account of this. A more accurate portrayal of the equity of funding is perhaps provided by APAs. In aggregate these total £17 million for Para athletes for Tokyo against £44 million for aspirant Olympians, so a 28 per cent share for the prospective Tokyo Paralympians. On this measure they still appear under-recognised by UK Sport. Is the funding agency really saying that success at the Paralympics is less valuable to the nation? With many more medals on offer at a Paralympics, given the variety of disability classes it caters for, one could even make an argument for Para sport to be more heavily funded than Olympic programmes. After all, ParalympicsGB provided sixty-four gold-medal thrills for the British public in Rio compared with twenty-seven from Team GB at the Olympics. And this is before considering the fewer opportunities for Paralympians to supplement their sporting earnings when compared with their Olympian counterparts.

Within the two parallel Games programmes UK Sport certainly preaches a mantra of medal equality: the twelfth British Olympic cycling medal, if a bronze, is of equal value to the sole bronze medal in badminton or judo. This seems fair, but one consequence is that if a big sport that already wins many medals is deemed to have a greater likelihood of adding to its medal tally at the next Olympics, then it might edge a smaller sport reckoned to have lesser marginal medal potential out of the funding list. This probably explains the fate of badminton, in spite of the bronze medal for Marcus Ellis and Chris Langridge in the men's doubles at Rio.

Such an approach to funding can only be justified if the medals table is an end in itself. Economists often argue that there is diminishing marginal utility from each additional unit of a good that a person consumes. The same could be said of medals in any particular sport. We know that Britain is the dominant global power in the cycling velodrome; one medal either way from Team GB's current overall medal count does not change that. By contrast, a sole medal from a smaller sport, especially one without much history of success, can be a cause of disproportionate celebration. Almost half a million people over fourteen years old play badminton in England every week. How inspirational is an Olympic medal for them? And would the two million people who cycle in England every week begrudge them that if it meant British Cycling having to tighten its belt just a touch?

Ultimately a funding model that backs past success with a greater share of available monies would collapse under its own inherent absurdity. There are already indications that one or two of the better-funded sports struggle to work out how to spend all the funds that are made available to them. One wonders just what economies might be available without compromising medal prospects, if only a truly honest, thorough review took place.

There are examples of UK Sport sustaining support for a sport that has fallen short and being rewarded with a subsequent revival. British Swimming is the highest-profile recent example, its six Rio medals, double the number it won in London when it was just sixteenth in the swimming medal table, being bettered by only four other nations. In between, as well as cutting its funding by 15 per cent, UKS helped orchestrate a series of changes, including the British Swimming chief executive relinquishing his long-held parallel post in control of the sport's grassroots to focus solely – and as it turned out, successfully – on the elite programme.

Team sports create a kink in the funding architecture. At most only two medals are available in team sports, one for each gender, but they require squads of players that are expensive to fund. If medals are deemed equal across sports, then on any value-for-money exercise team sports would receive nothing. GB Basketball's complaints after it was dropped from funding in 2012 helped cement a recognition that team sports needed to be treated differently, even if basketball itself was not ultimately saved from the chop. Buoyed by its women's team's gold medal in Rio, hockey received a 12 per cent funding increase for Tokyo, to £18 million, making it the seventh-best funded sport. It still had only two medals it could pursue and a men's team who finished fifth in a pool of six in Rio, so failing to qualify for the quarter-finals, nevertheless eighty hockey players will receive APAs for the Tokyo cycle at a cost of over £5 million.

It is little wonder then that David Pond was so shocked to find his sport cut from funding. The men's hockey squad's APAs alone would see his entire performance programme through a four-year cycle. And his team were far closer to a medal in Rio.

UK Sport rebuffed attempts by each of the sports culled from funding to overturn the quango's decision. Less than a month after the reaffirmed rejections were communicated, three hundred people from across the funded sports – chairs, chief executives, performance directors and heads of communication to the fore – were invited to the cavernous Business Design Centre in north London for UK Sport to set us on our way to the Winter and Summer Games in PyeongChang, Tokyo and Beijing. This so-called Mission:East summit was a lavish affair, but the funding agency's leaders failed to overcome the downbeat mood engendered by their own struggles to cope with the fallout from the bullying and doping allegations that were at the time engulfing British Cycling. They stood accused in the court of media opinion of failing to exercise due oversight of the investment of public funds into cycling, blinded by the sport's repeated successes at Olympic Games. The accusation had an air of credibility to those of us accustomed to dealing with them.

Liz Nicholl began her introductory presentation by promising to 'get the elephant in the room on the table' and went on to talk about 'a number of reviews that have exposed fractures in our system in some sports. It's not a fracture in our system. It's very detailed fractures in some sports' and to warn us that 'it could happen in another sport tomorrow. It could be your sport.' Surprisingly she claimed that the UK Sport board had wanted some years ago to stop using the oft-cited phrase 'no compromise' to describe its investment philosophy because 'there was a potential for it to be misunderstood'. But she said it had given up the attempt because the media and others simply kept on using it to describe the organisation's approach to the pursuit of medals. Hardly the reaction of an organisation whose 'backbone' she claimed 'kept it strong'. This was all about post-event rationalisation rather than a policy U-turn. Backside covering rather than backbone stiffening. 'For the avoidance of doubt, it is not a message about winning at all costs. It's not just about winning, otherwise it's not going to inspire anybody. This is a minor tremor, but it is not going to shake our confidence in what we do, and it certainly hasn't as yet shaken government's confidence.'

The audience was decidedly underwhelmed, and the 'as yet' was a warning caveat. Lavish surroundings weren't what the moment called for, however much we were assured that they had been paid for by an insurance company's partnership with UK Sport and its Mission:East event. Just a month before, a YouGov survey had shown that just 7 per cent of Britons polled said they had been inspired to take up sport by the Olympics. Not only had the much-heralded system we were all a part of been shown to have fractures, but it also was failing to deliver on its primary objective, that of inspiring the public to become active. Only 4 per cent of those asked by YouGov backed UK Sport's funding strategy for Tokyo 2020. If the imperative to look at alternative sources of finance for future cycles hadn't already been clear to us all, it certainly was now. Just at the moment of its greatest success ever, elite sport in the UK appeared on borrowed time, vulnerable to any shift in public or political sentiment that might bring an end to its gilded age.

On the stage at Mission:East was rower Katherine Grainger, Britain's most successful female Olympian. A month later she was appointed UK Sport's new chair, and in her first interview, conducted with the BBC, she did not shy away from the issue of finance. 'The funding we have is finite. It's not stretching, and as more sports are successful the irony is that the money can't go as far. I think everyone's aware that we can't continue to rely on those sources to the extent we have done. What UK Sport has enabled me to do is to live this incredible opportunity as an athlete at international level. That takes money, and if we don't have an ongoing source of income then it will be a problem for athletes.'

9

OLYMPIAN OPPORTUNITY COST

The 800 metres final for women at the 2009 World Athletics Championships in Berlin was all about Caster Semenya. The South African's sex was the subject of intense debate among coaches and athletes at the training track, spectators in the Olympic Stadium and global media chasing the story of an athlete who might not, biologically, be what she purported to be. Rising above the barrage of scrutiny, Semenya powered home to win the gold medal. Realising belatedly that they owed a duty of care to the young woman, the IAAF's media officers spared her the ritual of a post-race press conference, and Britain's Jenny Meadows, bronze medallist, found herself facing a press whose only interest was in her views of the absent winner's eligibility to compete. Meadows' medal was her first at global level. In the maelstrom she barely had time to reflect on the bonus she was due from her kit sponsor for her success, the princely sum of £750.

Jenny Meadows stands five foot one and a third inches tall. 'I always thought I was five foot one and three quarters, but I'm not apparently. I've lost a little bit,' she tells me, hinting at an attention to detail common among high-performing athletes, but also at an awareness of the adversity that was a motivator throughout her career. The Pocket Rocket regularly surprised by bursting out of packs of taller runners to take a race by the scruff. Hers was a career of consistent promise and medal success, forged in her own fashion often outside the system, blighted by drugs cheats and marked by a degree of lost financial opportunity that makes her equanimity on retirement all the more remarkable.

When we meet to reflect on the cost of pursuing an Olympic dream, Meadows is in what she planned to be her last season on the track, taking on the role of pacemaker to athletes still capable of chasing records. She had paced Britain's Laura Muir to a European record and had back-to-back races in Doha and Shanghai, the first of them pacing for Caster Semenya. Any of the animus reported between the two athletes was clearly either a thing of the past or a figment of the press's imagination. Meadows believes it very much to be the latter.

Pacemaking had come as a (pleasant) financial shock. When her race agent told Meadows the fees on offer, the scales fell from her eyes. She could earn more leading out a race and only partially completing it than she had often been paid as a regular entrant. 'Let me get this right. I don't run all of the way. When the race gets tough I stop. If that job exists, I'll take it. Because if I don't do it then somebody else will.' Part of her motivation was financial – 'I'm getting some really good money, it's a joke' – and part the natural desire to help the athletes in her slipstream. The hard work continued. It took five months of training to pace Muir in two races. 'I almost begrudge having to go out and do the training sessions. I can't say I enjoy it, apart from the buzz on the day. Then I love it.'

To understand how one of the foremost middle-distance runners in the world should have come to this specialist role in the twilight of her track career, we must jump back to the young athlete who started in the sport at the age of seven. On her first night at the local athletics club the coach asked her what she wanted to do, meaning, run, jump or throw? Her answer was, she says, either 'To win the Olympics' or 'To go to the Olympics'.

She blossomed a little late and never quite thought she belonged in the British team, even when she broke through into the senior ranks. In her teenage and student years she represented her country, winning a Commonwealth Games relay silver in Manchester in 2002, but she never really embraced her own ability. 'As you get older you realise that you are just one of many. You realise just what a hard task it is. On finishing university I thought the natural thing is to just get a job.' Meadows started work as a part-time teaching assistant. She did this for a year but baulked at studying to qualify as a teacher because the demands would get in the way of her training. She moved instead into sports development as an athletics officer working in schools.

As with many young sportspeople, parental support was essential. When a teenager she once needed expensive physio treatment. Her mother opened her purse and fished out the seventy pounds required. 'And there might have been only eighty in there. I knew it was a massive sacrifice. At the same time, I knew it was justified. My mum and dad had bought into me doing well. I tried hard.' Indeed, Meadows describes her mother as 'almost like the performance director in her own little element. She sorted the physio out. She took on the job of the agent, to sort my races out.' Meadows commuted to Liverpool University from her home in Wigan. Her parents supplied the car. She relied on volunteer coaches and in time married one, Trevor Painter, who coached her throughout her senior career. They still live in Wigan today, Meadows never having strayed from her home town.

Meadows and Painter, wife and husband, were as she sees it 'trying to live two lives'. Their salaries in sports development effectively funded Meadows' pursuit of an athletics career, and the costs stretched well beyond physio sessions. A spell of warm-weather training might set them back £2,000. They had a mortgage, a car, an average wage, and took no holidays – all of their vacation allowance was used for overseas training.

The year 2007 proved to be pivotal. Meadows was then twenty-six. On returning from warm-weather training that spring, the reality of returning to work hit her hard, so she and her husband made a financial reckoning of the cost of her becoming a full-time athlete. Her father rarely proffered advice, but when she set out to him her concerns that she could not afford to give up work and focus entirely on athletics, his reply tipped the balance: 'But can you afford not to do it?' That summer she made the British team for the World Championships in Osaka. She had been picked for the 4 x 400 relay, but an injury to another athlete on the eve of the team's flight opened up a slot in the 800 metres. She reached the semi-finals of the 800, running a personal best to boot.

That autumn the progress she had demonstrated in Japan got her onto the bottom rung of the Lottery funding ladder, as a Category F athlete receiving an award of £2,000. The associated perk of medical support could have helped ease her financial burdens a little further, but she preferred to pay for her own treatments near home with her trusted support team, rather than travel a hundred miles to Loughborough to be looked after. The biggest benefit was mental: 'Psychologically I'd almost always perceived lack of funding as lack of belief in me.' She was certainly very old to be in receipt of her first Lottery award.

Although Meadows was now formally in the funding system, and firmly on the athletics radar, the spoils were few. She looked at other athletes in their Nike kit and wondered, *How do you get that?* Reluctant to use agents she wrote letters to potential backers herself. 'I met some agents and thought I just don't trust them. This is something I don't want to get into. I'd hear horror stories. Kit that went to the agent first and by the time it got to the athlete there would only be a small percentage left.' She hadn't had her own kit sponsor for about five years. In 2009 one of her letters paid off and she signed to Asics, the source of the £750 bronze medal bonus in Berlin. 'I think they just put it in the contract thinking, *She's not going to get one.*'

One sponsor certainly got good value from its investment. Meadows' signature Oakley sunglasses were always wrapped around her face, whether under the indoor arena lights or whatever the weather on an outdoor track. She had 'literally been given a free pair of sunglasses' by the company, found they helped her focus when she first wore them in a race, and stuck with them. 'Putting them on, it was my way of saying, *OK, stop being the nice Jenny and believe in yourself.* To hear her talk, she would probably have paid Oakley to carry on wearing them, regardless of the brand recognition the manufacturer derived from her competitive success.

It was only after her bronze medal, however, that she really began to appreciate what she might have been missing out on by ploughing her own furrow rather than plugging into the industrial machinery of the athletics world. The first time she was told her appearance fee for starting a race on the circuit she was shocked to discover that it was higher than the prize money for finishing first in the event. *What about all the poor others?* she thought. 'I had no idea...'

If giving up her own job was a gamble that she could not afford not to take, husband and coach Trevor's career decision to relinquish his day job was a dimensionally greater roll of the sporting and financial dice. At the end of 2010, focusing their joint efforts exclusively on her athletics career seemed the logical next step in discovering the limits of her capabilities. Looking back, Meadows recalls, 'I said to Trevor – I wish I wouldn't had done now – "I think you should give your job up" and he says, "What?"' At its most prosaic, this meant Painter the coach could be at all fourteen of his athlete's weekly training sessions, rather than the four he could fit in around his work. 'We just went really professional in 2011. We were so on top of everything. It was that attention to detail.'

Wiser now to the economics of the sport, the pair set their sights on the Diamond League event series as a means of compensating for the loss of Painter's salary. The target was the $40,000 prize on offer to the winner of the League's series for her event, the 800 metres. Meadows ran a time below two minutes – the benchmark of a very good performance for a woman over two laps of the track – seven times that year. Painter's meticulous planning paid off. Meadows was sleeping alone upstairs at home in her altitude tent. 'Trevor had a lovely time downstairs chilling out.' They paid £300 excess baggage to take the tent with them to Shanghai for the Diamond League meeting. She won that race. And she won the Diamond League series too. In their eyes, the $40,000 prize had paid Painter's wages for the year.

For all her success on the invitational circuit that year, Meadows fell short of her ultimate objective of winning a medal at the World Championships in Daegu (South Korea's fourth-largest city, in case you didn't know). Indeed, she failed to progress beyond the semi-finals, the fastest athlete not to make the cut. Having seen her Lottery funding jump to Category A and a grant of £26,000 a year in 2010 and 2011, it was now halved as she was knocked two rungs down the ladder. Such is the structure of the system, she could even have been removed from the list entirely. 'They had every right to chop me altogether.' As a senior athlete she needed to keep meeting high achievement targets to be sure of retaining her place. This time the selectors exercised their discretion to keep her on.

That December Jenny Meadows suffered her first ever injury, while training in South Africa. 'I literally tripped over a brick. It was a really minor injury. I'd been in the sport for twenty-three years and never even pulled a muscle.' The injury to her foot was

a freak occurrence but the exact problem went undiagnosed for
some months. Meadows had fulfilled her ambition of competing
in the Olympics in Beijing in 2008, but now a home Games in
London was fast approaching, she was Diamond League champion, and she was unfit. Reluctant as ever to leave Wigan, Meadows and Painter had built a team around her that they were
paying for themselves: nutrition, sports science, physio, strength
and conditioning. The last alone was costing £300 a month. She
had made a decision to plough her own furrow, believing that
set-up worked for her, but it came at a price. Her £13,000 Lottery award was not stretching very far. 'The people I was using
were world class. Any money I generated I was using to pay these
other people.'

Meadows couldn't race at all in 2012. London came and went
without her. Surgery on her Achilles followed at the end of August. The next year dawned a little brighter and she made the
final of the European Indoor Championships. But injury ruled
out the summer season. In the autumn Painter took a call from
UK Athletics' performance director, Neil Black. Jenny Meadows
was dropped from Lottery funding. This time the selectors had
gone the other way. 'I think it was the right thing for Neil to
phone Trevor and not me. I'd been taken off at the discretion of
the panel. I could have been kept on. I felt totally rejected.'

The Commonwealth Games in Glasgow 2014 had long been
identified by Meadows as her point of retirement. Now she had
no funding, and no Diamond League income as she couldn't get
a lane in races. An epidural in her back to enable her to compete
in the Commonwealths cost her £2,000. Meadows made only a
couple of thousand pounds from racing that year. She says it felt
as though she was leaving university all over again. Her family
were helping out with the costs, and a philanthropic backer was
paying for warm-weather training, but he was her only remaining
sponsor. There was only one sub-two-minute performance in

2014, and sixth in the final of the Games was not the way Meadows wanted to bow out. So she didn't.

A German TV documentary in December 2014 turned the world of athletics upside down. Its allegations of systematic doping by Russian athletes proved to be just the first crack in the informational dam. In time the torrent of evidence of cheating would engulf all Russian Olympic and Paralympic sports. Documentary maker Hajo Seppelt began, however, with a single 800-metre runner and her husband. Yuliya Stepanova was a direct competitor of Meadows, while husband Vitaly Stepanov had worked for RUSADA, Russia's anti-doping agency. Both had now turned whistle-blower.

Stepanova, at the time running under her maiden name of Rusanova, had won the semi-final in Daegu in 2011 that had seen Meadows finish in a not-quite-quick-enough third place. Eighteen months later abnormalities in her athlete biological passport led to Stepanova being banned from the sport for two years, and her results over the prior two years annulled. Her last place in the World Championships final was struck from the record books, but of course the race could never be re-run, nor her place on the start line reallocated to Meadows. Four years later, as a result of the revelations from Stepanova and her husband and the inquiries these triggered, the event's gold medallist Mariya Savinova had all of her records expunged going back to July 2010, wiping her victory from the record books. In all, three of the eight Daegu finalists in the women's 800 metres, each a Russian, now have a DQ (disqualified) against their name.

Hajo Seppelt, Vitaly Stepanov and Yuliya Stepanova did sport a huge favour, but it is no surprise that athletes denied by a doper-turned-whistle-blower should suffer conflicting emotions when reflecting on what has gone before and what might have been. Jenny Meadows had long had suspicions about some of her Russian competitors, their sudden appearances at the highest level, the spots on their backs. Now her suspicions were proved well founded. A medal upgrade came her way: now she was a European Championships silver rather than bronze medallist from 2010. But she remained in silver behind Savinova's gold at the World Indoor Championships earlier that year. The Russian's record annulment didn't go back quite far enough for Meadows to become a retrospective world champion.

Meadows recognises that sport is fickle. 'You can literally just get a cold and it can take away all that you've worked for.' It is impossible, though, for her not to indulge in a degree of fantasy athletics. She believes she would have won maybe eight medals had Russian athletes run honestly, instead of the four in her possession. She thinks she would now have a couple of golds, which would have put her 'on a totally different level, up with some of the greats' with all the financial benefits that would have entailed. 'It cuts me.'

Asked to put an overall number on her loss of earnings across her career because of doping in athletics, Meadows gives a ballpark range of £100,000 to £150,000. 'It's massive!' Probed to justify this estimate, she rattles off details that show she has given it considerable thought. Her Lottery funding chop cost her £13,000 a year; a kit sponsor's bonus would have been £4,000 higher had one silver become gold; no prize money from the IAAF paid out to the eight finalists in her Daegu event; she might have earned a few thousand pounds a race on the Diamond League circuit for three or four years running more races and finishing higher up the order than she did in reality. And the great unknown is what her commercial value might have been had she had a global-level gold medal to her name while she was still competing at the height of her career. 'I probably don't want to really add it all up because then I'd feel . . .' She tails off with a groan.

With a couple of pacemaking outings ahead of her, a masters degree in sports marketing and business management to complete, and life after an elite athletics career to craft, Jenny Meadows reflects that 'being a full-time athlete to pursue my goals has cost me financially. Definitely I'm in a worse financial position than if I'd just gone down the normal route. Definitely. But I wouldn't have been able to live with myself. That phone call I had with my dad when he said, "You can't afford not to."' And this from an Olympian with records and medals to her name. She chose to operate at the margins of the central system. Her husband threw his lot in with her professionally. Both decisions raised the stakes for her financially. The pay-off was sporting but certainly not pecuniary.

'If I am really brutally honest, I wish sport wasn't a business. I really believe that if it was like it was in my mum and dad's era, where everybody works full time and just those really committed people go to the track in the evening and choose to sacrifice other things in their lives, and whoever's got the most staying power is the best, I believe I could have been the best in the world.'

10

LIGHTS OUT IN LONDON

Twelve seconds after the ball hit the back of the net the floodlights went out. Frank Lampard's goal was West Ham's second, the home team coming back from 2–0 down on a chilly November evening in 1997. I was standing behind the goal with the rest of the Crystal Palace fans. Our early elation turned to frustration, first with the Hammers' comeback, and then with the lengthy delay while the lights were fixed only to fail again and the match be abandoned. Exactly a month later we were back at Upton Park to see Palace soundly beaten in the restaged fixture. We left the ground feeling cheated, victims of supporters' perennial 'what might have been' syndrome. As it transpired, we had all been cheated, home and away fans alike. The floodlights hadn't failed; they'd been sabotaged by a criminal Malaysian betting syndicate.

The Upton Park sabotage was not an isolated incident. A game at Crystal Palace's own Selhurst Park was also targeted, the lights going out when Palace's tenant at the time, Wimbledon, was level with Arsenal. In February 1998, three days before Charlton Athletic was due to play Liverpool at the Valley, police made arrests at the ground just as a circuit-breaker was about to be installed in the lighting system. Two Malaysians, a Chinese man and a British security supervisor employed by Charlton were convicted and sentenced to between eighteen months and four years in prison. It was reported that the syndicate could have made £30 million had it succeeded in rigging the match at the Valley. The key was that in the event of a game being abandoned, the score at the time was deemed to be a final result in the Asian markets that the syndicate operated in. If it knew it could pull the plug whenever the scores were level, the odds of the syndicate profiting were dramatically improved. The criminals must have been sweating when Neil Shipperley's double put Palace two goals up, and again when the floodlights were temporarily repaired, but the scam worked. At least until their loose-lipped British conspirator inadvertently alerted the police.

Betting is now part of the Premier League furniture. Half its teams sport gambling brand logos on their shirts, the majority from Asia. Most teams have official gambling partners and the digital boards around pitch perimeters routinely parade advertising for the firms' products in both English and Asian languages. Two decades ago, however, the prevalence of betting on English football in the Far East was barely known and its possible ramifications very little understood.

It is notable that the big six Premier League clubs do not have betting businesses as shirt sponsors. This is unlikely to be distaste on their part, but simply a function of the money involved. Shirt deals for clubs outside this upper echelon are routinely reported as having a value of only a few million pounds a year, whereas Chevrolet's deal with Manchester United is reported to be worth £53 million a year, and Yokohama's with Chelsea £40 million. Indeed, the big six account for three quarters of the estimated value of shirt deals in the Premier League. One betting industry insider believes that the global financial crisis a decade ago was instrumental in opening the door to his industry's use of Premier League players as billboards. As corporations worldwide tightened their belts, and the financial sector in particular scaled back its spending, so the lesser clubs were left with fewer places to turn to for sponsorship. At the same time, the explosive growth in Internet gambling and the accompanying fascination with football provided an obvious alternative for clubs and gaming companies alike.

Football has largely escaped betting controversies, in spite of the weight of money staked on matches worldwide. Indeed, those cases that have made the headlines have tended to cause more titillation than consternation. Years after his retirement, Southampton's Matthew Le Tissier revealed in his autobiography, *Taking Le Tiss*, that he and teammates had attempted to profit from a spread bet on the time of the first throw-in in a match, but that he under-hit a pass that was intended to fly out of play direct from the kick-off and no money was made. 'With so much riding on it, I was a bit nervous and didn't give it enough welly.' Police decided it would be a waste of their resources to investigate after Le Tissier's book was published.

In 2017 non-league Sutton United's glorious run in the FA Cup ended with a 5–0 defeat at home to Arsenal and global headlines after its substitute goalkeeper was filmed eating a pie on the bench. This triggered payouts for his friends who had placed bets with the bookie that had temporarily taken over the club's shirt sponsorship for the game and set up the pie bet as a publicity stunt. The outcome of the game was unaffected as Sutton had already used its permitted three substitutes, but the keeper was sacked and Arsenal's generosity in donating its match fee to Sutton was swept away in the media frenzy.

The Gambling Commission's Sports Betting Integrity Unit reveals, however, that football tops the list of sports that are reported to it on suspicion of corruption. In the first three months of 2017, 33 per cent of reports it received related to soccer, followed closely by tennis on 30 per cent and more distantly by horseracing and greyhounds on 9 and 7 per cent respectively. Four fifths of reports were made by betting operators and specialist bet monitoring companies, with sports governing bodies and the public making most of the remainder. Also in early 2017, Joey Barton, then of Burnley FC, accepted a Football Association misconduct charge for placing 1,260 bets on football over the course of a decade. He was banned from the game for eighteen months, subsequently reduced to thirteen months on appeal. The tip-off to the FA came from a betting company.

Although admitting the charges against him, Barton railed against what he perceived to be an unjustly harsh sentence. His public statement on the day the ban was announced held a mirror up to the FA and football more generally.

> Surely they need to accept there is a huge clash between their rules and the culture that surrounds the modern game, where anyone who watches football on TV or in the stadiums is bombarded by marketing, advertising and sponsorship by betting companies, and where much of the coverage now, on Sky for example, is intertwined with the broadcasters' own gambling interests. That all means this is not an easy environment in which to try to stop gambling, or even to encourage people within the sport that betting is wrong. It is like asking a recovering alcoholic to spend all his time in a pub or a brewery. If the FA is serious about tackling gambling I would urge it to reconsider its own dependence on the gambling industry. I say that knowing that every time I pull on my team's shirt, I am advertising a betting company. I say none of this to justify myself. But I do want to explain that sometimes these issues are more complicated than they seem.

Two months later the FA severed its sponsorship agreement with betting company Ladbrokes only one year into a four-year contract. It seemed Barton had been heard.

The standard measure of the scale of the gambling industry in the UK, as employed by its regulator, the Gambling Commission, is the gross gambling yield. This is the amount retained by betting companies after paying out winnings but before the deduction of their costs of operation. In 2016 the Commission assessed this yield across all gambling activities in Britain, including casinos, lotteries and bingo, as £13.6 billion. Sports betting made up £5 billion of this total, roughly a third of it remotely via the Internet or telephone, and two thirds through physical bookies, either on- or off-course. Over half of the licences to operate remote betting activities were held by businesses domiciled outside the UK. Football was by far the largest generator of gross gambling yield for remote operators at £580 million.

This, though, is only to scratch the surface of the industry worldwide. With so much sports betting unregulated, reliable estimates of the size of the global market are hard to establish. Some report the industry's gross gambling yield as being in the hundreds of billions of dollars, with Asians the dominant players. Others have mooted a yield of a trillion dollars or more, much of it illegal. Talk to anyone operating in this sea of money, and the threats to sporting integrity, real and imagined, will loom large in your discussion.

The advent of online betting exchanges with all the sophisticated functionality of financial exchanges has facilitated the growth of automated computerised gambling. Syndicates of gamblers deploy their statistical analysis of probability using super-fast computers to exploit anomalies in the pricing of sporting odds. Often these anomalies appear only fleetingly, before the weight of computerised money then closes them down, and often during the course of sports events themselves, so-called 'in running'.

One syndicate head described to me his operation, which has bet on over three million markets in its fifteen years as a customer of the leading exchange, Betfair. With fifteen people scattered across the world, including a clutch of computer programmers, and employing skills first acquired on trading desks in the financial markets, the syndicate has generated tens of millions of pounds in profits. In turn, it has paid around forty pence for every pound of profit it has made in exchange fees to Betfair. The syndicate is constantly learning and refines its activities accordingly. 'If we turned on our original programme now it would lose money as it would be obsolete,' its head observes. His syndicate bets on all sports except golf. 'In golf there's one syndicate in the UK that's got absolutely everything sussed. They win absolutely all the money in the world in golf. They supply major bookmakers with prices, all on a profit share. Every time you bet with Coral or Ladbrokes, for example, you are taking on them. They know every single course backwards, how the players will putt on every course. They know the weather. They really do very well at it.'

Knowledge is crucial, and can be acquired if you have the money that goes with scale. This syndicate does far less in-running betting in football than it does pre-match. Its head cites five syndicates that have each made more than $1 billion gambling, two of them focusing on football and based in London, two on horseracing with one of these based in the United States. 'The two in London dominate in-running football betting and before-the-off. They have enormous bets, three or four million pounds. They buy the services of a company that has scouts at every game. We're talking Ethiopian football they'll have a scout at. The syndicates themselves have 200 or 300 employees each. The investment needed to compete with them is just too much.' The data business is RunningBall, which claims a network of 1,500 scouts in a hundred countries and bespoke technology 'which provides faster than TV live and push data feeds for in-running prices'. For our syndicate head, the danger of lagging behind the biggest syndicates with the wherewithal to employ such a service is too great. 'If you are even a second behind them, you are not able to be at the front of the queue pricing it up. But that doesn't mean that if we had scouts at every game we would make money. The real investment all these groups have made is in pricing and computer programmes, the scouts are just the icing on the cake.'

This player does see evidence of corruption in football. 'There are examples of suspicious activity. At the end of a season in Italy when two teams need a draw, these always go off odds-on and it will be a draw. A draw should always be a minimum price of 2–1. The money also suggests it is corrupt. Some of those can be the best value bets you get because you've got no chance of losing.' He sees far more suspicious activity elsewhere, however. 'Every one of our bots has a too-good-to-be-true scenario, and we have automated exposure limits which control our downside. And if it looks too good to be true, we just turn the computer off. In horseracing there are 300 horse races around the world a day, and we turn off maybe once or twice a week. And that doesn't mean the race is corrupt. It might just mean our prices are very inaccurate or the market is very inaccurate. Or something bent is going on.'

Greyhound racing is a bread-and-butter staple of the syndicate's activity. 'Dog racing, with so many races you don't need so much edge and you don't need so much stake. It's all computerised. I couldn't name a single dog in the UK now, but that doesn't stop me betting on every single dog in the country. I couldn't even really name a horse, I don't think. But that doesn't matter. They are numbers on the database. There's very little human resource wasted. Our margin on dog racing is 0.15 per cent and the turnover comes not from having it all on one market, but on having it on eighty markets a day and others in Australia or in New Zealand.' With 480 dogs racing each day in the UK, the syndicate finds that the too-good-to-be-true scenario kicks in on average a couple of times a day and the computer switches off. 'You only need one dog, so that's two dogs out of the 480 racing that day, and it doesn't necessarily mean it's bent. It means someone knows more than we do. A dog may have put in a particularly good training time that is publicly available information but our computer hasn't found it, that's also a possibility.'

His syndicate is one of the sources of information about suspicious activity reflected in the Gambling Commission's statistics. 'Corruption is very bad for us as we model everything by computer, and the computer has a perceived idea of value, and the more the market is away from that perception the more we bet. I talk to the ICC. We keep records of all the prices. Whenever they have a cricket match they think is dodgy, they ask me what the prices were and what I think the prices should have been. It's very easy to spot someone having a terrible day at cricket. They drop a couple of catches. They bowl five wides. They shell an easy catch into the covers. They could just be having a bad day. But if there's a movement in the price just before they come in to bat and their performance is then bad, you can identify when – not that they are necessarily cheating but when it's worth investigating. The money from India appears very, very quickly in the Betfair market. Yesterday's IPL game had £50 million traded on Betfair. And that's usual for an IPL game. It's not suspicious. For me, I want to help the ICC.'

Cricket's problems with corruption have centred on spot-fixing, in which individual moments within a match are fixed for corrupt gain rather than the outcome of entire contests. Hansie Cronje's sacking as South Africa's captain in 2000 for match-fixing and his subsequent life ban and then untimely death in a plane crash that fuelled myriad conspiracy theories, serve as a reminder that even the greatest sportspeople are not beyond the reach of bookmakers. However, that scandal also emphasised the perils of fixing an entire match with so many variables. Cronje, for example, took a bribe to set up a run chase with England captain Nasser Hussain in a rain-affected Test at Centurion Park. England duly won the Test with only two wickets and a mere five balls to spare. With Hussain and every other player on the pitch unaware of Cronje's motives in setting up the chance of a thrilling finish in a match otherwise heading for a stalemate, the outcome could just as easily have mirrored Matthew Le Tissier's fluffed kick to touch.

Spot-fixing is easier to implement and to control, and need only involve a single player without affecting the outcome of the game. It can also be hard to prove unless you have clear evidence of financial gain. As the syndicate head observes, 'It's easier to persuade people to spot-fix than to throw away their wicket. So say you want to spot-fix a Test match and you want an opening batsman to go slow for ten overs, you just tell him, "Make sure you don't get out and then build an innings from there." Now that's uncatchable, and the batsman hasn't done anything to harm his team's chances of winning. And no money may have changed hands. And what about the groundsman talking honestly about the state of the pitch? How do you educate someone not to do something that comes naturally to them?' Only weeks after we spoke, Indian police arrested three men on suspicion of using a groundsman to tamper with the state of the pitch for an IPL match.

The *News of the World* exposed spot-fixing to the glare of publicity in 2010 when it paid a Pakistani agent £150,000 to ensure three no-balls were bowled in a Test at Lord's at preordained moments in the match. The no-balls duly ensued, and the agent and three cricketers, included Pakistan's captain Salman Butt, were subsequently jailed and banned from the game. Their bans expired in 2015 and each has subsequently returned to the game. The youngest, Mohammad Amir, is back in the Pakistan national side, playing a key role in its 2017 Champions Trophy victory against arch rivals India.

While the *News of the World* received a demonstration that an international match could be corrupted, spot-fixing is much more likely to have been prevalent at lower levels of the game. And that remains the risk, facilitated by the sheer number of matches available on various broadcast platforms. This is just as true of tennis, which is widely regarded as having a corruption problem, consistent with the number of suspicions about matches that are reported to the Gambling Commission.

Australian Scott Ferguson is the former head of education at Betfair. He identifies tennis as the sport facing the biggest challenge to its integrity. This is a function of its perfect storm of head-to-head matches involving only two players, a circuit that can only financially support a small fraction of those trying to make a living, and the widespread prevalence of live streaming of games in the lower echelons of the sport. And the publicity that has accompanied apparently corrupt events means that suspicions now far outweigh actual malpractice.

'There's plenty going on, but there's plenty going on that people aren't noticing and plenty that people are accusing of being fixed but isn't. You can see a pattern but unless there's money behind it, it's just a natural thing,' Ferguson observes. 'The difference between someone ranked two hundred and someone ranked five is that the person ranked five will keep hitting the lines. The most that the guy ranked two hundred can do is occasionally win a set but that's it. But if the guy ranked five starts missing the lines by that much, he can be just having a bad day. Today a hell of a lot of pressure is thrown on players. The whole heap of crap that social media piles on players these days. They say, "You lost, but you were only a break down." But it's the natural cycle, it happens. It's natural volatility. Go back and look at results from before betting really took off. It happened then. On social media there are just mugs who don't understand probability. They think a match must be fixed instead of factoring in the emotional swings, the tactical swings that happen.'

Low-ranked players are the most vulnerable to financial temptation. The ITF may have moved to restructure its tours to reduce the number of full-time professionals on the circuit, but it is unlikely to be able to sweep away the many aspirant players who believe they can climb the ladder of success. Scott Ferguson highlights the collision of opportunity and need. 'At the lowest level of tennis you've got people watching on streams and betting point by point. They'd rather bet on that than on a gaming machine. The bookmakers' prices are all made by a model. There are so many unknowns. These guys aren't professionals. They might be sleeping on the floor of a hotel or in a car. The Futures Tour is supposed to be aspirational. It's not your aspiration to stay there, but the gap between that level and the top ...'

The betting syndicate head we met earlier concurs. 'Tennis players who are ranked one hundred in the world are often losing money by being on the tour. They pay a lot of money to be there. It's only the Federers of this world who make fortunes. In the Challenger events there are often people who need to win money to be able to get to the next event, and often that will be dodgy. There used to be a very common one – not so much now – when the winner of the first set and the winner of the second set were known, and the players then played the third set for the match. Which is a much easier sell to the players to be corrupt, because they still play one set for real to see who goes through to the next round. And so you could take a big position on player A to win the first set and a big position on player B to win the second. And it would look a lot less suspicious to the authorities. You can see – soft psychology – why people might be willing to do that. It's probably one in two hundred or three hundred matches which are bent.'

The match which blew open the issue of corruption in tennis involved Russian world number four Nikolay Davydenko retiring hurt in the third set of a match against an opponent, Martin Vassallo Arguello, ranked eighty-three places below him at a tournament in Poland in 2007. Davydenko won the first set, whereupon money poured onto the Betfair exchange in favour of his Argentinian opponent, who promptly won the second set before the Russian's final-set withdrawal. Mark Davies, son of legendary sports commentator Barry, was Betfair's spokesman at the time. He had been one of its very first employees when the company was in embryonic form. Davies led the decision to void all bets on the match and alert the ATP to its concerns. For him, there was a red-flag combination of a change in the odds accompanied by a heavy weight of money. 'The price moved dramatically, and we went very public on it and we suspended betting.' Millions of pounds had been placed on a relatively minor contest, backing an unexpected outcome that then came to pass in an unlikely fashion.

Tennis was short of investigatory resources at the time and relied on experts from horseracing to conduct an inquiry into the affair. A year later, both players – who had denied any wrongdoing – were exonerated. The ATP said that the inquiry team had 'exhausted all avenues of inquiry open to it'. The case emphasised the difficulties facing the authorities. As Scott Ferguson states, 'It's very difficult to police. A player may be from one country. His mobile phone may be from another country. The people he's been talking to may be from another country. It would be great if it was two English players playing in England with phones on a Vodafone contract. But it's not.'

A year after the Davydenko–Arguello match, the Tennis Integrity Unit was established, funded by the various governing bodies. It has since rooted out a few handfuls of mainly low-ranked corrupt players from the sport. Its highest-profile scalp was that of former world number fifty-five, Daniel Köllerer, in 2011. Five lifetime bans were handed out in 2016. The TIU has memorandums of understanding (MOUs) with betting companies and regulators that provide it with alerts about suspicious matches, backed up by supporting data. In 2016 it received 292 alerts, the majority relating to the ITF Men's Futures circuit. There were 114,216 professional matches that year. Either the betting syndicate head's estimate of one in 200 or 300 matches being bent is wildly incorrect, or the TIU is as yet only scratching the surface of the problem. Shortly after Wimbledon 2017 it announced that one match at the Championships and one at that year's French Open were under investigation, emphasising that this was an indication at that stage only that something may have been awry, not that there definitely was corruption involved.

The single event that attracted the most betting volume on Betfair during the London 2012 Olympics was a tennis match, the Federer–Del Potro semi-final with $31 million wagered. The Games saw total volume of $568 million on the exchange, more than half of it on tennis. In the context of the overall sports betting market this is small. One insider argues that the Olympics does not face a betting problem because the vast majority of its constituent sports are not routinely followed by gamblers between Games. The IOC is not taking anything for granted, however, and has a partnership with Interpol to protect the integrity of competition. At the Rio Olympics in 2016 three boxers for Britain and Ireland were severely reprimanded for betting on the sport at the Games, and the British Olympic Association and its Irish counterpart were both taken to task for failing to educate their athletes about the IOC's ban on betting.

MOUs were a weapon employed heavily by Betfair as it fought to carve out a position for its novel exchange in the face of opposition from the betting and sporting establishment. Mark Davies remembers, 'We got heavily kicked by people with the accusation that we were a threat to the integrity of sport generally – as if it's the betting piece that's problematic, rather than corrupt people. It's corrupt people who use it as a tool. People in the racing industry would ask, "Why would I want to bet on a horse to lose? I want my horses to win." What do you do about the stable lad who gives a horse an extra pail of oats before it goes out to run and no one knows anything about that apart from the stable lad? And that's where all the betting to lose allegations came from. The racing industry saw that we were going to decimate bookmakers' margins and they were being paid a percentage of bookmakers' profits. They saw a massive threat to their revenues. So they attacked us as being a threat of corruption in their industry.'

Betfair signed an MOU with the Jockey Club in 2003, enabling it to pass on information about betting on horseracing that complied with data protection requirements. This codified the flow of information that had already begun from the exchange operator and allowed its data to be used to pursue cases of apparent corruption. In autumn 2004 sixteen people were arrested on suspicion of race-fixing, including jockey Kieren Fallon, whose licence was suspended pending the outcome of proceedings. Betfair's provision of information on its betting markets had been instrumental in the investigation that led to the arrests. Fallon's trial alongside five other defendants collapsed three years later, the judge ruling there was no case to answer. In 2011, however, the authorities had greater success. The British Horseracing Authority handed out bans to eleven people for conspiracy to corrupt races, including four jockeys and two trainers, in a case initially triggered by suspicious activity on betting exchanges.

Mark Davies is no longer in the betting industry. Like others involved at Betfair's inception and through its early years, its success has enriched him and he pursues other interests, within and outside sport. He recently became chair of GB Archery and supports the Cambridge University's crews in their Boat Race preparations. Betfair itself is now embedded within the conventional bookie Paddy Power, a FTSE 100 company.

Davies looks back at the exchange's formative years through the lens of the financial markets where he spent his early career. 'People don't think about betting in clinical terms in the way they would a share price. I can love that stock but think it's overvalued. I can love that eventuality but don't think it's as likely as that one. I can even think it's going to be the outcome that's going to transpire, but its likelihood is overstated.' This may be because punters believe they can somehow intuit the outcome of sporting contests involving human (and animal) endeavour, or that there is no concept of inside information in sport, as there is in finance, so gamblers can fruitfully search for the insight of a cricket groundsman or a masseur treating a top player. 'One racing commentator absolutely hated us. Why did he hate us? Because on the night before, when the bookies made their first show, over the years he had always been better informed than they had, so he could pick off their bad prices. And then we came along and stopped that happening because their prices were suddenly based on a much broader spread of information and often weren't as anomalous as they had been.'

Scott Ferguson, Mark Davies and the syndicate head all defend the betting industry, or at least their corners of it. Ferguson would rather not see televised football matches engulfed in gambling ads when he is watching with his kids, but believes the industry is now too fragmented to 'put the genie back in the bottle'; Davies argues, 'If you shine a light into a dark room and see a lot of rats, it doesn't mean you put all the rats there in the first place'; and the syndicate head believes, 'The bodies involved are catching up faster than the criminals are coming up with new and clever ways to corrupt people.'

None of these arguments are likely to shake the determination of the American authorities in their long-standing resistance to sports betting in the United States. The American Gaming Association lobbies relentlessly for a relaxation of the Interstate

Wire Act of 1961 and the Professional and Sports Protection Act of 1992, which together ensure legal sports betting remains restricted to only four American states: Delaware, Montana, Nevada and Oregon. Of these, only Nevada is able to offer a full suite of sports betting products. The AGA estimated that $4.7 billion would be wagered on Super Bowl 51 between the New England Patriots and the Atlanta Falcons in 2017, 97 per cent of it illegally, the remainder in Nevada. The Association estimated overall sports betting by Americans at $154 billion in 2016, 'nearly all of it through bookies and offshore, illicit websites'. Hoping it will convince by demonstrating that the cat has long since slinked out of the bag, it argues that a regulated industry would 'generate tax revenues and jobs, protect consumers and leverage cutting-edge technology to strengthen the integrity of the games we all love'.

American officialdom's antipathy to sports betting can largely be traced to one event, the Black Sox scandal of 1919, in which Chicago White Sox players took bribes to lose baseball's World Series against the Cincinnati Reds. After a grand-jury investigation, eight players went to trial, were acquitted but then subsequently banned from the game for life. Their bans were never rescinded, and the cloud of a corrupted contest at the pinnacle of a major sport hangs over the American psyche to this day. The NFL, for example, bars its employees from gambling on any sport whatsoever, not just football. With the bar set so high, it seems unlikely that this century-long prohibition will end any time soon.

11

JUST A LITTLE PRICK

The British Athletics Writers' Association lunch in 2008 featured a slide show of photos of various members of the Fourth Estate going about their business at athletics meetings around the world, hard at work in press boxes, mixed zones and trackside. In the middle of the sequence, up popped an image of Dwain Chambers after winning the 100 metres at the British Championships. He was surrounded by a gaggle of beaming journalists thrusting their Dictaphones at him in apparent adoration. The returning drugs cheat had cocked a snook at UK Athletics and, whether it was for love of the man or the story, the journalists' pleasure was plain to see.

There can be little doubt that performance-enhancing drugs have kept a certain strand of the media in business in recent years. Cheating in sport is as much a certainty as life's inevitable duo, death and taxes. And just as newsworthy. It is only fair to record that the majority of journalists who have covered doping regard it as a scourge, although some seem to have been converted to this opinion over time. As awareness of drug abuse in sport has increased, so journalistic abhorrence has grown, at the same time both fuelling and mirroring that of the public that they serve. A decade on, Chambers' return from his two-year ban and his successful legal challenge to the British Olympic Association's lifetime bar on drugs cheats now appears a period piece. With all that has since transpired, it seems unlikely that today a British offender would constitute a novelty at a press jolly.

Dwain Chambers writes of 'the "get even" gremlin ... shouting ever louder' in describing his decision to take performance-enhancing drugs. This belief, whether genuine or confected – that an athlete has to cheat to be competitive because their rivals are doping – appears frequently in cases that are exposed. The most unpleasant example in British athletics in recent years involved sprinter Bernice Wilson, who served two bans – the first lasting four years – and her coach George Skafidas, who was banned for life from the sport in 2016. Theirs is a tale of an abusive relationship. Skafidas confessed, 'I ruined her career and not only, her life.' Embedded in the tribunal's decision on the case is Wilson's evidence, stating 'Dr Skafidas made clear to her that track athletes needed to take banned drugs in order to succeed.' In a sport where thousandths, hundreths and tenths of seconds really matter, any sense that rivals are stealing an advantage constitutes a stern test of moral resolve.

When I meet Bernice Wilson she is eleven days away from her first competitive race in six years, a North of England League Division Three meeting in Derby. She is running for a new club which does not have its own track, has been training on grass, largely by herself, and is hoping to run around a second slower than her personal best over 100 metres. She had wanted to continue to compete for her old club, the prestigious Birchfield Harriers, 'but understandably they rejected me'. Wilson's only senior British vest came at the European Indoor Championships in 2011, four months before her doping was unmasked. As she contemplates her return, her ambitions are shrouded in a rose-tinted hue. 'I don't know if I'll get to where I was, but I've always believed I can get somewhere in athletics. I would love to represent Great Britain again, but maybe I'm just kidding myself.'

The tribunal that banned George Skafidas for life also handed out a second ban to Wilson, who had failed a drugs test shortly before her four-year ban expired. Her second sanction was cut to only ten months to reflect the assistance she had given the authorities – it had become clear to them that the sprinter was being abused by her coach, with whom she had an on-off personal relationship. First time around Wilson knew what she was doing, under the guidance of her coach. The second time Skafidas had been swapping the vitamins she'd bought from Holland and Barratt for clomiphene – a drug that can help boost testosterone levels – and then had intercepted and destroyed the letter from UK Anti-Doping that informed her of the failed test. 'He was telling me, "Take this vitamin at this time," and I forgot once, and he wasn't very happy about it and afterwards I realised why, but at the time I didn't think anything of it.' Eyes fully open at last, Wilson provided the evidence that proved Skafidas's guilt. 'I was really sneaky. George was in Greece, and while we Skyped I had my phone on record and he admitted it all.'

The physical, emotional and financial consequences of Bernice Wilson's experience were stark. 'It made a difference,' she remembers of her first period of doping. Her failed test in 2011 showed use of the steroid clenbuterol and testosterone. 'I was sometimes training for three or four hours. It was quite intense. And even though my muscles would get tired, I could just keep going. I could lift things I couldn't believe I could lift. I was lifting heavy weights. And then I saw my body was changing and I didn't like that. I was getting bigger, and people could see it, but they didn't really say a lot. It was a really, really bad side effect. Especially as a female, I like to have a good image, and that was not a good image. My appearance changed. I think my mum suspected. I didn't say anything to my mum, but she knew.' The clomiphene she took unwittingly four years later is usually prescribed to stimulate ovulation and treat infertility, and the tribunal highlighted its attendant dangers. 'Now looking back on it I'm thinking, *Has it affected me? When I stop athletics, when I want to have children, can I?*'

The ban cost Wilson her job as a sports development officer for the council, 'because I was seen as a bad example to kids'. Even now, although back in work, she is still paying off debts from the time, including her solicitor's bill. 'It's a bit tricky.' She does not know exactly where the drugs she took came from – she suspects Greece and Bulgaria – or how Skafidas paid for them, although he had access to her accounts and so she probably paid for them herself indirectly. Money wasn't the issue at the time; being competitive was.

'I was always there but not quite there. It got to the point where it got annoying. I'm training, training, training, and then George came along and there was this temptation, that if you take this you are going to do well. And it was like, maybe I can get into the British team, be successful, be good, if I do.' Her coach convinced her that she was simply levelling the playing field. 'Once we started in a relationship, there was pressure from him, domestic-violence pressure. I kind of thought that he was right in everything he said. Which I know sounds stupid, but I did. It was basically, "You need to do it, you need to do it, and you're not going to get anywhere if you don't. And all the training that you're doing is going to be a waste of time." It made me see athletics differently, because I was thinking, *Oh my God, everybody is on drugs!* On the start line I was thinking if I'm not going to be taking anything, I'll be at a disadvantage.'

A month before her first race back, Bernice Wilson passed an online course to become an anti-doping adviser, and is happy to share her experiences. 'The first time after I spoke to people about it in London, I remember driving back. I was nearly at my home, and – this must sound very cheesy – this big rainbow came out and I remember thinking I felt really good about myself for getting it all out and I thought this is some sort of sign to say, "You did well." There might be people in my position, that are being coached by some man, and they may think the same as me – because George was quite a lot older than me – and maybe think that he's everything, and are easily influenced. And I just want to say, "Don't get sucked in," and if they are saying, "Take something," don't. Just don't.'

The cost of obtaining drugs does not appear to be a major factor in the decision-making process of those tempted to cheat. The risk of discovery, in contrast, looms large. Bernice Wilson says her coach told her, 'It's baby portions. You're not going to get caught.' Dwain Chambers' own account makes clear the importance to him at the time of the assurances he was given by his supplier, Victor Conte, that the drugs he was given were undetectable. If money features, it is in the lure of the rewards for greater success with the assistance of illegal drugs. And also the non-monetary rewards – the recognition and the glory that comes with being a winner.

It is possible to buy Kenacort online for only $3.98 an injection dose. This is the corticosteroid triamcinolone that Bradley Wiggins used on account of his asthma, and which became one element of the doping rumours that swirled around British Cycling and Team Sky in 2016. The anti-doping authorities granted Wiggins a number of Therapeutic Use Exemptions for the drug, effectively time-limited permissions for its use. These TUEs were necessary because Kenacort was judged capable of causing rapid weight loss and power gains, both very handy for an endurance cyclist, and so the drug was on the authorities' restricted list.

Search online for any banned substance cited in an anti-doping rule violation and you will find multiple websites claiming to be able to supply it. These might charge only a few dollars a pill or syringe for drugs with legitimate applications for those not looking to compete in elite sport – or only doing so with a TUE. On the other hand, if you want to boost your red blood cell count by injecting yourself with EPO, you might have to spend a few hundred dollars on each injection and deal with an illegal supplier to get your hands on it. Either way, the risks appear more to the body than the wallet.

UK Anti-Doping was founded in 2009 to deliver the drugs testing programmes in British sport, investigate possible cases of illegal drug use and educate athletes on the merits of clean sport. Its predecessor organisation was a unit within UK Sport. Under this previous structure, the governing bodies of each sport had the responsibility for deciding whether an attempted test by the anti-doping unit constituted a missed test to be placed on an athlete's record. Three such missed tests in an eighteen-month period and the athlete concerned would be banned for a year.

At UK Athletics I had the responsibility of opining on each possible missed test. It was a depressing role, and a deeply conflicted one. Depressing because the explanations and excuses given by athletes for missed tests were so workaday – almost invariably believable, but insufficient to rule that they were not actually missed tests. Conflicted because I naturally wished that our star athletes hadn't missed a test and thus taken one of three steps towards a ban. Quite rightly, UKAD's creation took responsibility for this initial judgement away from the governing bodies, leaving us to focus on educating athletes about the importance of keeping on top of their obligations under the drugs testing system – and keeping close tabs on those who had already missed tests and were at risk of a ban if they slipped up again. Tales of last-minute decisions to stay at a girlfriend's, of changes to training plans, of the sudden need for a medical appointment, of broken doorbells, were all now for UKAD to evaluate.

What my brief period as arbiter of excuses did reveal to me was the stacking of the odds against the anti-doping authorities.

The wilful cheat does not need much of a gambling mentality to reckon that the chances of being caught, with all their economic and reputational consequences, are slim. At UK Athletics we monitored the percentage of attempted tests on British athletes that were missed. When UKAD was first established, this statistic was typically 3 to 4 per cent on average. With vigorous education of athletes and frequent reminders to those who had already missed one test, we managed to reduce this to pretty consistently between 1 and 2 per cent. Viewed as one in fifty or a hundred tests being missed, this still left work to be done. It was an indication of human frailty and complacency, and indeed the challenges posed by the online system, ADAMS, that athletes have to use to log their whereabouts for the testers.

It is no surprise that athletes frequently cite the number of times a year they are tested as an indication of their commitment to clean sport. Indeed, where once the likes of Andy Murray complained about the intrusiveness of the whereabouts system, requiring a one-hour slot in which to be available for testing every day, over time they have come to embrace it as another indicator of their honest approach to competition. For some the realisation that they failed to maintain their data but were not targeted to be tested that day will come as a great relief and a spur to do better in future. For others, however, this will be a crack in the credibility of the testing system, reinforcing the belief that cheats can prosper. This is no different to divided public attitudes to parking offences – most are relieved when a mistake doesn't result in a ticket and a fine, but a minority are spurred to gamble on the non-appearance of a traffic warden when they park illegally.

In 2013 a pair of academic scientists at the University of Adelaide, Aaron Hermann and Maciej Henneberg, highlighted the short window post-doping in which a drugs test can identify cheating, and even within that window the low success rate many tests have in detecting doping – they cited an average test sensitivity of only 40 per cent. Their conclusion: that if a cheating athlete is tested monthly with no prior warning of the tests, there is only a 33 per cent chance that they will be unmasked as a doper. Testing carries a cost, and few athletes are tested as frequently as a dozen times a year. They might, though, need to be tested far more frequently for the system to truly work. Hermann and Henneberg estimated that the annual cost of implementing an effective testing programme would be at least $25,000 per athlete.

The Australian Sports Anti-doping Authority, ASADA, publishes a list of charges for its testing services. A full screen urine test, including collection, transportation and testing, costs AU$922, provided it is one of at least four tests being undertaken on a single mission by the agency. Add in a blood test and the charge rises to AU$1,337. That's approximately £565 or £820. Fees are negotiable for customers conducting programmes involving series of tests, and ASADA, which is effectively a near-monopoly provider of services in its local market, will have built a profit margin into its prices to assist in the funding of its other activities.. Taking all these factors together, it's fair to assume that the underlying cost per test is lower, but still significant for those seeking to test sport sufficiently rigorously so as to ensure its cleanness. In the UK private figures indicate that UKAD charges £440 plus VAT for a urine sample collection and analysis and £419 plus VAT for a blood sample, so not dissimilar to its Australian counterpart.

ASADA's annual income in 2015/16 was AU$15.8 million (£9.7 million). Like many government agencies in an era of global austerity, its public funding had been reduced. After covering its overheads, including the bill for its forty-eight full-time staff, ASADA managed to conduct 6,022 tests that year, and this in one of the world's most passionate and highly developed sporting nations – think Aussie Rules, cricket, both rugby codes, swimming and the growing soccer scene, and an impending Gold Coast

Commonwealth Games. That's not a lot of money, staff or drugs tests to go round.

This financial constraint is not unique to ASADA. Indeed, it hamstrings anti-doping agencies worldwide. UK Anti-Doping spends £8.1 million a year, just over a third of it on staff. It generates £2 million from conducting testing that it can charge for (typically at major events in the UK and overseas), and relies on a government grant-in-aid of around £5.5 million to balance its books. Staffing aside, its two major outgoings are £1.5 million in fees spent at the Drug Control Centre at King's College in London, a laboratory accredited by the World Anti-Doping Agency, and £1.8 million in administering the athlete testing programme in the UK, which includes the costs for the doping control personnel who collect the samples. Or occasionally run up against broken doorbells.

In 2015/16 UKAD attempted to conduct 7,771 tests, of which almost 9 per cent were unsuccessful. These tests cover all athletes across all major sports whose status requires them to submit to the whereabouts regime, plus all those below this elite level who UKAD deem necessary to test at any time. The list of sportspeople funded by UK Sport alone runs to 1,100, to which can be added those athletes in the Olympic and Paralympic sports who are just below the funding cut-off, plus the thousands competing at the top level in the wide range of non-Games sports, including all of the major team sports.

Data published by America's anti-doping agency, USADA, provides a similar picture of activity. In 2015 it conducted 10,514 tests on a total of 5,214 sportspeople across more than eighty sports (counting disability sports as separate entities within this total). Sixty per cent of these tests were part of USADA's core programmes, with the remainder paid for by client sports. The breakdown by sport is indicative of the focus on Olympic Games disciplines and is reflective of where risk has been high and is likely to remain so. Able-bodied athletics (track and field in US parlance) accounted for 20 per cent of all tests conducted, with cycling, triathlon, weightlifting and swimming following behind. American football was subject to only fourteen tests, baseball sixteen, and basketball twenty. Cheerleading, with twelve in-competition tests, was only just behind these three iconic American sports in USADA's testing list.

The lack of tests of major team sports by USADA is not indicative of a lack of interest, nor even of a belief that these sports are clean. Instead, the sports conduct their own testing programmes, with frameworks that are the subject of lengthy negotiations with the players' unions. Major League Baseball, for example, conducted 8,158 tests in 2015, not far short of USADA's grand total. Players know they will have to provide urine samples at the start and end of each season, and be subject to random tests for human growth hormone. The number of sanctions against players has increased as testing sophistication has improved and as the MLB has secured greater frequency of tests in its negotiations with the union.

Highly structured agreements between the leagues and the players' unions militate against the effectiveness of these anti-doping programmes. Surprise, off-season tests are the most effective, but these remain a minor part of the negotiated deals. There can be little doubt that they are necessary, as any student of the Bay Area Laboratory Co-Operative (BALCO) affair would testify. Victor Conte's BALCO supplied performance-enhancing drugs to a series of high-profile stars, including Dwain Chambers, across a range of sports, notably baseball, athletics and American football. A federal investigation assisted by USADA and brought into the public arena by a pair of journalists at the *San Francisco Chronicle* eventually broke the scandal. Conte was jailed. Some stars were sanctioned. Others avoided punishment for lack of hard evidence of doping, but had their reputations tarnished with a mental asterisk against their names in the minds of the sporting public. *Game of Shadows*, the book chronicling the scandal by the two journalists, Mark Fainaru-Wada and Lance Williams, still stands as a sobering reminder of the scale of the challenge facing the anti-doping authorities.

If testing programmes were entirely randomly administered, it would be easy to conclude that a drugs cheat has a very minimal chance of being detected. That may indeed be the case, but the anti-doping authorities improve their odds of success by directing their scarce resources towards those athletes deemed to represent a higher risk. This category obviously includes the successful stars, because they might have cheated their way to success but also because the public needs to be confident that the success it sees is honestly won. Top athletes are indeed tested often within competitions, and are likely to be sought out unannounced by doping officers at other times. It is these out-of-competition tests that are most likely to detect doping, as only a naive or inept cheat is likely to fall foul of an in-competition test that they know is coming their way if they compete successfully.

The authorities also direct their scarce resources according to the intelligence they gather from a variety of sources about possible doping violations. In the UK investigatory work by UKAD, often in harness with the police, has turned up the use of performance-enhancing drugs in a number of cases away from the top end of sport. It is no coincidence that UKAD's first chairman, the impressive David Kenworthy, is a former policeman. His successor had been head of both the National Crime Squad and its replacement the Serious Organised Crime Agency. Such investigative work, however, is expensive, and UKAD's slim resources only stretch to employing a couple of full-time investigators. In consequence, the authorities have often appeared to lag behind the media in the hunt for doping cheats. The media, in turn, have found whistle-blowers, both public and covert, a fruitful source of leads. With the authorities having a necessarily high burden of proof to establish, and lengthy investigative processes, it is not surprising that those with whistles to blow often choose to go to the press in search of an accelerated outcome.

USADA's annual revenue is just under $17 million, three quarters of it in the form of a federal grant and a contractual arrangement with the US Olympic Committee. America is a nation with a population almost five times the size of the UK's; its anti-doping agency's budget is less than twice Britain's, although their differing scopes make comparison an inexact exercise. Before the UK's Department of Digital, Culture, Media and Sport thinks to congratulate itself on the scale of its investment, however, it should remember that UKAD's grant-in-aid support from the British government amounts to only about 4 per cent of the budget of UK Sport. This could be viewed as a 4 per cent insurance premium paid by the government to protect the integrity of the nation's direct investment in elite sport. So modest is this premium, it is easy to conclude that it has bought an insurance policy that offers only a bare minimum of cover. Moreover, the US government does not invest directly in elite sport in the same way as its UK counterpart, so may not be deemed to have the same direct financial imperative to ensure sufficient doping detection and prevention mechanisms are in place.

The BALCO scandal broke in 2003. Systemic cheating across a range of sports was laid bare, at its centre one individual and one laboratory. A dozen years later, the systematic corruption of sport on a far greater scale was revealed, at its centre one nation and notoriously one hole in the wall of a testing laboratory. To this day, Victor Conte's motives in creating his cocktail of drugs – dubbed the Clear – remain opaque. They probably in part mirrored those of the athletes he supplied: a mix of monetary and reputational reward laced with a desire to exercise power and influence. Today, the sporting world is similarly left to speculate as to the motives behind Russia's wholesale corruption of competition. Reputational reward, power and influence are again likely to be to the fore. Money, however, may be no object, making it especially hard to construct punishments to fit the crimes.

Investigators were first put on to BALCO by the receipt in the post of a syringe of liquid from an anonymous source, later found to be track and field coach Trevor Graham, who numbered triple Olympic gold medallist Marion Jones among his athletes. The Russian scandal was similarly revealed by an individual at the heart of the corruption. The collaboration between Yuliya Stepanova, the banned 800-metre runner, and documentary maker Hajo Seppelt triggered an investigation into systemic cheating within Russian athletics. In turn, assisted again by a whistle-blower, this led to the discovery that the testing laboratory at the Sochi 2014 Winter Olympics and Paralympics had a hole in the wall through which Russian athletes' samples were swapped for clean urine in order to avoid failed tests. First, the IAAF suspended the Russian Athletics Federation from competition; then the International Paralympic Committee took the same step with the Russian Paralympic Committee, so barring Russia from the Rio Paralympics.

The formal investigations into Russian doping in athletics and at Sochi were undertaken by independent panels commissioned by the World Anti-Doping Agency (WADA). The first was led by Dick Pound, WADA's first president, the second by Richard McLaren, a prominent international sports lawyer. Their work, and more particularly its reception by the IOC, highlighted the inherent financial tension within WADA's construction, a tension which might yet prove a fatal flaw in the battle between dopers and advocates of clean sport. Where the IPC banned Russia wholesale, the IOC handed responsibility for deciding whether the country should be barred from Rio over to individual sports.

The result was a mish-mash, with some sports banning Russia outright, some imposing bans on selected Russians, and others no bans at all.

WADA was founded in 1999 and four years later published the World Anti-Doping Code. The Agency is effectively the global coordinator of anti-doping activity. It polices adherence to the Code, manages the ADAMS system so that athletes on the testing register can be tested wherever they are in the world, pursues scientific research, delivers athlete education programmes on doping matters and works to assist law enforcement agencies in the pursuit of offenders. It describes itself as 'an international independent agency'. But in the eyes of many that is not strictly true.

At its creation WADA was conceived as an equal venture between the Olympic movement and governments worldwide. Its funding is split equally between the two groups; its thirty-eight-member Foundation Board is also evenly divided, and its presidency alternates between a candidate nominated by the governments and a candidate from within the IOC family. In 2017 it invoiced governments around the world for $15 million, with the IOC matching this dollar for dollar. In addition, WADA receives a grant from the city of Montreal in return for basing its activities there. In 2016 the Agency had total income of $30 million, enabling it to employ eighty-eight staff.

The intuitive reaction – that this is not a sufficient sum of money, nor enough personnel, to coordinate the anti-doping movement worldwide – is reinforced by the costs of the various investigations into systemic doping in Russia. By early 2017 one reckoning put these at $3.7 million to date. WADA's balance sheet at the end of 2016 showed reserves equal to just over 80 per cent of a year's spending by the Agency – not an unhealthy balance but insufficient to allow it to take much risk in its relationships with its paymasters.

The Agency's key relationship, that with the IOC, was tested
as never before in the run-up to the Rio Olympics. WADA's president, Craig Reedie, is an IOC vice-president, and he found himself in charge of an organisation out of step with many of his
IOC colleagues, including its president, Thomas Bach. Money
was talking, with the largest wallet having by far the loudest voice.

The United States, Japan and Canada are by a clear margin
the biggest individual governmental contributors to WADA's budget, at $2.2 million, $1.5 million and $1.1 million respectively.
Five major European nations, including Russia and the UK, each
contribute $0.8 million. Reflecting its relative inability to pay, and
no doubt realism on the part of WADA negotiators past, Africa
as a whole is invoiced for only $74,312. The major developed-
world sporting nations, those with a material stake in the sporting
game, therefore provide virtually all WADA's budget, but no one
country contributes a game-changing sum of money. Britain's
contribution, by the way, comes out of UKAD's grant-in-aid
from the government. Of the eight largest governmental contributors to WADA's income, five currently have seats at the Foundation Board table. While it is safe to assume that the IOC WADA
Board members are unlikely to have homogenous views on any
issue, it can nonetheless be seen that governments are not well
placed to exercise influence, nor given the rather trivial sums
involved are they likely to have the stomach for a bloody struggle
against IOC interests.

If it is assumed that all parties on the WADA Board are mo-
tivated to protect their investment in sport, then it has to be
asked both whether they consider their investment anywhere
near sufficient and whether the Agency's governance structure
is fit for purpose. The IOC's unrestricted reserves at the end of
2016 stood at $1.5 billion. That's enough to cover a hundred
years of its contributions to WADA at the current rate. Indeed,
they could probably fund the entire spend on anti-doping by

agencies worldwide over a full four-year Olympic cycle. The thirty-four WADA-accredited laboratories around the world analysed 328,000 samples in 2016, suggesting that probably only a few hundred million dollars a year is spent on the global battle against doping.

If the IOC truly believes that demonstrably clean sport is vital to the health of its brand, then it needs to have the courage not only to increase its financial contribution to anti-doping, but also to establish a firewall between its funding of WADA and the organisation's governance. The IOC proclaims its not-for-profit status, but the pressure it appeared to exert on WADA at the height of the Russian crisis in 2016 was indicative of a deeply commercial enterprise that had fallen into the trap of allowing short-term considerations to blind it to its own long-term interests. In early 2017, assailed by criticism of its role in the fight against doping, the IOC claimed that the total spend on anti-doping by all parties around the globe amounted to around $300 million a year, so emphasising that critics should not focus solely on its direct contribution to WADA. But one might still ask whether this figure is sufficient.

If WADA was reconstructed so that the IOC was deemed a major customer rather than effectively a co-owner, then WADA could be held to account in the delivery of cleaner sport according to agreed objectives and standards of delivery. Of course, WADA would never want to jeopardise its existence by losing its major customer, but if governments stood ready to make good any lost revenue should the IOC behave unreasonably, then WADA's leadership would enjoy a freedom of movement currently curtailed by an overbearing Olympic movement. It would also be healthier for WADA if the contribution of Olympic sports was made directly by each discipline rather than by virtue of their being part of the collective Games. If the IOC were not WADA's sole dominant customer, but was joined by a set of major sports, then the Agency's ability to set its own course would be strengthened.

In the absence of a material change in funding structures, national anti-doping agencies are on the prowl for alternative sources of income. UKAD was contracted to step into the shoes of RUSADA on the suspension of the Russian anti-doping agency and to operate drugs testing within Russia after the WADA-approved laboratory in Moscow lost its accredited status. This was the highest possible endorsement of UKAD's existing consultancy work around the world, both with anti-doping authorities and sporting events. Such a contract was not without its risks given the febrile environment, replete with aggressive posturing, that surrounded the Russian suspensions. The decision to accept the contract was apparently not an easy one for the UKAD Board to make, with one of the decisive factors in favour the high profit margin that the UKAD team had factored into their pricing of the project, such was its imperative to find extra income.

UKAD will have entered into its Russian contract hoping that it would prove relatively short-lived, and with an eye on how it could engineer an eventual withdrawal from Moscow with its reputation and finances both intact. Neither are a given. History does not relate whether USADA was given the opportunity to bid for this work. The American agency has, however, capitalised on its reputation for noisy advocacy of the benefits of clean sport to secure a long-term contract with one of the newest arrivals on the sporting scene, the Ultimate Fighting Championship.

UFC mixed martial arts is very much a millennial phenomenon, although its foundation dates back to 1993. In mid-2015 USADA became the global independent anti-doping administrator for the UFC, responsible for all aspects of anti-doping in the sport, from the education of athletes to testing. In its first six months of operation it conducted 353 tests and handed down one sanction on a fighter. Here we can see a sport that understands the significance of a rigorous independent anti-doping regime for credibility in the eyes of its public, and is prepared to pay for it on an arms-length basis. Doubtless there are discussions between UFC and USADA about standards of delivery, just as there would be in any commercial arrangement, and it might just prove to be a model for an enlightened future relationship between the IOC and WADA, if only both were prepared to step outside their current overly engineered arrangements for the good of the sports they serve.

The final of the 100 metres at the 2017 World Athletics Championships wasn't the send-off that Usain Bolt had hoped for as he headed into retirement. Justin Gatlin, twice convicted and banned for doping offences, won gold with Bolt an unaccustomed third. You will doubtless have your own perspective on the morality tale woven around Dwain Chambers, Justin Gatlin and other sportspeople who have been found guilty of doping. I knew instantly, as Gatlin crossed the finish line, that our event would make global headlines overnight, but the spontaneous booing that broke out from the crowd was a surprise and became the journalists' focus. Commentators worked themselves into a lather about the rights and wrongs of jeering an athlete who had served his time for cheating, but as a damning public judgement of the performance of the authorities in their battle against drugs cheats it couldn't have been clearer.

12

LONDON'S COLISEUM

The marquee gleamed white in the unseasonably bright November sunshine. Press and VIPs had been ushered through the layers of security, a general sense of bonhomie in the air. The London Games were a little under five years away and we were gathered for the unveiling of the design for the Olympic Stadium. Even the hardest of hearts couldn't fail to beat faster when we were told that we were seated on top of the finish line for the athletics track. As ever, LOCOG's spin machine had sweated the fine details.

The design concept was as much a surprise to me as it was to the rest of the audience. UK Athletics had been consulted on the technical requirements of our sport. Could the long- and triple-jump pits be inside the track rather than outside it, for example, so bringing spectators closer? (Yes, but it messes badly with the competition timetable as you have to work around the dangers of flying implements from the field events.) We had also been quizzed on the basic requirements for future hosting of major international events, in particular the stadium capacity that the IAAF and European Athletics ask of host cities. But we'd not been engaged in any meaningful discussions about the practicalities of operating the stadium, in particular how it might be used by us and others during the summer athletics season, so I was as pregnant with expectation as anyone in the marquee that morning.

It's fair to say that the big reveal from LOCOG Chairman Seb Coe and London Mayor Ken Livingstone was a jaw-dropper – and not at first sight in a bad way. Conscious of the long history of white elephants from Olympics past, they had opted for what they described as a demountable stadium with a capacity of 80,000 at Games time, reducing to 25,000 for posterity. The audience and by extension the wider world were told that they hoped to sell the remaining 55,000 seats and their supporting infrastructure – the upper tier and roof of the stadium – to a future host of the Games. Chicago was the city that tripped off most tongues in the hurly-burly after the formal launch had concluded. This was billed as a £496 million solution to the stadium challenge, and that before anything recouped from the sale of its upper two thirds – barely used, one careful previous owner.

Looking back at the BBC's report of the launch with the benefit of more than a decade's hindsight, and with all that has transpired subsequently, the quotes attributed to the three major players make salutary reading. 'No one can say we've compromised on design, on sustainability or on the legacy potential.' (Olympics Minister Tessa Jowell) 'A stadium for a new era.' (Seb Coe) 'We made a commitment there would be a permanent athletics facility and we have honoured that commitment. For West Ham, we have identified a site much better suited to their needs.' (Ken Livingstone)

Spool forward to the London Stadium, as it has been renamed, and the concept of a demountable stadium now seems risible, or at least the belief that this particular stadium's upper bowl could have been deconstructed and shipped across the Atlantic, then inland to the Windy City for replanting atop an identikit lower bowl ready for a 2016 Games. With hindsight I wonder why it wasn't instantly obvious to all of us that this emperor was in the buff.

The Olympic Stadium saga stands as an object lesson in how grand sporting ambitions can have unwelcome financial and reputational consequences. In this instance, taxpayers were left to pick up an unexpected bill years after the Games circus had folded its tents and left town. The success of a highly ambitious urban regeneration project was overshadowed by the failure both to plan intelligently for its flagship property and to deal effectively with the deficiencies in the original plan when they became apparent. This tale of woe deserves retelling, to illuminate the scale of the economic and logistical challenges facing cities who wish to rise to the status of Olympic host, and to help explain why the list of those expressing that ambition is becoming ever shorter.

The first person to blow the whistle to me on the folly of the stadium design was the redoubtable Margaret Ford, who was appointed the first chair of the London Legacy Development Corporation in spring 2009. The LLDC was created by London's mayor to plan and manage the development of the Olympic Park, the physical legacy of the 2012 Games. It did not take its board of directors long to realise that it had been handed a poisoned chalice, nor that its decisions on the stadium would likely define its own reputation, regardless of any successes it might have elsewhere in the Park in the years ahead.

Margaret Ford invited me to her office in Stratford a few months into her tenure. In a style I came to know and respect, but which was disarming encountered for the first time, she told me that the 25,000-seat scaled-down stadium would become a windswept piece of rubbish – or words to that effect. There was only a slim budget in the LLDC's plans for the reconfiguration of the stadium, and that would certainly not stretch to providing a roof against the vagaries of an English summer for athletics meetings – or more importantly winter weather should any low-er-division football club show interest in becoming a tenant too. Moreover, the hospitality facilities for the Games in the stadium's west stand would have to come down as they did not have planning permission to become permanent, even though they were being constructed to a standard to provide the utmost security for Olympic dignitaries, from the Queen downwards. And without hospitality, the economics of using a modern stadium are severely compromised.

Already blame was being attached to the trio of decision-makers, Livingstone, Jowell and Coe, who had left Ford and her colleagues with the colossal headache, and to athletics for being a sport incapable of supporting a more economically viable solution. I had a good deal of sympathy for Ford's position. Athletics is indeed a sport that can only sell a few days of action to substantial crowds each summer – and before 2012 substantial meant 15,000 spectators at Crystal Palace, barely a respectable crowd for a Championship football team. However, UKA had never cavilled at sharing the stadium with a football club and the decision to eschew Premier League soccer was as perplexing to us as it was to many others. We were, though, determined that we wouldn't be denied a physical legacy that could transform the opportunities for our sport, however much we might be pressured to do so. Atlanta 1996 had left behind a baseball stadium in lieu of an athletics facility, depriving the entire United States of an athletics venue of true substance. We could not abide the thought of a similar Games legacy in Britain.

Apologists for the decision to exclude top-flight football from the Olympic Stadium design and long-term plans for its usage point to the change in ownership of West Ham United as pivotal. Before the takeover by David Gold and David Sullivan, it is claimed that West Ham's owners had no interest in a tenancy in Stratford. Ken Livingstone was also quoted back in 2010 as believing that a bid to host the Olympics based on a football legacy for the main stadium would not have succeeded. We will never know if that would have been the case, but what we do know is that the new West Ham owners' first high-profile public pronouncement on the stadium had all the appearance of an attempted coup.

The deal to buy West Ham was announced in January 2010. In February David Gold told the BBC, in confirming his club's interest in striking a deal to move into the Olympic Stadium, 'One other possibility is to abandon the athletic idea altogether and maybe build a small athletics stadium that can be used for ever. Not as an Olympic athletics stadium but a regional stadium with seating facility commensurate to their requirements which would be about 5,000.'

It seemed the size of the athletics legacy stadium was shrinking at an accelerating rate. I hit back publicly at the 'patronising' attitude of football and in return received a phone call out of the blue from a West Ham director who asked me not to take any notice of David Gold but to listen instead to their chief executive Karren Brady, who had a very different view. Whatever Brady's private thoughts about athletics, it became clear at our first meeting in March 2010 that she had an entirely pragmatic view of what might be necessary for her to secure a tenancy of the Olympic Stadium and with it a transformation of West Ham's financial prospects. Then, after a sudden intervention from Tottenham Hotspur, itself wrestling with meeting demand for tickets and hospitality provision that far outstripped the capacity of its existing ground, the battle lines were drawn.

Early in 2010 we hatched a plan with Seb Coe to bid to host the IAAF World Athletics Championships in London in 2015. What better way, we figured, to cement a spectator legacy from the Games for track and field and demonstrate the continuing viability of an athletics track in the Olympic Stadium? It was also

clear by then that Coe intended to take a tilt at the post of president of the IAAF, which might conceivably become vacant in the
summer of 2011, although the incumbent Lamine Diack was
proving typically Delphic in pronouncements about his own future. Coe was highly unlikely to stand against the sitting president, but he needed to be ready, and the prospect of a London
World Championships would have the corollary benefit of enhancing his credentials in the eyes of the IAAF electorate. Making clear our intention to bid for the World Championships,
which had an autumn 2010 deadline, very deliberately added a
twist of tension to the debate about the Stadium.

The stakes for West Ham and Tottenham could be measured
against the cost of Arsenal's Emirates Stadium, which the club
had moved into in 2006. The 60,000-seat venue, by Arsenal's
own account, cost £390 million. Some £260 million of this was
financed with a debt facility, the remainder from other sources
including the residential development of its old Highbury Stadium site. The Emirates is almost universally regarded as the gold
standard of new football stadiums in Britain – certainly it has the
ancillary facilities necessary to maximise matchday revenues and
cater for the conference and hospitality markets at other times.
Any London club in particular would need to aspire to similar
quantity and quality of provision in the understandable belief
that over the very long run in football money breeds success.

To this day Tottenham's intervention in the Stadium saga remains perplexing, although to its credit the club's plans were
unambiguous. It wanted to raze the Olympic arena to the ground
and start from scratch with a purpose-built football stadium in
the belief that in the UK athletics and soccer could not co-exist
effectively within one stadium, given British fans' desire to get up
close to the pitch. Continental European grounds often have a
running track between spectators and players, but this viewing
experience doesn't appeal to Britons used to tight, intense stadi-

ums. What is strange is that, at least as far as I could see, Tottenham made very little effort to address the politics of the Olympics, in particular the legacy questions, which were so prominent at the time and which have subsequently proved a millstone around the neck of the Olympic memory in all manner of ways.

It is highly probable, of course, that Tottenham's chairman, Daniel Levy, and his colleagues were doing all their work behind the scenes in addressing the need for an Olympic legacy in any stadium planning. I took one brief phone call from Levy, who asked whether we would consider a commitment to redevelop the stadium at Crystal Palace in lieu of a UK Athletics tenancy at the Olympic Stadium. This suggestion was reinforced by a meeting in early 2011 with Keith Mills, a non-executive director on the Tottenham Hotspur board but more significantly also the deputy chairman of LOCOG and a key player in the Olympic project from its early days. At his office in St James's he showed me plans for a football ground on the Stratford site and in a persistent but gentlemanly fashion pressed home Tottenham's view that athletics meetings in the Olympic Stadium were simply not viable. The irony of the second-in-command of the London Games advocating the removal of its athletics track was not lost on me. Impeccable financial analysis it may have been, but in a dark corner somewhere the soul of the Olympics was weeping.

By now our plans to bid for the 2015 IAAF World Athletics Championships had been scuppered by the Stadium farrago. Any bid needed a government financial guarantee – an IAAF requirement – and Hugh Robertson, the sports minister of the day, had made clear to me just before the formal bid deadline in October that one wouldn't be forthcoming while the future of the athletics track at the Stadium was in doubt. We had already submitted an indicative bid to the IAAF by then, in part to keep up pressure on government and the LLDC, in part to ensure that the IAAF was vocal in its support for our lobbying. We knew the IAAF would never grant us the Championships while there was such uncertainty. It had been badly bitten in the past by British promises that had turned to dust – a planned stadium at Pickett's Lock (just down the road from Tottenham as it happens) for the 2005 Championships which at the very last minute became a proposal for Sheffield to host the event. The IAAF had not been amused, and its corporate memory was more than long enough for any promises this time to have to be forged in steel, whether from Sheffield or elsewhere.

Meanwhile the politicians and bureaucrats within any meaningful distance of the Stadium decision were in a state of seemingly constant nervousness, as if a judicial review was always just around the next corner – which it probably was, to be fair. Even Seb Coe was apparently reluctant to speak out on the subject, to our mounting frustration. Salvation came from an unexpected corner in the shape of IAAF President Lamine Diack. Stung by memories of the Pickett's Lock snub to his organisation, and mindful of the lesson of Atlanta 1996 for athletics, he weighed into the debate at the start of 2011. Britain would have told 'a big lie' in its bid for the Olympics if football took over the Stadium at the expense of athletics. 'You can consider you are dead. You are finished.' Within days, Coe too had found his voice, to our great relief. The timing was everything. Just over a year and a half before the Games, avoiding embarrassment was a major priority for the broad church of interested parties in the UK. Had the debate been taking place after the Games, the effect of Diack's intervention would have been far weaker.

West Ham United was chosen as the preferred football tenant in February 2011. (Who knows what happened to former Mayor Ken Livingstone's site 'better suited' to them?) The big guns had voiced their support very late in the day, but there was a plethora of positive statements once the decision had been made. I was invited by West Ham to a reception at Forman's on Fish Island, overlooking the Olympic Stadium, to hear the LLDC's decision announced on screen. I watched as David Gold told the assembled press of a school cross-country run when he was a kid and his delight that day that his club would be moving into the Olympic Stadium. I'm sure I saw a tear roll down his cheek, although it might just have been a trick of the sunlight which was bouncing around the room.

That summer the cards continued to fall athletics' way, even though the LLDC's decision remained open to challenge and review. The IAAF had opened the bidding process for its 2017 World Championships a year earlier than would have normally been the case. Some colleagues at UKA, spooked by the political machinations of the IAAF, believed this was the work of anti-British IAAF Council members looking to minimise the chances of London winning while uncertainty prevailed over the Olympic Stadium's future. I preferred to look at it as a godsend to hammer home our position with the decision-makers at the LLDC and in government.

In April, with the Games fast approaching, we engineered a meeting between London's mayor, Boris Johnson, and Lamine Diack at the annual Sport Accord beano for governing bodies, businesses, event organisers and host cities, held that year in London. We needed Diack to understand from Johnson that London was serious in its intent to host the Worlds. Unsurprisingly, the Stadium was pretty much the only matter at issue.

Six months later, with our formal bid presentation only five weeks away, the IAAF sent its Evaluation Commission to London to kick the tyres of our bid before heading off to Doha to do the same to our only rivals. Its reports were unlikely to make much of a difference to the IAAF Council's final decision, unless it found a fundamental flaw in either. We knew what ours might be and decided to address it up front, straight after breakfast on the first morning of the Commission's visit.

We gathered a small group in a meeting room at the St Pancras Renaissance Hotel, including Margaret Ford, Seb Coe and Hugh Robertson. We were only missing Boris Johnson, who we were told was just minutes away on his bike. The mayor swept in, sweaty, with only seconds to spare, and we settled down with the Commission members to square away any doubts they might have about our ability to deliver the Olympic Stadium with a track. Seb Coe set the scene for his IAAF Council colleagues. Hugh Robertson, with due reverence, then slid a letter across the table from the government setting out its commitment to the track, accompanied by soft words of reassurance. The presentational baton was now passed to Johnson so that London could back up the commitment. The mayor apologised for not having a letter, grabbed a pad of hotel-branded paper from the middle of the conference table and told the visiting dignitaries that he'd write whatever letter they wanted him to. I thought it might be all over for us and looked for the exit, but there was no need. Cue laughter, and the evaluation visit was now on the road.

Once the decision in principle to rebuff Tottenham had been made, a succession of LLDC leaders dug in with their lawyers and saw off a series of challenges to their choice. At the same time West Ham engaged in an attritional battle to finalise the terms of a ninety-nine-year lease of the stadium during the football season. You don't have to be an expert in game theory to realise that almost all the cards were in the Hammers' hand once the decision had been made to retain the athletics track. As each nuance of the club's tenancy agreement has found its way into the press, the recognition that West Ham secured a stellar financial deal has grown. It's not just the basic rent, a mere £2.5 million a year, or the modest nature of the anti-embarrassment clause that Boris Johnson secured for himself in the event the club was sold, or even West Ham's contribution of just £15 million to the conversion costs, but the fine details about what was or was not included. The media got particularly exercised on discovering that West Ham did not even have to pay for its own corner flags.

The real value to West Ham lies in the opportunity provided by the renamed London Stadium to grow its income. Arsenal's financial accounts for 2015/16 show gate and matchday revenues from its 60,000-seat stadium of £100 million. This equates to just under £1,700 per seat per season. West Ham's old Boleyn Ground had a capacity of 35,000. The club's financial accounts filed at Companies House show income from 'match receipts and related football activities' of £27 million in 2015/16, its last season at the Boleyn. The numbers may not be strictly comparable, but this equates to under half the per-seat yield generated by Arsenal. In order to fill its new home, West Ham will have had to sell a large number of low-price season tickets. On the other hand, hospitality opportunities will have increased given the breadth of provision created in the new arena. However one models the possible uplift in likely income, the addition of at least 20,000 new seats (the final maximum capacity continues to be adjusted) means that it must dwarf West Ham's annual rent. Indeed, the club's £15 million conversion cost contribution may well have been recouped in the first season in the London Stadium with something to spare.

UK Athletics' tenancy deal is even cheaper, and for its size just as important to it as West Ham's, although the numbers involved are much more modest. As noted earlier, athletics is a sport with a short summer season with few opportunities to generate a substantial audience. UKA has been granted a ninety-nine-year lease for a few weeks each summer, with a break clause after fifty years. In effect it pays no rent, merely the marginal costs of opening up and using the Stadium such as security. The financial benefit of this arrangement for an organisation with total revenues of around £24 million is critical. In the summer of 2014 the Olympic Stadium was closed for redevelopment and UKA posted a loss that year of just over £0.5 million. When it was open again in the summer of 2015, hosting a two-day Diamond League meeting and one-day IPC Grand Prix Final, the governing body made a profit of a little more than £1.2 million. Although there were a number of relevant factors, it's fair to say that the difference of almost £1.8 million was pretty much entirely the result of being able to stage our showpiece events in a much larger venue. And not just a larger one, but a modern one with excellent transport links, unlike the crumbling arena in Crystal Palace Park.

The last card that West Ham played in its negotiations came when there really was no other show in town. It insisted on the installation of retractable seats so as to overcome the problem of fan resistance to a continental-style viewing experience across a running track to the football pitch. And so tenders were invited for the Stadium's conversion that not only included a new roof and permanent back-of-house facilities to replace the empty and temporary spaces that existed for the 2012 Games, but also movable seats in the lower bowl of the arena. The Stade de France has such flexibility, so the announcement that the same arrangement would be used in Stratford was interesting but set no hares running, aside from a further rise in the overall conversion costs. The adjectives used to describe the seating solution by those leading the project also lulled observers – dreaming no doubt of hydraulics and other mechanical solutions – into a sense of security.

For the LLDC, reaping little return from West Ham each year and next to none from UK Athletics, it was vital that the lower bowl seats not only moved, but did so quickly and cheaply. Squeezing events into the Stadium in the few weeks between the end of the football season and the start of the athletics season is central to its economic model. The London market for hosting major rock and pop gigs is fiercely competitive, because it can be highly lucrative. Twickenham has tight restrictions from Richmond Council on the number of such events it can host each year; Arsenal occasionally uses the Emirates for concerts; the FA is a major player as it continues to address the financial challenge of the cost of building the new Wembley, even a decade after it opened. With the conspicuous success of indoor gigs at the O2, there is clearly scope to attract big audiences to the right outdoor venue in the east of London. Johnson's successor as mayor, Sadiq Khan, also had his eye on bringing a Major League Baseball fixture to the capital, as well as a pair of matches in cricket's 2019 World Cup. The boundaries had been measured and found to be distant enough from the planned drop-in wicket – as long, of course, as the seats were fully retracted.

The first hint that there might be a problem with the seating came at the UK Athletics Diamond League meeting in July 2016. The seats along the back straight of the track remained forward – in 'football mode' to use the LLDC's parlance – covering the long-jump runway that we had intended to use. We were told they hadn't quite had time to move them. A few weeks later they informed us that they thought this seating configuration had worked so well they intended to leave it like that for the two World Championships the next summer. The logistical ramifications were substantial for us, and the decision could only be rationalised if there was a problem with the seating, which indeed there was.

Sky News broke the story of the immovable, movable seating. Its sports editor, Paul Kelso, was filmed in the bowels of the London Stadium standing underneath the seats in the lower bowl of the east stand. To the untrained eye he appeared to be on a building site, surrounded by scaffolding poles and breeze blocks. And not a hydraulic anything in sight. The cost, he claimed, of moving the seats each season was up to £8 million, and just as importantly it was an exercise that took weeks not hours, or even a couple of days as was generally believed. The immovable seats were also blowing a hole in the plan for monetising the Stadium between the two sporting seasons.

The position of chair of the London Legacy Development Corporation appears to have been cursed, or subject to the bitterest politics. Margaret Ford was unceremoniously removed by Boris Johnson only weeks before the London 2012 Games. She was replaced by Daniel Moylan, whose tenure lasted a mere three months. When Moylan moved on his seat was filled by the mayor himself, although the heavy lifting was undertaken by his aide Neale Coleman, who in time was bumped up from deputy chair to chair. Late in 2015 he left to work, very briefly, as an adviser to new Labour Party leader Jeremy Corbyn. The LLDC reins were then assumed by one of its non-executive directors, David Edmonds. Just under a year later the retractable seating fiasco led to his resignation. To all intents and purposes he lost a game of Pass the Bomb.

With a degree of ill-disguised relish, Mayor Sadiq Khan launched an inquiry into the escalating costs of the Stadium conversion, joining the list of such investigations into the projects of his predecessor, the proposed Garden Bridge being the most prominent. A statement from his office at City Hall revealed that the total bill for the London Stadium was now £752 million. Remember, the Emirates cost £390 million. The new Wembley, on the other hand, set the FA back almost £800 million, although the contractors had to bear approaching £200 million of additional cost overruns on their own account. The report that was then produced by auditors Moore Stephens for the Mayor concluded that the transformation of the Stadium had cost £133 million more than originally projected, and that it was operating at an annual loss of £20 million. In an attempt to staunch these losses, Khan announced he was taking full control of the venue and would attempt to renegotiate the deals with its tenants that were providing him with so little income.

The three stadiums are now head to head in the capital's events market. The LLDC has the advantage over the FA and Arsenal of being able to fall back on public funding, although clearly a call to City Hall about money is not great for job security for its leaders. It is, however, saddled with unremunerative tenancy agreements for the bulk of the year and an operating configuration that is far from ideal. This after all is a stadium originally designed to be reduced to its lower bowl only. And a fixed lower bowl at that.

At the height of the battle between West Ham and Tottenham over the Olympic Stadium's future, the president and CEO of Spurs' bidding partner, AEG, predicted that the Olympic Stadium would be 'bust in ten years' if the combined football and athletics option prevailed. Had it not been for the protection of public ownership, it looks from subsequent events as though he would certainly have been right.

13

POSSESSION OF THE LAW

The offices of the Uganda Athletics Federation are tucked away in a row of backstreet shops in downtown Kampala, just off the Entebbe Road. A couple of rooms cluttered with files, old copies of track and field magazines and sporting mementos are home to the handful of elected volunteers and staff who administer athletics for a nation of 35 million people, Africa's tenth-largest population. Six miles down the road is the cavernous Mandela National Stadium, a 40,000-seat concrete bowl that is home to the national football team, the Uganda Cranes. It was a gift from the People's Republic of China, built to a standard blueprint as part of a campaign to cement international influence. Although it only opened in 1997, it already looks much the worse for wear. The Mandela National Stadium contains Uganda's only modern athletics track.

On the day I visit this track is teeming with children being schooled by trainee coaches as part of UK Athletics' international influence programme. In bidding to host the World Athletics Championships we had promised to fly coach mentors around the world to tutor teachers in how to coach athletics to youngsters. Our budget didn't run to building new stadiums, but we did have human capital to deploy in the developing world. Uganda was the first stop. Teachers had arrived from across the country for a week of tuition, some taking more than a day to complete a journey that made a mockery of Western conceptions of distance. Their inspiration, and that of the children they schooled, was Stephen Kiprotich, Ugandan winner of the men's marathon at London 2012. It made me smile inwardly to learn that Kiprotich had a sometimes delicate relationship with the Uganda Athletics Federation; problems between star athletes and their governing bodies are truly a global phenomenon.

The home of the International Association of Athletics Federations is altogether more lavish. Located on the quayside in Monaco a short jog from the Fairmont Hotel – at which the IAAF's previous president maintained a permanent suite – the offices were hailed by Prince Albert on their opening in 2015 as evidence of the long and prosperous relationship between the principality and the international governing body. Towards the bottom of its press release heralding the opening, the IAAF noted that it continued to maintain a separate executive office for the president, the Villa Miraflores on Avenue Saint-Michel overlooking the Casino.

Subsequent events, including the arrest of President Lamine Diack by French police investigating claims of corruption, might provide a clue as to why this second office was kept apart from the IAAF's operational staff in their shiny new billet. Out of sight and out of mind. It may be, however, that Diack was simply loath to leave the villa's sumptuous embrace. Villa Miraflores was one of the attractions that helped lure the IAAF from London when it relocated its operations to the shores of the Mediterranean in 1994. The Nazi Party had similarly recognised and utilised the villa's charms when the Germans occupied Monaco. One of Seb Coe's symbolic early acts on succeeding Diack was to hand the keys to Miraflores back to the principality and to cancel the suite at the Fairmont. At the time of writing in 2018, the French police investigation remained ongoing.

Uganda is one of the 214 member federations of the IAAF, ranging from Afghanistan to Zimbabwe via Aruba, Micronesia, Surinam and Vanuatu – more than the 193 member states of the United Nations. Each has an equal vote in electing the IAAF's president and the other members of its ruling council. The contrast between the riches at the centre and the penury of most of the organisation's member federations is most stark during the lobbying ahead of each quadrennial election congress. The presidency and council seats are unpaid positions, but the trappings of power can appear considerable, especially to those on the outside who rely heavily on largesse from Monaco to support their work in the sport. Votes are swung by electoral promises that can appear very modest to those from the larger nations with little appreciation of the travails of the vast majority of their counterparts. There are some who carp that all the member federations have a say in the selection of the sport's leadership. Many of the minnows may send no more than a single athlete to a major competition and don't even have a track facility. But that is the constitution, and it is this that maps out the battleground on which elections are contested.

The 2015 IAAF presidential election was a hard-fought affair. Lamine Diack was bowing out after four terms of four years. Incumbent presidents tend not to have their re-elections opposed (not necessarily a good thing for sporting democracy or administration), so this was a rare opportunity to get one's feet under the desk. Seb Coe and Sergey Bubka, vice presidents both, were the two candidates. With three months to run, the Briton's electoral intelligence, part-funded by UK Sport's international influence budget, suggested the outcome was too close to call. In a hotel suite in Doha, looking out over the shimmering waters of the Gulf, I sat with Coe and IAAF Deputy General Secretary

Nick Davies hammering out a plan to distribute a chunk of the IAAF's reserves to its electorate. If it is a once-every-four-years occurrence for an organisation like the IAAF to truly remember it exists for its members, then it was only at a moment like this that wealth redistribution was ever likely to be considered and enacted.

At the end of 2012 the IAAF's balance sheet sported reserves of $89 million. This was a high point in the quadrennial cycle of its resources, as it had received its dues from the International Olympic Committee on the back of that year's Olympics. The IOC pays a fee to each of the sports that take part in its Games according to a formula designed to gauge relative popularity. In 2012 that fee amounted to $47 million for the IAAF. Typically, athletics' global governing body lived beyond its means in non-Olympic years and restored itself to health in each Games year. Not the way a prudent business might approach its budgeting, but that was the way it was. As the 2015 election approached, best estimates were that the IAAF's reserves would total around $65 million by year end. This compared with annual expenditure of about $55 million. Just over a quarter of this spending was on development, undeniably a key role for the body to undertake, but much of the rest was sucked up by administrative costs representing considerable fat just waiting to be cut.

It was clear that Nick Davies's loyalties lay with Coe in the contest for the presidency, and his insight into the IAAF's costs in Monaco was invaluable. Two years later he was expelled from the IAAF after an Ethics Board investigation into his receipt of a cash payment from President Diack's son. The Board's decision included the revelation that IAAF staff had taken $500,000 in cash to the Beijing World Championships to cover 'various expenses' including the per diems paid to members of the IAAF 'family'. This merely confirmed the widespread perception that this was an organisation with an unconventional approach to financial management, and ripe for an efficiency drive.

Out of our deliberations popped the Olympic Athletics Dividend, a key late addition to Coe's manifesto. His pledge was that half the income received from the IOC would be distributed to the IAAF's member federations on an equal basis, a grant amounting to around a total of $100,000 for each of them over a four-year cycle. There were strings attached, in essence to ensure the funds were deployed for the benefit of the sport, but the message was clear: the IAAF existed for its members, and those members were best placed to nurture athletics on the ground. The sums involved were relatively trivial for the larger nations, a number of whom pledged to waive their Dividend or to ensure it was deployed in international outreach. For the bulk of the smaller nations, however, the money was anything but. Coe won the election by a mere eight votes. Anecdotally, it seems the promise of hard cash from the Monaco mother ship tipped the balance. Gianni Infantino won election to the presidency of FIFA only a few months later on a manifesto which included a hike in development grants for its member nations from $2 million to a total of $5 million each over a four-year cycle. Same election tactic, just a far bigger budget inside a much wealthier international federation.

The question of ownership of a sport is a fraught one, particularly in relation to who makes the decisions and how any spoils that it generates are shared out. Typically, international federations and national governing bodies default to a one-member-one-vote model, but inequalities of contribution create inevitable frictions. To be considered a 'member in good standing' in athletics, for example, a federation must send a delegation to the IAAF's congresses and athletes to its competitions. The latter is facilitated by an entry slot being available for every nation regardless of qualification standards. The result is the sight of ath-

letes from remote atolls finishing seconds after the winners in the
preliminary rounds of the 100 metres at world championships.
Often a nation's VIP delegation will outnumber its team of competing athletes, or athlete.

A core responsibility of an international governing body is
to be the custodian of the rules of its sport, and their policeman. It is also typically the record-keeper, which is of particular significance in a measurable sport such as cycling, swimming, weightlifting or athletics. None of which is a revenue
generator; indeed, each constitutes a financial burden. The
opportunity to monetise governing status is through competitions, provided the ruling body can hold on to the prestige
events in its sport. Some have. Others can only look with envy
at third-party organisations that have commercialised their
sports either independently of the governing organisation, or
at financial arm's length.

The International Olympic Committee is the ultimate thievish
sporting magpie. Over the course of a century it has persuaded
the watching public that its compilation of games constitutes the
pinnacle event for the vast majority of the constituent sports
without being the governor or regulator of any of them. The
competing sportspeople are not paid directly for their endeav-
ours, and the National Olympic Committees (NOCs) and sports
bodies which organise the athletes into teams have to fund their
costs by competing in a commercial marketplace from which the
IOC has withheld the juiciest fruit for itself. Host nations and
cities bear most of the costs of organising the Games, their revenue opportunities restricted essentially to ticket sales and local
sponsorship deals, again having to work in the shadow of the
IOC's own headline sponsors. And yet every four years the athletes and their NOCs come back for more. The format of each
sport might be identical to that of the world championships in
the intervening years, and the competitors the same, but the ca-

chet of an Olympic medal trumps all. You don't get knighted in the UK for merely being a multiple world champion.

The IOC generates revenue in three ways: it bears the cost of providing broadcast footage but keeps all the rights revenues that this imagery facilitates; it manages its headline programme of The Olympic Partner (TOP) sponsors; and it enjoys the benefit of its official licensing deals. Of total revenues over the 2003–16 cycle of $5.7 billion, $4.2 billion came from broadcasters and $1 billion from the TOP programme. Broadcast income is clearly key to the IOC's success and the health of its Games, and it has trebled over the past four quadrennial cycles. Sponsorship income has almost doubled. At the end of 2016 the organisation was sitting on unrestricted reserves of $1.5 billion, more than sufficient for many rainy days.

Games organisers, NOCs and international sports bodies are beneficiaries of IOC support, in return for their contribution to the show and for having to work around the restrictions imposed by the IOC's own sponsorship programmes – although these do provide doors for NOCs to knock on in search of TOP sponsors willing to spend extra money in national territories. The organisers of the London Games in 2012 received $1.4 billion in financial support. The Rio 2016 organising committee got $1.5 billion. At the end of 2016, $600 million was sitting in the IOC's accounts – separate from its unrestricted reserves – earmarked to support continental and national Olympic bodies over the coming four years through the IOC's Olympic Solidarity programme, much of it in the form of activities and grants aimed at those with the greatest financial need. During 2016, by the completion of the Rio Games $540 million had been distributed to the international governing bodies of the participating summer sports – the source of Coe's Olympic Athletics Dividend.

While athletics received $47 million from the IOC after the London Games, the seven sports immediately below it each received $22 million from the IOC. The majority of the summer sports were in a fourth tier, the lowest, and were granted only $14 million each. After London, the IOC rejigged its categorisation of sports according to their perceived popularity. Media statistics, such as TV viewing figures and Internet traffic, were the most important determinant, but public surveys and ticket requests also carried weight in the analysis. Athletics lost its status at the head of the rankings, no longer standing alone above the crowd. In future it would have to share top billing with swimming and gymnastics – both previously in the second tier – for the first time, with consequent financial implications. The IAAF's accounts show that its income from the IOC for the Rio Games fell by around 15 per cent, to under $40 million, when compared to London. The restructuring for Rio also created a fifth tier. Modern pentathlon was placed in the lowest of the five bands, alongside Olympics newcomers rugby and golf. As an indication of lacklustre public interest, it would appear that modern pentathlon survives in the Games largely by virtue of its heritage status, which goes back to Baron de Coubertin's personal interest in the sport.

Football, tennis, rugby and golf can appear strange bedfellows at the Olympics. The fees from the IOC to their international governing bodies would barely touch the sides of their vast coffers, and star players can prove reluctant to sign up to the Olympic Village experience or even to the Games themselves. With no prize money on offer, and more prestigious accolades to be won elsewhere in their sport, the world's top male golfers seemed a little too keen to be scared off by the Zika virus ahead of Rio 2016. The seduction of the Games can be insidious, however, and it may be that attitudes soften over coming cycles as they have in tennis. The Olympics has gradually cemented its place in the affections of the top tennis players, the IOC and host cities securing considerable sporting stardust for comparatively little financial outlay.

Golf and tennis are both sports run, at elite level, directly for the benefit of the players themselves. The ATP, which describes itself as 'the governing body of the men's professional tennis circuits', presides over three tiers of tours around the world, including the four Grand Slam events. The WTA fulfils an equivalent role in women's tennis. These two bodies for top professionals are affiliated to the International Tennis Federation, but the ATP's pride in the circumstances of the birth of the ATP Tour makes clear where power truly resides. Founded in 1972 to represent the leading players, the ATP channelled frustrations with the existing circuit, presided over by the ITF, into plans for an independent tour. In 1988, in a car park press conference at the US Open, the ATP's leaders launched their breakaway circuit. Support from the stars of the game gave the bandwagon momentum, and power was effectively seized from the ITF. Without the talent, leading tournaments would have been empty vessels, and all soon fell in line with the new world order.

The ATP's plans were modelled in part on the structure of professional golf. Where the ATP Tour split from the ITF, golf's PGA Tour had been a 1968 breakaway by the top players from the rank-and-file club professionals who made up the bulk of the membership of the Professional Golfers' Association. Both the ATP Tour and the PGA Tour, as well as the latter's European counterpart, are managed for the players. This is reflected in their governance structures. The ATP board comprises a chairman, three player representatives and three tournament representatives. The PGA European Tour has a board heavy with players past and present, only recently introducing a coterie of independent appointees. Its accounts emphasise the importance of hosting a home Ryder Cup once every four years. In 2014 the PGA European Tour Group made a profit of £17 million from revenues of £231 million, that year having hosted the Ryder Cup at Gleneagles. The following year, a fallow one in Ryder Cup terms, turnover dropped to £154 million, which created a loss of almost £8 million. In 2016 the Cup was held in America, and although revenues rebounded to £199 million the organisation still posted a small loss.

Golf is governed under a joint arrangement between the R&A in Scotland and the United States Golf Association. The R&A also owns the annual Open Championships, one of golf's four global majors and a material revenue generator for the governing body. In 2016 the R&A generated turnover of £73 million. After funding its governance functions and making grants to the sport, it made a profit before tax of £9 million, while its reserves totalled £110 million at the end of that year. The PGA European Tour by contrast, a bigger enterprise but a much younger organisation, had reserves of only £15 million. However, the rise of player power is unlikely to abate. New tournaments tailored to the players' interests are taking root and are likely to help shift the riches in sport away from traditional bodies to the players' collectives. The end-of-season ATP World Tour Finals, rebranded and relaunched in 2008, has grown in appeal as its roots have taken firmer hold in the public consciousness. What was once an afterthought now ranks just below the four majors in significance.

Britain's governing body for tennis, the Lawn Tennis Association, is in many respects a bystander in the professional game. Britain won the Davis Cup for the first time in seventy-nine years in 2015, but within twenty-four hours star player Andy Murray and team captain Leon Smith had both publicly criticised the LTA, the organisation responsible for the team. 'I feel like you waste time because nothing ever gets done, and I don't like wasting my time. I don't speak to any of the people who are in a high-up position about that. I haven't really spoken to them about anything,' Murray was reported as saying. There could be no doubt whatsoever that the players wanted credit to be handed out only where they themselves believed it was due.

The LTA is not short of cash; indeed, it is able to luxuriate in the riches generated for it by the Wimbledon Championships, which take place each summer three miles away from its sprawling headquarters in Roehampton just off London's South Circular Road. Opened in 2007 at a cost of around £40 million, the LTA's HQ is wrapped around a courtyard containing an enormous centuries-old plane tree. Its twenty-two tennis courts were originally intended as a performance hub for elite players, but a change of leadership triggered a change in strategy, and the concept of a National Tennis Centre that drove elite success withered. Now the Centre's courts and accommodation are available for hire by anyone willing to pay for the experience. The original plans for Roehampton were criticised by those whose stardom gave them a voice in the media. So in turn were the new plans. But the £40 million building isn't going anywhere in a hurry. The LTA, now more heavily focused on nurturing the grass roots of the sport, is damned either way. It is simply too wealthy for its own good.

Just as the LTA was denied credit for the British team's Davis Cup triumph, so it gains no accolades for the perennial success of the Wimbledon Championships. These are managed under an arrangement between the LTA and the All England Lawn Tennis and Croquet Club that extends out to 2053. A joint committee of management comprises twelve members from the All England Club and seven from the LTA. The All England Club makes clear that it is the organisation that conducts the day-to-day operations of the Championships, and it is certainly the public's perception that the Club is responsible for their success. Importantly, though, 90 per cent of the surplus generated by the Wimbledon fortnight is invested back into tennis through the LTA. In 2016 the Championships turned over £203 million. The 90 per cent profit distribution to the LTA, which amounted to £38 million, accounted for 58 per cent of the LTA's overall revenues. Not surprisingly, the possibility of any future hiccup in this income ranked at the top of the business risks identified in the LTA's accounts.

The ultimate ambitions of the All England Club may be altruistic, as reflected in the distribution of profits from Wimbledon, but that is not so for other competition organisers. Whereas the stars have secured commercial control over some individual sports, such as golf and tennis, in team sports the links between governance and the hosting of competitions vary in strength. Player power is far more fragmented than in individual sports that have continuous, observable world rankings, and national bodies are unlikely to risk being ostracised by the sport in setting themselves against its established competition structures. FIFA and football's continental governing bodies continue to control the flagship competitions for both international and club sides. It is hard to envisage a disruptor launching a credible attempt to create a rival to the World Cup when the whole world wishes and is invited to participate in that competition. Whatever the complaints about FIFA's governance and the probity of its leadership, past and present, the organisation continues to have a firm lock on the pinnacle competition in football.

At the end of 2015, which new president Gianni Infantino described as 'an incredibly tough year for FIFA', the organisation had reserves of $1.3 billion. The ruling body had lost money that year, which it blamed in part on 'unforeseen costs such as legal fees and costs for extraordinary meetings' – hardly a surprise given the leadership turmoil it had endured. Infantino's predecessor Sepp Blatter had been suspended in October on suspicion of financial impropriety and then banned from the sport for eight years in December, a penalty subsequently reduced to six years.

A year later, however, and FIFA's losses had grown. Again, exceptional legal expenses weighed on the result, as did the costs of dealing with what FIFA described as 'ill-considered investments' under the previous regime, including its newly opened

World Football Museum in Zurich. However, the governing body forecast that over the four-year cycle 2015–18, culminating in the World Cup in Russia, which would account for the bulk of its revenues over the period, it would make a $132 million profit, leaving it with reserves of over $1.6 billion. FIFA forecast that in the World Cup year it would have revenues of $4 billion and invest $1.9 billion in the tournament itself. Financially, this is the gift that simply must keep on giving.

Where a governing body does retain control over the sport's flagship event, the distribution of power among its membership can be highly contentious. The IAAF's four-yearly bonanza comes from an event outside its control, the Olympics, so the principle of equal voting rights across federations is not subject to significant challenge. The international governing body in cricket, by contrast, controls its one-day World Cup competitions, and is heavily reliant on the monies that they generate. The past few years have been marked by a struggle for control of the International Cricket Council and the profits from these flagship events. To the fore has been India, the home of the IPL, the financial monster that threatens to engulf the global game.

The ICC is a company registered in the British Virgin Islands, but its operational headquarters is in the United Arab Emirates. The shift in power in the sport towards India was reflected in a move in HQ from Lord's Cricket Ground, its home in London for almost a century, to Dubai in 2005. The ICC's financial affairs had been conducted in the tax-efficient climes of Monaco, but these too were now transferred into the new home for the sport in the UAE. 2014 was a World Twenty20 year, and the tournament generated a $158 million profit for the ICC and by extension its membership. 2015 was a World Cup year. This competition delivered profits of $289 million. The overall financial surpluses the ICC produced in those two years were $129 million and $263 million respectively, emphasising its almost total reliance on the success of the sport's one-day showpiece competitions. The ICC paid dividends to its members of $52 million in 2014 and $343 million in 2015. In the subsequent year, 2016, the surplus was slimmer at $92 million and no dividends were declared.

Whereas the IOC, FIFA and the IAAF all adopt a paternalistic attitude to the development of their sport in disbursing their income – or perhaps, cynically, a self-preservationist approach – the ICC's direct development support is modest relative to the cash distributions to its members. The 2015 World Cup led to a $25 million payment into the ICC Global Cricket Development Programme, but a footnote in the governing body's accounts makes clear that in its latest rights cycle these allocations have been discontinued. Power, and the money that goes with it, has been devolved. A former South African Test cricketer, David Richardson, is the chief executive of the ICC. Its business model keeps the organisation lean, with only sixty-five staff in Dubai and a couple of handfuls more around the world. 'The members do take the attitude that *You need to be lean because you are spending our money*,' he observes.

Richardson explains that the structure of the ICC, and by extension the organisation of the sport internationally, can only be understood in a historical context. 'Cricket's governance model has evolved. It started off with Australia and England, and that was it. Then they added South Africa, and then slowly but surely they've added teams. So it's like it's almost a founding members club. And at this stage anyway they've gone as far as ten members, and the rest effectively, they're just there. It's taken a hundred years to get to ten. How long it will take to get rid of that membership class system? I think it will take a long time to evolve. And the financials follow that.'

The power struggle at the heart of global cricket reached a crescendo in 2014. And the financials were the focus of the struggle. The three biggest international players – India, England and Australia – forced through changes to the governance structure and distribution of dividends that were heavily in their favour. They were guaranteed three of the five seats on the key executive committee, and members' financial shares were to be based on their financial contribution to the success of the ICC's events, as well as their history in the game and the performances of their teams across its three formats. The board would be chaired by Narayanaswami Srinivasan, the president of India's governing body, the BCCI.

The ICC has 105 members, but in 2014 only ten of these had full member status by virtue of being eligible to participate in official Test matches – the ten becoming twelve with the addition of Ireland and Afghanistan in 2017. The remainder are either associates or affiliates with much lower influence. In effect, the big three had out-muscled the other full members. India, the commercial breadbasket of the sport, was widely regarded as the prime mover of the changes, while conscious itself of the increasing power of players to dictate terms and to demand their share of the spoils, as evident in the IPL. Cricket may be a team sport, but individual contributions are statistically plain to see, and the alchemy of a team and the tactics entailed are far easier to disaggregate – and reward individually – than in sports such as soccer or rugby.

The previous model for distributing the profits of the ICC was that the ten full members shared 75 per cent of the surplus and the associates the remaining 25 per cent. As profits grew, so tensions had increased between the largest countries, whose activities drove the ICC's success, and the smaller nations benefitting from the expenditure to develop cricket within their borders. But, Richardson emphasises, it was never originally intended to be like that. 'When the 75:25 per cent model came in it was a subscription. The full members must pay seventy-five and the associate

members the other twenty-five. It was only when we started organising our own events that we had a surplus. We've only got 1.5
million cricketers outside the ten full members. When we get to
ten million, then maybe we can justify more of an investment.'
The solution of the big three nations was for the first 32 per cent
of the ICC's revenues, not just its profits, to be distributed to
them. India would take the majority. Then the 75:25 model
would be applied to the remaining profits.

The changes proved short-lived, but not the accompanying
acrimony. In 2016 Srinivasan was forced out of office on the
back of an ongoing corruption investigation involving allegations of match-fixing. His successor as BCCI president and
ICC chair, Shashank Manohar, shepherded a set of proposals
reversing the big three's putsch to the verge of approval before
resigning from office himself after only eight months in charge.
He was persuaded to change his mind to see the reforms
through. David Richardson acknowledges that the solution arrived at is 'a bit of a compromise. It's a bit of a thumb suck.'
India will still receive the largest share of the ICC's surplus,
but it will no longer be a slice off the top of the organisation's
revenues. 'The proposal on the table is not a scientific formula.
It's too difficult. What should be your criteria? If we were to
give a weighting to what each country contributes we should
probably pay 75 per cent to India. But on the other hand, if
it's on the basis that we want to grow the game and make certain members sustainable then India should get nothing because they get enough money.' India was initially outvoted thirteen to one when the ICC board approved a revised structure,
but it refused to back down. Under the agreement finally
thrashed out, India was slated to receive $405 million over
eight years from the ICC. England was to be the next-highest
recipient of funds with $139 million, the other major Test-
playing nations enjoying $128 million each.

A key proposal within the governance and financial reforms was that the ICC chair would not be able to hold a position in one of its member bodies, to avoid any conflict of interest. That Shashank Manohar should initially choose to implement that by resigning from the ICC rather than the BCCI, albeit citing 'personal reasons', came as something of a shock to the politicians within the sport, although one did describe him to me at the height of the political battle as 'a bit of a reluctant administrator' who operated without a mobile phone and didn't like to travel. 'He even hates going to Delhi because it's full of smog.' With the spoils of world cricket distributed to its members rather than spent at the centre, perhaps they should not have been too surprised that one of its bureaucratic grandees would prefer to be in control at home – where the cash is spent rather than where it originates.

The chain of cause and effect from fan to president is a long one, such that it is all too easy for sports administrators to lose sight of the ultimate source of the revenues that they preside over. Global competitions drive broadcast revenues and sponsor income – the principal sources of international federations' wealth – but these are entirely reliant on the consumption habits of sports fans worldwide. The greatest protection the leaders of world sport have is the quality of their events and the interest that they generate, because it is this that keeps fans tuning in and the dollars rolling in.

14

TEN MILLION POUNDS A VOTE, OR FLEXING PUTIN'S PECS

The crowds on Buttertubs Pass testified to the success of Yorkshire's weekend annexation by the French. Team Sky's Richie Porte tweeted, 'The crowds were just massive. It's like nothing I have ever seen anywhere before.' For a county notoriously proud of its own identity, so much so that until 1992 you had to be born in Yorkshire to play cricket for the county side, the Grand Départ of cycling's 2014 Tour de France was a triumph for regional marketing and an exhilarating sporting celebration. So much so that Yorkshire returned to the well of goodwill it had generated to secure the right to host the Union Cycliste Internationale's 2019 Road World Championships.

The success of the weekend and the serried ranks of people lining the key stretches of the course (key from the perspective of the pictures seen by international TV audiences) will have come as a relief to the Grand Départ's organisers, who had struggled and failed to control the event's budget. Until the crowds arrived they can only have speculated as to the success of their venture. With the event free to watch, spectator dynamics had been very hard to forecast. As no money was changing hands, fans' commitment to attending was tenuous. But the people of Yorkshire and beyond came out and did their part.

Leeds Council, supported by its partners in the venture, published an impact report after the event. It estimated that 3.3 million people watched the stretch of the Tour in Yorkshire and a further 1.5 million on its subsequent run through Cambridge, Essex and into central London. More significantly for the council, the report guesstimated that the overall economic benefit for Yorkshire of hosting the event was £102 million out of an overall total of £128 million. More than adequate justification, you might think, for the £31 million spent by public agencies in hosting the event, £10 million of which was committed by UK Sport's Major Events team. Some £27 million of that £31 million was included in the overall assessment of economic impact, as it was spent within the UK (the balancing £4 million being paid to the Tour as a rights fee to become the host), but even stripping that out, the ratio of outcome to financial input appears impressive.

As a textbook exercise in Keynesian economics, John Maynard himself would surely have been impressed. Why set unemployed men to digging holes in the road to stimulate the economy when you can host a cycle race instead?

Your answer may depend in large part on your political philosophy as well as your preferred macroeconomic model. The bulk of the boost to Yorkshire's economy is said to have been in visitor spend – £88 million in total, of which a quarter was on accommodation and three quarters on other casual expenditure. Is this an appropriate use of public funds, whether local or national or Lottery? Should hoteliers and B & B owners expect the authorities to use scarce resources directly to boost their trade, or would that money be better spent on improvements to the tourist experience that would have a more lasting impact?

If you are of a sceptical mindset, you can of course challenge the impact estimates too. The survey followed a methodology developed by UK Sport called eventIMPACTS, and essentially involved face-to-face interviews with spectators. Such sampling is understandably blunt as a modelling instrument. Small adjustments to the numbers plugged into the model as a result of the interviews can have very magnified effects on the final conclusions. And as with any analysis of the real world, we can never know what the Yorkshire economy would have been like had the Tour instead departed from a different European venue keen to flaunt its international sporting credentials.

That a sub-industry exists of statisticians who weigh the benefits of hosting events bears testimony to the sheer scale of the global sports competition business. Consultants A. T. Kearney calculate that in busy years, such as the four-yearly coincidence of Olympics and UEFA European Championships, major events can account for as much as 8 per cent of overall global sports industry revenues, falling back to around 1 per cent in quieter years.

Impact assessments now routinely form a part of the process of corralling support for bids to host major international events. Yorkshire's original intention to bid for the Tour would have been informed by a projection of its impact, thereby enabling politicians and bureaucrats to persuade their budget holders to open wallets and commit funding to the venture. After the event, the assessed final impact was above the £100 million anticipated effect reported in the run-up to the Tour. This projection is likely to have played some part in persuading UK Sport to commit its £10 million, but it is notable that it only came to the party late when the organisers were rumoured to have hit financial difficulties. The BBC reported Nick Clegg's lobbying as playing a part in the reversal of the initial decision not to support the event, the deputy prime minister recognising the importance of playing to his Yorkshire constituency interests and reaping a perhaps unexpected reward for his role in the coalition government.

Thirty-one million pounds is not a sum to be sniffed at, although neither is £102 million of local economic uplift. In context, however, the sums suddenly appear piffling. The Yorkshire economy has been estimated at £88 billion a year, of which tourism alone is worth £7 billion. Viewed in this light, major events must be justified on other grounds, whether sporting legacy (however measured), international image or local goodwill and positivity.

Our bid to host the IAAF World Athletics Championships had its own assessment of expected economic impact behind it. Commissioned by a specialist agency trusted by London & Partners, the Greater London Authority's arm that exists to promote the capital internationally, it concluded that the 2017 Championships would boost the London economy by around £100 million. The GLA invested a maximum of £8 million towards the overall cost of hosting the event – enough of a multiplier for the mayor to feel comfortable in signing the IAAF's Event Organising Agreement alongside UK Athletics.

Privately, however, the GLA's people admitted that economic impact was largely irrelevant to their decision. Partly because they recognised the unavoidable weaknesses in any such modelling, but more importantly because London was so large and so well known that it didn't in isolation need either a specific economic boost from a single event such as this, or even the global recognition of the city's attractions that would ensue. I'm sure there were many times during the planning and preparation for the Championships when they must have asked themselves why they were bothering, such were some of the demands on their time and emotions, but they did so to justify their decision on the future of the Olympic Stadium (the GLA being its major shareholder) and because bringing events to London is a continuous part of what the authorities do to sustain the city's global reputation.

The GLA's decision to part-fund the Championships rested on government not only providing funding itself, again through

UK Sport's Major Events team, which deploys Lottery and exchequer monies, but also underwriting the overall event. As
underwriter, the government would have to meet any losses the
event might incur after any funding committed by the GLA,
UK Athletics and UK Sport. Such underwriting is a requirement of the IAAF of any hosts, as it is for many global sporting
events. The IAAF justifies this requirement as protecting its
member federation – in this case UK Athletics – from the blow-
back of any shortfall. More significantly, it recognises that cities
also often operate on constrained budgets, and it wants to ensure it has the highest possible financial protection both for itself and against the risk that the event collapses or is delivered
below specification. It is not just for a photo opportunity that
the president of the IAAF signs the event contract alongside the
newly chosen hosts within minutes of announcing his Council's
choice of city. No time can be allowed for second thoughts or
renegotiations.

Securing government support for our 2017 Championships
bid was a relatively straightforward exercise. After Sports Minister Hugh Robertson's foot-dragging of a year earlier, when
Olympic Stadium uncertainty had politicians running scared,
this time around the Stadium was our trump card in arranging
the necessary underwrite. Budgets were drawn up, although there
was a sense that few people believed them given experiences elsewhere, in particular with London 2012, and the impact assessment commissioned. This event was to be the biggest financial
commitment to date from UK Sport to a single event – later
eclipsed by the Grand Départ – but the quango had a process that
it believed in regardless of event size. Having employed all the
dark arts we could to persuade our partners to get to this stage,
we were more than happy to run with whatever process was required to get our bid submitted in time with all requisite commitments in place.

More curious, though, was the manner in which the GLA later decided that it wanted to host the IPC's World Para Athletics Championships alongside the IAAF's event in 2017. In the months leading up to the London Paralympics we conducted a tender process to find a British host for the World Championships. In bidding for the IAAF Championships we had made a public commitment to host the IPC event in the UK should we be successful. There were some moves afoot to bring disability athletics closer to the IAAF. A memorandum of understanding had been signed between the IPC and the IAAF, albeit with few meaningful obligations on either side. We supported this initiative and were keen to showcase the world's elite Para athletes, although we doubted that this would actually make any difference in the bid battle with our rivals for the IAAF event, Doha. As it was, we won and so turned our attention to our promise about the IPC Championships.

In spite of a number of enquiries as to its possible interest, London declined to participate in our tender process. It was never entirely clear whether this was a matter of money, human capacity to work on the event, simple sloth or something more insidious. So, the tender proceeded and we awarded the IPC Championships to a different British city.

On the last day of the Paralympics in London, the sun beating down fiercely on the Mall at the finish line to the final event, the wheelchair marathon, Mayor Boris Johnson arrived in his habitual flurry to watch the last couple of laps of the race. Between asking for updates on the race standing, David Weir eventually prevailing for his fourth gold medal of the Games, Johnson asked why on earth London wasn't hosting the World Para Athletics in 2017. His bafflement that his staff had declined to submit a tender proposal suggests simple sloth was indeed the explanation. Or maybe no one, from the mayor downwards, had believed the Paralympics would be such a success until they actually were.

Within days, Johnson's regular fixer Neale Coleman had been deputed to fix this latest mayoral problem, and within weeks we had managed to help the other city agree to step aside in favour of London. The GLA became funder and underwriter of the Championships, securing the opportunity to burnish its credentials for inclusivity and diversity. And all, apparently, on a mayoral whim, assisted no doubt by the Weirwolf's triumph in the sunshine on the Mall.

The financial stakes for the GLA in underwriting the World Para Athletics Championships were much less than those for the government in standing behind the IAAF Worlds. Although both stretched over roughly the same amount of time in the same stadium with the same presentational production values, the overall budgets were very different. Athlete numbers were fewer for the IPC, around 1,000 against more than double that for the IAAF – which had some cost benefit, although the IPC event had more competition sessions. Scale alone couldn't explain why the IAAF Championships had a cost budget of £55 million and the IPC event one of only £11 million.

The difference lay in the respective demands of the owners of the two events, the IAAF and the IPC. The former, for example, requires the hosts to pay for the accommodation of the competing athletes and their support staff, as well as an enormous entourage from the IAAF and its 200-plus member federations from around the world. At the Para Athletics Championships, competing nations pay their own way. This alone accounts for a £7 million cost differential between the two events. In winning the IAAF bid we had also made a promise to foot the bill for athlete prize money, which would otherwise fall to the IAAF itself. Our competitor Doha had previously made this promise, and on the morning of the bid itself we thought it necessary to remove this difference between us. This was a $7.2 million commitment – £4.6 million at 2011 exchange rates.

The IPC does not pay athletes any prize money, leaving the sport closer to the original Olympian ideals. Over time this is likely to change, but only once the IPC has managed to grow global awareness of Para sport away from the quadrennial Paralympics themselves to such an extent that cities are eager to compete to host its championships. That day is still some way off. For now, the IPC often makes a direct financial contribution to assist host cities as it has to work hard to find them. Low spectator numbers for the events means slim ticket income and thin revenues from commercial partners. London 2017's crowds point to the possibility of a more robust financial model in years to come, with eventual funding for competing nations' travel and accommodation and even rewards for athletes. Unless, that is, the IPC can find a short cut via wealthy emerging nations keen to display their sporting prowess and commit funds sooner.

The IAAF has ridden this tiger of aspirant nations itself over the past decade or so, all in the name of the development of athletics. In the process it has garnered sponsor revenues, seen its championships played out in front of half-empty stadiums and had seemingly no developmental benefit. Osaka 2007, Daegu 2011, Moscow 2013 and Beijing 2015: each fitted the cash-rich audience-poor model. And there is Doha 2019 to come. The short-termism of the IAAF hierarchy is laid bare by the transient nature of the sponsors that have been dragged aboard the athletics bandwagon by host governments looking to embellish their bids. Samsung popped up around the championships in Daegu. It became the inaugural sponsor of the IAAF's Diamond League series, but didn't renew when the contract expired and Daegu was in the past. Russian bank VTB emerged as a global partner around the time of Moscow 2013, and China's Sinolube was unveiled as 'the official lubricant of the IAAF' in 2015, just in time for Beijing. Neither proved a long-distance runner.

Chastened wannabe hosts of international sporting events have often suspected that a very different lubricant is needed to win bid battles against the new wave of emergent nations. Cries of foul play regularly accompany bid decisions, and the press has fun with tales of brown envelopes, designer handbags, fancy watches and fancier cars being pressed into service by winning cities. And sometimes losing ones. England's failed bid for the 2018 FIFA World Cup deployed Mulberry handbags as gifts for the wives of voting FIFA councillors, to widespread derision and embarrassment. Richard Caborn, an excellent former sports minister and ambassador for the bid, defended the FA's team as operating within the rules of the contest. But within the rules or not, handing a propaganda opportunity to Trinidad's Jack Warner, widely regarded as the very embodiment of football corruption, was a calamitous own goal. Warner very publicly handed back his wife's handbag. In 2017 the UK's Serious Fraud Office was said to be examining a newly published FIFA report into the 2018 and 2022 World Cup bidding processes.

When the stakes of the game are so high – after all, there can only be one winning city – you can be sure that minor corruption or marginal flirting with the bidding rules will be indulged in. The Football Association returned from Zurich in 2010 a chastened organisation, securing only two of the twenty-two votes available. The bid team and its advisers read like a dream ensemble, from football royalty in the guise of David Beckham and actual royalty in the form of Prince William to a plethora of grandees from sport, business and politics. The bid had cost £21 million. Given we can assume that England won the vote of its own member of the electorate, that's £21 million to win one vote. Even now, it's hard to imagine how it could have spent that much money. Handbags aside at £230 a pop, what ways can one conceive of spending that amount of money, £6 million more than originally planned?

What the winning host, Russia, spent on its bid, or exactly how it spent it, who knows? The 2018 World Cup has become the latest in a series of sporting events to go to Russia, intended, it would seem, to puff up the nation's collective ego and enhance its standing in the eyes of the world. The 2013 IAAF World Athletics Championships, the 2014 Winter Olympic and Paralympic Games, an annual Formula 1 Grand Prix from 2014, plus a string of events in other sports, especially in Sochi. It would be hypocritical, however, of Western nations to criticise self-aggrandisement as an objective in hosting competitions. After all, UK Sport's funding of major events has just that objective on behalf of the nation, and what was Leeds Council's funding of the Grand Départ if not in large part about putting Yorkshire on the global sporting map?

When a host nation already has a sporting heritage, pressure builds to ensure local victories on the field of play. This explains the success of UK Sport's chair, Sue Campbell, in securing a major uplift in funding for British Olympic and Paralympic sports ahead of London 2012. Rival nations have characterised this as tantamount to financial doping. We now know that Russia has pursued chemical doping in recent years in search of medal success at events hosted within its borders. The IAAF took evidence of systematic state-controlled doping ahead of Moscow 2013 as grounds for banning Russian athletes from the Rio Olympics. The IPC took the same line for all Russian sports at the Rio Paralympics after it was shown that results at the Sochi Paralympics had been corrupted.

Nations without a base of sporting capability to build on, whether legitimately or illegitimately, have resorted to talent recruitment. One bizarre moment at the World Indoor Athletics Championships in Istanbul in 2008 was an infield interview with Turkey's İlham Tanui Özbilen after he won the silver medal. He was interviewed in English rather than Turkish as only a year earlier Kenya's William Biwott Tanui had emigrated to Turkey, changed his name and received accelerated permission from the IAAF to switch nationality. Turkey has since got a taste for international imports, causing much complaining on the margins of European-level competitions in particular, where their acquisitions have propelled the country up the medal table. Kenya provides rich pickings for such transfers of allegiance. With enormous strength in distance running and only three places per nation available at each event in an athletics championship, many top Kenyan runners have little hope of making their own team in spite of being competitive at the highest level. As they come from a relatively impoverished nation, it does not require much investment to transform the financial prospects for an athlete who is just outside the Kenyan team.

Some countries are so far below international sporting standards that imports are almost their only realistic prospect of achieving local success on the stages that they have built at such great expense. Qatar is the most obvious example. A nation underpinned by huge natural gas reserves of just under two million people, the vast majority transient expatriates, it has the highest per capita income in the world. As the economy has developed and its single city, Doha, sprung up from the desert as a forest of skyscrapers, so its ruling Al Thani family has bought trophy financial assets around the world and brought the world's trophy sporting assets to Qatar. Its stunning Aspire Dome indoor complex has hosted athletics, fencing, gymnastics and handball, among other sports, at international level; the World Para Athletics Championships was held in the city in 2015, as was the UCI's Road World Championships a year later; the IAAF World Championships arrive in 2019 and, the cherry on the top of this gilded cake, the FIFA World Cup in 2022. There won't be much Qatari success to celebrate at the end of this run, but they do at least have Olympic silver medalist and world champion high jumper

Mutaz Essa Barshim, who was Doha born and bred. Prospects on home soil for the Qatari football team in 2022 appear less rosy.

Qatar's success in winning the rights to host the FIFA World Cup created more of a stir than Russia's. The bids were decided at the same time, and – England's ignominy for its home press aside – it was the decision to go to a nation not regarded as a football powerhouse and with a brutally hot summer climate that really grabbed the global media's attention. However hard the now disgraced FIFA president Sepp Blatter attempted to spin the decision, it made little sense to those outside the machinations of the bureaucrats who made the choice. How could FIFA create a new audience for football in a nation of under three million inhabitants? How could it make sense to ask the world's greatest footballers to be at their best in forty-degree heat? Why would you then contemplate moving the World Cup to later in the year, thus disrupting club competitions across the world and alienating the clubs who hold the contracts of the star players who make your tournament?

I went for a run in Doha at the crack of dawn one March morning and soon realised the error of my ways, turning tail and heading back to the air-conditioned relief of the hotel lobby. Later that day, in a break between sessions at the World Indoor Athletics Championships, I ventured outside the Aspire Dome to see the outdoor Fan Zone. There were only two fans to be seen, both stalwarts of the British Athletics Supporters Club, huddled together in a tiny patch of shade. Mad dogs and Englishmen. Little wonder then that we believed that what was in the best interests of athletics should be on our side when we entered the bidding contest for the outdoor 2017 World Championships, scheduled to be held in late summer with Qatari temperatures near their annual peak.

The bidding contest was nevertheless a tight one and run, on our side at least, on a constrained budget that ran to only a few hundred thousand pounds. Separating what mattered from the inevitable noise, gossip and misdirection was never easy. Bid consultants would have had us see ghosts behind every door. A poll of readers on one apparently influential sports business website had Doha constantly in the lead. We did not know everything contained in the formal Doha bid, but we did know of its offer to pick up the athlete prize fund, a straight benefit to the IAAF's own balance sheet.

Bid consultants are viewed by many as a necessary weapon in the bidder's armoury, providing continuously updated assessments of the likely voting intentions of the electorate. Theirs is an existence lived in the world's hotel lobbies, with the Olympic and FIFA World Cup circuits by far the most lucrative. The 2017 New Year's Honours List included one leading British exponent of the art, with a citation 'for services to International Trade and the Sports Sector'. In the event, we chose to leave our lead consultant at home when we travelled to Monaco for the final round of lobbying. This didn't, unfortunately, do much to reduce the noises off that distracted the bid team from its work.

The day before the IAAF Council's choice of 2017 host city, we were taken aside by a senior employee of the IAAF who hammered home the message that unless we matched Doha's prize money offer our bid was sunk. IAAF Council members were telling us the same thing, in particular some from Europe who we counted among our strongest supporters. That evening we convened a meeting to decide whether our budgets for the event would allow us to take the financial hit and to assess whether our bid was genuinely in jeopardy. The sports minister and representatives of the mayor of London and UK Sport huddled with us and we decided to push the button and offer the prize money.

We printed out individual letters to each of the twenty-six Council members to leave at each of their places in their meeting room at the Fairmont Hotel during the first coffee break the next morning. Then Seb Coe was deputed to check that President Lamine Diack was happy to sanction this circumvention of the bid rules as we were well beyond the deadline for any change to our proposals. We were given the green light. When we made our presentation to the Council the next afternoon the watching press in an adjoining room were genuinely surprised at our last-minute offer and, as we emptied out of the meeting room with victory under our belts, pounced on the politicians on our team to ask how the prize money was to be funded. Their off-the-cuff answer was that none of it would come from the public purse. This wasn't what had been discussed, let alone agreed, the night before, and so the new organising committee was saddled with a funding problem before we had even had time to take our first celebratory sip of champagne. It took many months of protracted negotiations between our funding partners to find a solution that fitted the carefree answer that had been tossed to the media.

In the years since the November 2011 award of the Worlds to London, suspicion has grown that the bid playing field may not have quite been level. The night before the award we were told of rumours that IAAF Council members were being called up to a room in the hotel to be given brown envelopes. Although our sources were high within the IAAF hierarchy, at the time I was keen to dismiss them as yet another distraction from the task at hand. More than four years later, after indications surfaced that there may well have been skulduggery behind Doha's subsequent successful bid to host the 2019 World Championships, I reported the earlier rumours of brown envelopes to the IAAF's Ethics Board, chaired by that doughty commercial silk Michael Beloff. It transpired that others' memories did not match mine, and Beloff's team didn't manage to talk directly to everyone who had been with me at the time, so the matter was shelved pending the emergence of any corroborating evidence.

That evidence may yet emerge. Veteran Kenyan athlete, IAAF Council member and president of Athletics Kenya, Isaiah Kiplagat was suspended on suspicion of taking delivery of two cars as an 'apparent gift' from Doha at around the time of its bid for the 2019 Worlds. Kiplagat died in the summer of 2016, still under suspension. More substantially, as French prosecutors worked through allegations of corruption against now-former President Diack and his son Papa Massata Diack, it was reported that the son had asked Qatar for $5 million in 2011. Later, *Le Monde* published details of alleged payments totalling $3.5 million. Whether these actually occurred, and if they did what their purpose might have been and whether that purpose was legitimate are all, presumably, for any court case that might eventually ensue to decide.

I now look back on 2011 with far less affection that I might have expected to had you told me ahead of time that we would be victorious. Bidding is a grubby business, however much you try to rise above the muck. One small example. The website poll of the likely winner that Doha kept stubbornly ahead in really bugged me. So much so that I doubted its veracity. I begged a favour from a City technology contact who set his automated trading robots to see if he could boost London in the poll. Briefly he managed it before Doha pulled ahead once more. His conclusion: their robots were at least as good as his.

There are more aspiring nations than there are major established events to go round. Baku's answer was to host an entirely novel multi-sport competition, the 2015 European Games, the new child of the European Olympic Committee. This featured twenty sports, some representing top-level competition, others token events from big sports, and some novelty acts such as beach soccer and 3 x 3 basketball. Russia topped the medal table with Britain third. The watching European public paid at best passing attention, and articles about the Games focused on oil-rich Azerbaijan's poor human rights record as much as the sport taking place in its

capital city. The future of the Games is uncertain. Minsk in Be-
larus is slated for the second edition in 2019, the Netherlands having withdrawn as hosts for financial reasons and replacement host
Russia then being bumped off because of its doping violations.

One of the prime movers behind the birth of the European
Games was Irishman Pierce O'Callaghan, a former race walker
highly regarded in global athletics and European Olympic cir-
cles. He and the European Olympic Committee were conscious
that the fifth ring of the Olympic rings was unemployed. Each of
the other four areas of the globe held their own multi-sport
games, creating an opportunity to exploit the commercial value
of the Olympic logo, whereas European ambitions in this regard
had foundered on the conflicting commercial interests of individual sports and nations. Sewing together European championships across the major sports had proved impossible. Now, though,
Europe had an aspirant nation with barrels of oil and gas wealth
and the desire to use sport to build its image.

Azerbaijan had sprung out of the old Soviet Union in 1991. In
its short independent history since then it had already made two
applications to host the Olympics in Baku. On both occasions it
had failed to make it onto the IOC's official candidate list. A
European Games presented the opportunity for Azerbaijan to
rent the Olympic rings with all their associated prestige, and so
O'Callaghan and colleagues were charged with corralling sports
to commit to hold competitions within the Games, and national
Olympic committees across Europe to back the concept. The
result was a hotchpotch of competitions at an unknown cost
which probably ran to many hundreds of millions of dollars, with
the organisers picking up most of the competitors' costs through
grants to the national committees. One result locals reported to
O'Callaghan was that 'they never saw the president [of Azerbai-
jan] as happy or relaxed as in those two weeks of sport'. Some
might consider that alone to be worth a billion dollars.

While it is no surprise to witness the Netherlands backing away from hosting an unproven event such as the European Games, the owners of the world's biggest competitions must by now be unsettled by the diminishing interest from prospective host cities. Rio's financial difficulties have undermined the already dubious attractions – at least economically – of staging the Olympics. Declining public support in opinion polls scuppered Boston's bid for 2024, and it withdrew its interest. On announcing that the city was pulling out, its mayor Martin J. Walsh declared, 'I will not sign a document that puts one dollar of taxpayers' money on the line for one penny of overruns on the Olympics.' Budapest backed out six months ahead of the IOC vote to choose a host, citing a similar lack of popular enthusiasm.

Los Angeles and Paris were left as the sole remaining competitors, a far cry from the nine bid submissions for the 2012 Games, five of which were eventually shortlisted. In the summer of 2017 the IOC brokered an arrangement whereby Paris would host the 2024 Olympics and Los Angeles the subsequent edition, so ensuring it snared both remaining cities. On the normal cycle, the 2032 hosts will not be declared until 2025. The IOC has therefore given itself plenty of time to address the dwindling attractiveness of its product in the eyes of potential hosts.

Other competitions are similarly blighted. Financial and political problems led to Durban being stripped of the right to host the 2022 Commonwealth Games, which posed a challenge for the Commonwealth Games Federation in finding future hosts for a competition that has struggled to establish a settled identity. When Durban lost the Games, a rash of Australian, Canadian, English and Malaysian cities quickly expressed an initial interest in stepping into the breach, suggesting that the allure of the competition retained some strength and that the attempt to move into Africa for the first time might simply have been a step too far. However, only one firm bid – from England in the form of Birmingham – eventually emerged from the Federation's hasty process to find a new host. Sports come and go from the Commonwealths, undermining the continuity that other major events have. In part this is an intentional flexibility designed to maximise the number of possible hosts, hence there was no velodrome cycling in Durban's original plans and no necessity for any city to construct a new venue specifically for that one sport. Nevertheless, the Welsh government conducted a feasibility study into Cardiff hosting the 2026 Games and concluded that it would not compete to provide the British candidate city for that year. It blamed Brexit uncertainties but more importantly projected costs of possibly over £1.5 billion, although these were derided by the CGF, which cited Glasgow 2014's final operating costs of 'only' £543 million.

Some of the difference between these two figures is necessary non-operational infrastructure spending, but the bandying about of numbers cannot disguise the salient fact that the inflated economics of major sporting events undermines their viability. Traffic chaos at the Rio Olympics became free-flowing roads at the Paralympics a few weeks later. The difference: that most of the dedicated Olympic lanes, notorious for clogging any city's highways, were only in place for the former and not for the Paras. Just one example of an expensive demand imposed by the International Olympic Committee that drains a city's funds and creates local ill will in the process. At the last count, the Rio Games were reported to have been $3.5 billion over budget. The arrogant assumption that the world needs the IOC, FIFA, the IAAF and other global governing bodies may get its comeuppance. If the current buyers' strike spreads much further, only the newly wealthy world will have the means and the appetite to pay, and if these nations cannot fill their stadiums then the financial models for bidding and hosting will have to be radically altered or the major event bubble will burst.

15

E-DREAMS AND BROKEN DREAMS

The Catford Tigers flared briefly but brightly in the early years of London's post-war recovery. Inspired by the spectacle of the return of speedway to New Cross and to Wimbledon's greyhound stadium on Good Friday 1946, a bunch of pre-teenage boys cleared a bomb site opposite Lewisham fire station so that they could ape the motorcycle stars on their pushbikes. While tens of thousands of spectators packed the speedway stadiums reopening across the country, cycle speedway fired the imagination of youngsters on rubble-strewn sites around London.

The Tigers were well down the sport's pecking order. The best teams, made up of older boys, boasted lightweight bikes with wide handlebars, not heavy pre-war roadsters, and enjoyed council support for their racing circuits. The local newspapers even gave them column inches to match the nearby professional football teams. The Catford Tigers had to find a new venue when the builders moved in to start a housing project, and were moved on again when some prefabricated homes were sited on their second circuit. The sport dwindled as London was rebuilt. Call-ups for National Service ate into the ranks of riders in the older teams. The Tigers themselves last raced in 1949, but the best teams continued to enjoy council support through the 1950s. Today, cycle speedway only exists in the UK as a small niche sport within the British Cycling portfolio, although with bank HSBC sponsoring an elite grand prix series as one element of its partnership with British Cycling, the sport may be in ruder health than the motorcycle big brother that spawned it.

Huge photographs of events at the old and new Wembley stadiums adorn the walls of the Club Wembley hospitality tier in the twenty-first-century edition of the home of English football. Alongside pictures of rock stars, daredevil Evel Knievel and rugby league matches are images of speedway riders sliding across the shale track at the old Wembley in front of packed crowds. The stadium was home to a league team in the immediate post-war years and then hosted major competitions up until 1981 when a crowd of over 92,000 watched the World Final, the last speedway at Wembley. Cardiff's Millennium Stadium took over as Britain's grand speedway arena of choice. Once a year, upwards of 40,000 spectators watch the British Grand Prix there. Below this big event glamour, however, the sport is crumbling.

Wimbledon's greyhound stadium closed for business in 2017, a victim of rising property values in south-west London and the enduring appeal of football. A new 20,000-capacity arena for AFC Wimbledon, a cluster of new homes and a leisure centre will take its place. A couple of thousand people attended the last dog racing in London. It's been reckoned that the capital has had as many as thirty-three greyhound tracks down the years, but that has now dwindled to none. Wimbledon's closure triggered reminiscences about the stadium's speedway past. The bikes had last raced there in 2005. At the post-war reopening that inspired the Catford Tigers, 30,000 had squeezed inside. Some of those lucky enough to make it in had queued for hours. Thousands were locked out.

While greyhound racing clung on in London until 2017, speedway had long gone. Its existence across the country remains perilous. The crowd that turns out once a year in Cardiff dwarves the aggregate attendances each week at the dwindling number of matches for the thirty teams that make up Speedway GB's three leagues. Viewing figures for those matches screened by BT Sport number in the tens of thousands, which might provide some indication of the sport's core fan base. There has been an inexorable inevitability about the financial consequences. Venerable names of speedway's heyday have disappeared. Not only the London teams, but more recently Coventry Bees were ejected first from the stadium they had used since 1928 and then from the Premiership. The team competed in only three challenge matches in 2017, while a supporters' club launched a JustGiving campaign to help its riders cope with their loss of income. Most shocking for the sport was the financial collapse of Manchester's Belle Vue Aces after the botched opening of the city's new National Speedway Stadium in 2016. The track was not fit for use on the inaugural night of racing, and 5,000 fans had to have their entrance money returned. The credibility of the operators was severely dented. The landlords of the £8 million facility, Manchester City Council, refused to renew the operators' lease, and their speedway licence was revoked by the governing body. The team started the 2017 season under new ownership, but the reputational damage continued to reverberate.

Attendance figures are not published for speedway matches. Introducing my wife to the sport as an evening out for our wedding anniversary, I estimate upwards of four hundred in the crowd for Eastbourne Eagles at home to Mildenhall Fen Tigers at the Eagles' home in the lee of Sussex's South Downs on a chilly Saturday in early May. Apparently, closer to a thousand had attended a Good Friday meet the month before. Few supporters are young. The smell of the methanol, the roar of the bikes and the sprays of dirt they throw up as the riders broadside around the bends instantly reconnect me to a sport I've not watched for almost four decades. This is a National Trophy match, so only a third-tier fixture, but the fact that so little has changed must in large part explain the demographic of the fans trackside. The action is snappy, the contest a close one. But the virtues of that evening's racing will have had no reach or resonance beyond the sport's dedicated aficionados.

Eastbourne speedway has been owned and operated by a single family since the 1930s, and four of its generations have ridden for the Eagles. The economics must be brutal for the team's highly experienced owners. At the end of the 2014 season they took the decision to drop out of the top Elite League down to the third-tier National League as a route to financial sustainability. One observer with a good insight into the decision believes that 'the lower cost base has enabled the Eagles to continue running. In the end it was National League or nothing.' Lowering rider costs, in particular the expense of flying foreign stars in from the continent for matches – the norm in the top flight – makes all the difference, especially as crowds are not much different now for the Eagles in spite of their reduced league status.

Cricket has its T20 format to counter paltry attendances at county championship matches; golf is trying out GolfSixes; tennis has Tie Break Tens; track and field is toying with Nitro Athletics. All are short-form versions of the traditional sport presented for a younger audience with fleeting attention spans. There is no indication that speedway, though, has found any answer to the changing ways in which today's public wants to engage with and consume sport. The National Speedway Museum is tucked away in a small building just inside the entrance to a vibrant wildlife park in Hertfordshire. The weekend crowds streaming in to see the big cats are oblivious of its existence. On the door is a postcard-sized notice: CLOSED. WHEN WE ARE CLOSED ENQUIRE. ASK AT WELCOME CENTRE.

The financial demands of elite competition are not confined to speedway, but extend across the sporting landscape. The organisational and infrastructure requirements imposed by league organisers combine with the thirst of fans for success in the arena to elevate the economic risks that team owners shoulder. High-profile casualties litter recent history.

Rugby union's London Welsh went into liquidation part-way through the 2016/17 season, unable to pay its debt to HMRC and citing a business model that was 'totally unsustainable' with crowds as low as 400 supporting a playing budget of £1.7 million. Expelled from the National Championship by the RFU, London Welsh regrouped as an amateur club with a five-year plan to work its way back into the National Leagues. It was only in 2015 that the club had been relegated from the Premiership.

Bradford Bulls went under just a few weeks before the start of the 2017 rugby league season. Reflecting on the RFL's scramble to establish a new Bulls in time for the start of the season, its then CEO Nigel Wood remembers, 'It was a big decision for us. Would you let a club of that magnitude go? We don't have enough clubs of that size, who play regularly in front of ten thousand people, just to give one away, just to casually let it go without a fight. Football can let Portsmouth get into a mess. Rugby union can let London Welsh disappear because it has got someone else to come up, but if we are saying that Bradford is not viable as a professional rugby league outfit then you are writing off, in my opinion, twenty-five clubs.' The operators of the new club were allowed to start at the same level as its defunct predecessor, albeit with a points handicap. 'The least worst option was to keep them in the championship but to give them a penalty of twelve points so it wasn't fatal, to give the new owners something to play for, to act as a galvanising force for supporters.' And what of the previous regime? 'The reason Bradford failed to my mind – and it's failed back to back; it had a long run of success and then it failed, failed,

failed – was just poor, poor local management and an absence of corporate discipline. Bradford just managed themselves extraordinarily badly.' Staff and players made redundant when the original Bulls folded subsequently launched legal actions against the various parties involved.

The ECB, similarly short of replacements for a failed team, provided Durham with a £3.8 million handout in 2016 in return for the imposition of relegation and points penalties for the following season, rather than let the county go bust, while Wood's observation about some sports' ability to rely on a strong pyramid of clubs to replace those that fall into financial difficulty is certainly evident in football. Portsmouth FC, the club he cites, suffered two administrations and two resultant points penalties. A nine-point deduction was handed down by the Premier League in 2010, and a ten-point penalty by the EFL was applied in 2013 as Pompey emerged from its second administration under the ownership of a supporters' trust. Constrained financial means, exacerbated by the points deductions, saw Portsmouth slide down three divisions over this period. The club topped League Two at the end of the 2016/17 to take a first step back up the divisional ladder, just as the former CEO of Disney, Michael Eisner, launched a takeover bid – ultimately successful – to persuade the supporters' trust to relinquish control. It won't be the last club to fall foul of poor financial management, nor the last to snare an investor new to the sport and attracted by the depth and breadth of interest in football.

The level of interest in esports, the new kids on the sporting block, has yet to rival that in soccer, but it is now impossible for conventional sports to ignore the threat this upstart industry poses to their fan bases, especially among the young. Skidding around bomb sites on bikes and using jumpers for goalposts have given way to virtual battles on laptops and tablets for Generation Z. League of Legends is the most popular multiplayer online battle

arena game (MOBA) worldwide. Its World Championship generated a global online audience of 36 million unique viewers in
2016, including a peak audience of almost 15 million. Overall
viewer hours across the fifteen days of competition totalled 370
million. The competing teams shared $6.7 million, almost half
of it contributed directly by watching fans into the prize pool.
And not all spectators were engaging from the comfort of their
own homes. Thousands packed arenas across the United States
for the privilege of watching video gamers competing on a virtual battlefield.

The growth of esports has been explosive. Newzoo is a business that describes itself as 'the leading provider of market intelligence covering the global games, esports, and mobile markets'.
Its annual global market report highlights both the scale of the
industry and the pace of its growth. Worldwide revenues of $493
million in 2016 were generated from media rights, advertising,
sponsorship, merchandising, ticket sales and fees to the publishers
of the games. The first three of these, representing investment by
brands in esports, made up $350 million of the total and reflect
conscious choices by companies to use esports as routes to market
instead of more conventional alternatives, including traditional
sports. In 2016 there were 424 events worldwide with prizes of
at least $5,000. Total prize money across all competitions was $93
million, almost $21 million accounted for by a single event, The
International. The global audience for esports is estimated at 323
million people, half of them said to be enthusiasts and half occasional viewers. Newzoo forecasts compound growth of 35 per
cent a year for the esports industry. If correct, it will be generating $1.5 billion of annual revenue by 2020.

Business consultants at PwC highlight the challenge esports
face in demonstrating their sporting legitimacy but see myriad
commercial opportunities for companies to jump on the bandwagon regardless. In a study of the industry they observe that 'the

esports community recognises that they have a long road ahead: to continue educating the public on why their sport is indeed, a real sport. It's entirely possible, though, that the growth or success of esports won't be tied to whether or not it's acknowledged as a sport, but rather whether the esports value pool is on par with traditional sports and other sectors. All the angst and uncertainty notwithstanding, esports has already proven itself a worthy competitor. It's here to stay.' One financial challenge companies face in seeking to monetise esports is its youthful audience's expectation that they can participate at little or no cost. Newzoo estimates that the average enthusiast will have spent only $3.64 on esports in 2017. The comparable figure for basketball is $15. Sporting fashions may change, but not the relative impecuniousness of the young.

The Score is a Canadian business which publishes what is probably the most popular esports app in the world. Andrew Calleja is one of the company's data coordinators. As an enthusiast as well as a professional in the industry, he is happy to share his personal insights. 'It's not hard to imagine that the average person would be shocked to hear the prize pool of The International, or be baffled after comparing their bank account balance with that of twenty-year-old Lee Sang-hyeok, known to fans around the world as Faker, the undisputed god of League of Legends. I believe that physical tournaments are crucial in lending legitimacy to the industry in the eyes of non-enthusiasts.'

A recent Cambridge music graduate is now seeking to carve out a dual career within both classical singing and esports. Sam Holmes began to take League of Legends seriously as a money-making opportunity while at university, triggered by something as prosaic as a new laptop. 'You are limited by your tools. It's like entering Formula 1 in a Toyota Yaris.' He 'optimised my gameplay' by watching video tutorials and other people playing live via the Twitch website, and found that he reached a level at which his own play was good enough to trigger ads on the site, earning him 'pennies compared to others' but just under the minimum wage nonetheless, £20 or so for three or four hours' play. 'I used to have a real attitude problem while playing. I literally used to scream,' but he's tamed that now as well as refining his mechanical skills and living a structured life – balancing music and gaming is part of that. His models are the professional players. Fnatic has always been the team he supported. 'The pro players live in a gaming house, have personal trainers, nutritionists, focus on their physical and mental well-being. I believe they are athletes.'

The next step for Sam Holmes is the establishment of a semi-pro league. His own team is associated with a gaming lounge in Chatham in the south-east of England that boasts a collection of retro games consoles from the 1980s onwards. When we meet he was flushed with the triumph of an inaugural 2–0 victory over a rival team the night before, which had 'opened my eyes that it's not just a bit of fun' and could be the foundation of a serious enterprise attractive to investors. He uses language redolent of conventional sportspeak. He's proud his team 'all stepped up to the mark' having been together only a fortnight whereas their rivals had competed for a year. They had contested the match from five different locations connected via headsets – 'Why leave the home?' Their opponents, by contrast, had been together in a single location.

Fnatic has the most popular roster of teams globally across a range of esports, claiming more than nine million online followers. Its founder Sam Mathews welcomes a packed audience of potential commercial partners and investors to the organisation's new, studiedly grungy HQ in the Shoreditch district of London that is so fashionable for new tech businesses. It is named the Bunkr. I am by far the oldest person in the room. I bump into a sports marketing executive who admits to feeling a generation too old himself at the tender age of thirty-one. Mathews is a couple of years his senior. He tells us the tale of his mother taking half of Fnatic when he founded it in 2004 and acting as the CFO for the first ten years of its existence. 'She kept in check the crazy visions you have as a nineteen-year-old.' He asks rhetorically how Fnatic make money. 'We don't, that's why we're here today!' If they are really not yet turning a profit, it seems only a matter of time before they do.

Mathews lays out Fnatic's mission. Their aim is 'to lead the new world sport into every household through content, products and experiences'. He adds that they 'really want to represent the community in an authentic way'. The continued success of the company's teams is crucial. Fnatic currently operate two gaming houses, in Berlin and Kuala Lumpur, attending to all their young pros' training needs under the guidance of a chief gaming officer, Patrik Sättermon, who is described by his boss as 'Alex Ferguson's Alex Ferguson', overseeing the managers of the fifty or so players across all of the ten esports Fnatic competes in. 'We want to give them the best-in-class facilities. We want to help them become stars.' Fnatic also manage the complete rights of the players – 'We have the ability to work with their YouTube, their Facebook, as much as we want' – a level of control beyond that in traditional sports.

Arguments about definitions of what constitutes a sport have filled hours of idle time in pubs. Should you include games played in pubs themselves, such as bar billiards or darts? Can an activity that only involves subjective judgement really be a sport? Think of diving or gymnastics, in which the opinions of officials entirely determine the outcome. What about motor sports? Are they sports in their own right? And if not, what is the difference between motorised propulsion for a driver and a horse carrying a rider?

These are not just debates of hypothetical interest. In 2015 the High Court in Great Britain ruled that the card game bridge is not a sport eligible for Lottery funding from Sport England as it does not involve physical activity, this being a principle underpinning the quango's objectives. In 2017 the European Court of Justice also ruled that bridge's characteristics were not such as to give it sporting status, thereby ensuring British players would continue to have to pay VAT on their competition entry fees. Had the ruling gone the other way, they would have avoided the tax. Speedway happens to be on Sport England's list of recognised sports, although it is not currently receiving any funding from the organisation.

Andrew Calleja believes the argument is moot. 'The definition of sport in the English language speaks about physical activity. How is throwing a dart weighing eighteen to fifty grams, or playing cards, any worthier of respect or [more] physically demanding than what esports professionals do? And in the end does it really matter? It has been my experience that most individuals arguing the "esports aren't sports" side of the matter act as if they feel threatened by esports – the ego is a precious and fragile thing. That legitimising esports will in some way delegitimise or demean their accomplishments in sports or that of the industry they love. It doesn't need to be that way. Can't we all just get along?'

There are no such doubts in the mind of Sam Mathews. He grew up playing rugby and video games, and draws parallels between the two. 'This is not about playing games to escape. It's about the thrill of competition. Suddenly, wow, I get the same thrill playing video games as I get on the rugby pitch, all the time, whenever I want it, as long as I can get an Internet connection and have a computer device.' He reels off the equivalencies. 'What is sport? It is an entertainment vehicle that people watch that is derived from a game that you don't script. It's a game of skill. Esports is that but with no limitations.' The only traditional sport that, to his mind, has the same universal appeal as esports is football. This is 'a new world order' to Mathews. 'It doesn't have the physicality. But we think it is the future of sport, because it is sport augmented by technology.'

The 'mind sports' lobby will have been heartened by the first signs of the Olympic movement's interest in esports. Within days of it becoming clear that Paris would be the host of the 2024 Olympics, the co-president of its bid committed to exploring with the IOC the possibility of including esports. The Asian Games in China in 2022 will feature them as fully fledged medal events with FIFA 17 and a variety of MOBA games such as League of Legends on the Games timetable. The Olympic Council of Asia (OCA) has either bowed to commercial pressure and cheapened the Olympic brand or shown remarkable foresight, depending on your point of view. The 2018 Asian Games will provide the first opportunity to compare sports meeting conventional definitions with those of the new technology era, esports having been scheduled as demonstration events in advance of their formal debut four years hence. Behind the OCA's decision lies a partnership with Alisports, the sports arm of Chinese online retailer Alibaba, which only a few months earlier had been unveiled as the International Olympic Committee's latest global partner alongside the likes of Coca-Cola, Visa and Toyota.

'As excited as I'd be to see esports in the Olympics,' Andrew Calleja observes, 'I don't expect to see it happen in my lifetime, mostly due to relatability. Physical activities are mostly universal, and in that way universally relevant to the majority of people on some level. I may not be able to run as fast as Usain Bolt, but I have run before. I understand how fast I can run, and that allows me to appreciate the speed, skill and physical conditioning it takes for him to compete at that level. Esports are much less relatable. Maybe I'm being short-sighted, pessimistic or too judgemental, but I fail to see many outsiders being interested in the map rotations of a Korean League of Legends team, the draft strategy of a Chinese Dota 2 team, the 1v4 clutches of a Russian CS:GO squad or the frame-precise predictions of a Japanese fighting game pro. Even to each other, many of the esports communities just don't care about the others. They live similar yet parallel lives. I have no doubt that if I didn't work in the industry that I would have little understanding and appreciation for the distinct skill sets of the different genres.'

One media outlet has reported Thomas Bach, IOC president, as believing esports run contrary to Olympian values. Where, though, should one draw the line with regard to a sport involving simulated death and destruction? Both Winter and Summer Olympics already award medals for skill with firearms, and Bach himself was an Olympic fencer who demonstrated his skill with a weapon whose antecedents were originally designed to kill when he won a gold medal at the 1976 Games. Bach also cited the lack of formal governance structures in esports, but it may be that he was unaware of the industry's development of an operating framework that in many ways apes that of traditional sports.

The World Esports Association (WESA) was founded in 2016 as a collaboration between a number of professional teams and the leading league organiser. Its launch press release proclaimed that 'based on similar traditional sports associations, WESA is an open and inclusive organisation that will further professionalise esports by introducing elements of player representation, standardised regulations, and revenue sharing for teams. WESA will seek to create predictable schedules for fans, players, organisers and broadcasters, and for the first time bring all stakeholders to the discussion table.' It subsequently established its Player Council and a code of conduct covering integrity issues, including doping.

The requirement for anti-doping controls might seem far-fetched, but in 2015 one player in the Cloud9 Counter-Strike team made an off-the-cuff comment that his team used the stimulant Adderall, the claim flaming online among followers of the sport. And why wouldn't esports be at risk of abuse of performance-enhancing drugs? Adderall is used to treat attention deficit hyperactivity disorder (ADHD), and is reported to be one of a number of prescription drugs used by students cramming for exams. The mental requirements of elite egaming are intense. Concentration and reaction times are critical. Where snooker players of yore were said to use beta blockers to slow their heart rates and steady their arms, esports stars who require intense focus might benefit from contrasting medication.

Andrew Calleja welcomes the establishment of formal structures. 'Unlike traditional sports, esports were created by and are the legal intellectual property of their respective game developers. For this reason, developers essentially have full control over their games. Each developer has their own approach to esports ideas and goals for the future of the industry. I believe that we're currently at a tipping point in the history of esports. How the next few years are handled will set the pace for the growth of the industry. As far as I'm concerned, the more rigorously regulated esports become, the better. The industry is still young, and as we – the fans – grow and mature, hopefully the industry will too.'

Just as the development of team, league and governance structures that parallel those of conventional sports can only encourage confidence in esports' durability, there is also growing evidence of a crossover between the old and the new. John Petter, formerly of BT, believes that 'there is an interplay between egaming and actual live sport which can influence the sports themselves. If I think back to my childhood, I knew the names of everybody in the First Division and a lot of Second Division footballers because you've got those Panini football stickers and you followed it really closely. Today's kids play FIFA soccer and they know everyone who plays for Barcelona and they look at it as a global game effectively. People are not buying *Shoot* magazine and swapping football stickers in the playground, they're playing FIFA. I think you do find that they are as happy watching a FIFA soccer game as they are an actual live game. All sports have to keep reinventing themselves.'

Premier League referees sport the logo of EA Sports on their shirtsleeves. The company behind the FIFA video game is the Premier League's lead partner and sponsor of its fantasy football game. The French football authorities, however, are one step ahead of their English counterparts. In 2016 Ligue 1 announced the formation of e-Ligue 1, an official French FIFA 17 league in partnership with EA Sports. The Bundesliga, La Liga and the Premier League are said to be close behind, with a Champions League competition for the national winners to follow. Separately, in what may simply be an exercise in football keeping its options open, Paris Saint-Germain purchased a League of Legends team. Learning a lesson from traditional sports, the Chinese League of Legends competition, the LPL, moved to a franchise system in 2017, removing the risk of relegation and so enhancing the value of its constituent teams for their owners and investors. Other elite league competitions are likely to follow suit. What is clear is that the balance of power between and within sports of all varieties is likely to shift markedly in future as the leisure habits of millennials dominate the continuing e-revolution.

WARM-DOWN

'If I am really brutally honest, I wish sport wasn't a business.' Jenny Meadows will never be granted her wish because, for her, sport is a contest at the highest possible level, a level at which it is a very serious business indeed. In the twenty-first century those sportspeople for whom the taking part and fighting well matter rather than the winning must choose either to compete at a lower level or to accept the reality that they are a curiosity in a sporting world in which success and financial reward are intimate teammates.

Football and the Olympics are the two Goliaths of this sporting world. No other movements have comparable universality of reach and appeal. One is a constant presence in the global sporting psyche, the other at heart a quadrennial event which is the culmination of an intense build-up of interest starting before the preceding circus has even finished. It is little wonder that esports aspire to the appeal of both soccer and the Games, and are modelling their structures accordingly. And who can say that esports won't dominate in the years ahead? The Olympics faced an existential crisis only a couple of decades ago. Football's appeal at that same time was a mere fraction of its current scale.

Many sports are now counting the cost of the two giants' resurgence. The sports market may have grown, but its size is not infinite and it is increasingly crowded. Broadcasting revenues are hard to come by. Sponsor dollars are scarce for those outside the gilded circle inhabited by the few true superstars in the most favoured sports, and it is hard to imagine any reversal of the haves and the have-nots. Franchise structures and collective wage bargaining may provide some protection for owners and players alike, but ultimately the harsh wind of public opinion – your opinion – will determine whether a sport and its various constituents can survive and thrive in the years ahead.

What you, the fan, currently have in abundance is choice – a multiplicity of broadcast and information channels, a wide variety of sports and a depth of leagues providing a range of engagement experiences from the showbiz of the elite to the intimacy of the amateur. None of this should be taken for granted. Sport is an expensive business, its economics distorted by the involvement of billionaires seeking playthings and aspirant nation states craving acceptance. These investors have raised the stakes across the sporting landscape. The cost of chasing success has gone up at every level because there is always just that bit more that could be spent to try and take a step up a ladder whose highest rungs are now spaced further apart than before.

The winners will be those sports that prove capable of moulding themselves to your likely future habits and finding a way into your wallet. New sports will offer immersive experiences with high levels of interaction between you and their stars, and formats that are broadcast-friendly, catering for short attention spans. Traditional sports are exploring equivalent ways of packaging their own fare, but it's as yet unclear whether their heritage will give them an advantage over new entrants in the competition for your scarce time. Meanwhile all the players in this fluid marketplace will want to ensure that their elite product is connected with the casual, everyday participant in their sport. One of the strongest claims that advocates for esports make on their behalf is that, whatever your ability, you can play the same game as the professional stars. Proponents of state funding for elite sports argue that national success inspires you to get off the sofa and get active. This latter claim doesn't stand up to statistical scrutiny, but the converse must be true – that engagement with elite sport is stronger if you, the fan, understand what it is like to play the game, however amateurishly.

As this contest between the old and the new intensifies, failure rates are only likely to increase, leaving you to wonder just what happened to the sport, the team, the athletes that over the years you have grown to love and grown to rely on emotionally. Just remember, as your sporting world morphs around you, there is little room for sentiment in the Sport Inc. boardroom.

PROGRAMME NOTES

Many of the sources of information and opinion used in this book are, I hope, readily apparent. The notes below are intended to fill in the gaps as well as provide signposts to further reading. I am grateful to all of those whose work I have been able to rely on, especially to the many journalists whose reports do so much to keep sports on their mettle.

Warm-up

3 The estimate of global sports industry revenues of $700 billion is from A. T. Kearney's study *Winning in the Business of Sports* produced in November 2014.

Chapter 1. Fifty-seven channels and nothing on

5 Cricket viewing figures are taken from Sean Ingle's Ashes blog on the *Guardian*'s website dated 12 July 2015.
6 Rupert Murdoch's 'battering ram' comment can be found on the *Independent*'s website dated 15 October 1996 in a piece by Robert Milliken.
6 The ECB's financial statements are available on the governing body's own website, and from the Companies House site.

7 Active Lives Survey and Active People Survey data is published by Sport England on its website.

8 The full extent of the problems in BT's Italian subsidiary became clear in an announcement by the company on 24 January 2017.

9 BT's financial statements are available on the company's own website. The claim of over one million viewers for almost all of the Premier League matches BT screens can be found in the company's 2016 annual report.

11 The Santander equity research report on BT Group containing its £775 million sports content estimate was published on 4 September 2015.

11 Details of Sky's Premier League TV rights deal can be found on the BBC website dated 10 February 2015.

13 The David Davies review is detailed in the media archive of the DCMS website in an article from 13 November 2009.

14 The *Telegraph* reported C4's £10 million London Paralympics deal in an article by Gareth A. Davies on 8 January 2010.

14 Discovery's sub-licensing deal with the BBC was reported by Owen Gibson on the *Guardian* website on 2 February 2016.

15 The BBC's revenues, including from licence fees, are available in the financial statements on its own website.

17 Audience figures and sports production costs for the BBC are my own understanding based on interaction with the Corporation. It reported its plans for 1,000 extra hours of sport on the BBC Sport website on 3 November 2017.

21 The *Guardian* reported the number of BBC staff that would be in Rio for the Olympics in an article published on 7 April 2016.

22 *SPOTY* votes were published online by the *Radio Times* on 19 December 2016. The *Mirror*, among others, reported the *X Factor* final votes on 12 December 2016.

22 Deloitte's 2016 edition of its *Annual Review of Football Finance* cites the Premier League's $1.1 billion annual income from international broadcasters.

23　The *New York Times* on 10 August 2015 reported the $1 billion value of the Premier League's rights deal with NBC.

Chapter 2. Bums on seats and the prawn sandwich brigade

26　A Deloitte press release on 14 December 2016 announced seventy million tickets sold for UK sporting events. Its 2016 *Annual Review of Football Finance* analysed sources of Premier League club revenues.

30　PwC's report, *At the Gate and Beyond*, published in October 2016, calculates premium seating income in the US to be $7.3 billion.

31　The insidethegames.biz website reported London 2012 ticket sales in an article posted on 13 November 2012.

35　The IPC trumpeted ticket sales for the 2017 World Para Athletics Championships in a press release on 23 June 2017. It is believed that the previous highest total sales for an edition of the Championships was around 15,000.

Chapter 3. Two worlds collide

43　The *Evening Standard* reported Boris Johnson's 'gangbusters' comment on 8 July 2015.

45　A. T. Kearney's emphasis on the importance of premium matches is contained in its *Winning in the Business of Sports*, November 2014.

52　Plans for a New York rugby league team to compete in England were reported on the BBC website and in other media on 15 October 2017.

52　Celtic PLC's financial results are available on the company's own website.

52　The Premier League's website details the distribution of broadcast revenues to individual clubs. It posted the 2016/17 figures on 1 June 2017.

54 The losses incurred by Randy Lerner through his owner-ship of Aston Villa are analysed by Bobby McMahon in an article published by *Forbes* dated 13 March 2016. The *Birmingham Mail* reported the *Forbes* analysis the next day.

56 The EFL's Owners' and Directors' Test can be found in the 'Regulations' section of its website

Chapter 4. The only time we feel like footballers

58 The PFA's objectives are contained on the 'About the PFA' page of its website.

58 The history of the minimum wage in football is described in an article on the EFL website by Phil Shaw dated 18 January 2016.

60 Arsenal FC's financial statements are published on its website.

61 Deloitte's *Football Money League 2017*, published in January 2017, ranks Arsenal the seventh-wealthiest club in the world.

61 The BBC Sport website has a useful explanation of the financial fair play rules posted on 25 September 2014.

63 The Premier League's 'short term cost control' regulations are contained within the *Premier League Handbook*, which is available on the League's website.

66 The totalSPORTEK.com website sets out the value of England cricketers' central contracts in an article posted on 11 October 2016.

66 George Dobell on the ESPNcricinfo website explained the new cricket salary cap in England on 23 January 2015. The PCA's own site lists the recommended minimum wages for cricketers by age.

69 NFL salary caps by team are available on the NFL Players Association website.

70 Liz Roscher lists the MLB luxury taxes for 2016 in an article on the SB Nation website dated 18 December 2016.

71 Premiership Rugby's salary cap is explained on its own website.

71 England international rugby players' new deal with the RFU was reported by Gavin Mairs on the *Telegraph* website on 2 November 2016.

71 BBC Sport reported the increase in the Super League salary cap on 5 April 2017.

72 Wimbledon prize money details can be found on the Championships' own website.

73 The ITF announced its restructuring of the tennis tour on 30 March 2017.

73 Athlete endorsement income can be found in an article written by Niall McCarthy on the Statista website, published 24 August 2015, and credited to Opendorse based on *Forbes* data.

Chapter 5. Twenty quid a coffee

76 Greg Rutherford was the Olympic champion defrauded by his agent (*Guardian*, 7 March 2017); Paul Pogba's transfer was being looked into by FIFA (*Independent*, 10 May 2017); and Terry Watson was the agent guilty of illegal inducements to college footballers (CBSSports.com, 17 April 2017).

77 The FA's website contains lists of all intermediaries, every player transaction between clubs that involved an intermediary, and the total fees paid by each club to agents. It also includes the regulations governing intermediaries' activities and guidance notes for both agents and players.

77 FIFA set out its new regulations on working with intermediaries in a circular dated 30 April 2014. It is available on FIFA's website.

77 The AFA's concerns with the new regulations were reported by Ben Rumsby on the *Telegraph* website on 31 March 2016.

86 George Ford's transfer was reported by Owen Slot on *The Times* website on 15 February 2017.

86 *Forbes* listed the world's most powerful sports agents in an article by Jason Belzer on 21 September 2016. It contains links to lists of both the most powerful agents and the most valuable agencies.

87 The altered NFL fee rates for agents are described by Kevin Kleps on the *Crain's Cleveland Business* website, 2 October 2016. The implications of the new regulations governing agents in the NFL are discussed by Michael Guisto on the website of law firm Neufeld, O'Leary and Guisto, 27 October 2016.

88 The MLBPA website sets out details of baseball players' salaries and the collective bargaining arrangements agreed with their clubs.

Chapter 6. Mr One Per Cent and the King of Shaves

90 Information about both World Championships and Diamond League prize money can be found on the IAAF's website.

92 Paris Diamond League meet director Laurent Boquillet cited a $300,000 appearance fee for Usain Bolt in 2013 that was widely reported at the time, for example in an article by Scott Douglas on runnersworld.com, 27 February 2013.

93 The HMRC's victory over Andre Agassi was reported on the BBC News website on 17 May 2006. Rafa Nadal's concerns with the UK tax system were reported by the *Guardian* on 13 October 2011. The *Telegraph* cited Sergio Garcia's similar position on 25 May 2006.

95 The report claiming only £7 million was raised under the UK tax arrangements of overseas sportspeople is cited in an article by Julian Hedley on the taxation.co.uk website, 10 September 2014.

96 The tax exemption for the 2016 Anniversary Games was reported in Hansard, 11 July 2016.

100 Image rights are explained in an article by lawyers Carol Couse and Chris Belcher on the Mills & Reeve website, 7 December 2016.

102 Jennie Granger's evidence to the House of Commons' Public Accounts Committee was reported on the *Guardian* website on 7 December 2016.

102 The 2017 UK budget reference to image rights was reported by Tom Herbert on AccountingWEB.co.uk on 9 March 2017.

102 The issue of José Mourinho's image rights and his arrival at Manchester United was reported in an article by James Ducker on the *Telegraph* website, 25 May 2016.

102 The HMRC raids on West Ham and Newcastle football clubs took place on 26 April 2017, and its accompanying statement about a suspected £5 million fraud was reported by, among others, BBC News.

107 The *New York Times* website described Nick Symmonds' battles over his rights as an athlete in reporting his retirement in an article by Jeré Longman, 3 January 2017.

Chapter 7. Toxicity out of the water

109 The decisions by Ryan Lochte's sponsors were reported by Matt Bonesteel on the *Washington Post* website on 22 August 2016.

110 Head's support for Maria Sharapova in spite of her doping ban was reported by the *Guardian* on 9 June 2016. The BBC Sport website reported Nike's support on 8 June 2016.

111 The £18 million value of the three-year Carabao Cup sponsorship deal was reported by BBC Sport on 4 November 2016. SportsPro reported the R$190 million value of Carabao's six-year shirt sponsorship of Flamengo on 3 January 2017.

115 IMR Sports Marketing's *Driving Business Through Sport*, December 2000, author Simon Rines, describes sponsorship as 'arguably the riskiest weapon in the marketers' armoury'.

115 IEG's estimate of the global sponsorship market is contained in its 2015 *Sponsorship Spending Report*.

116 A. T. Kearney's data on the sporting events market is contained in *Winning in the Business of Sports*, November 2014.

117 McKinsey's views on return on investment and activation spending are from the June 2014 article on its website, 'Is sports sponsorship worth it?'.

120 Deloitte ranks the social media following of leading football clubs in its *Football Money League 2017*, subtitled *Planet Football*, published in January 2017.

121 The rankings of Facebook likes of NFL teams can be found on the trackalytics.com website.

121 The *Forbes* NFL valuations were published on its website with an accompanying article by Mike Ozanian dated 14 September 2016.

121 Alva's analysis of Olympic sponsorship, *How should Sports Sponsorship effectiveness be measured? A Rio Olympics Case Study*, is available via the company's website.

122 One report about RBS's reduced appetite for sports, written by James Hall, was published in the finance section of the *Telegraph* website on 27 August 2010. The bank's sponsorship of rugby's Six Nations came to an end in 2017, although its NatWest brand then replaced Waitrose on the England cricket team's shirts as the ECB's 'principal partner'.

122 The *Telegraph*'s Ben Rumsby reported the McDonald's decision to end its IOC partnership on 16 June 2017.

Chapter 8. Release those big money balls

125 Praise for John Major after the Rio Olympics can be found in a number of places, for example in an opinion piece by the Institute of Directors' Simon Walker on the IoD's website, 13 October 2016.

125 Details of Gordon Brown's £300 million boost to elite sport funding ahead of London 2012 can be found on the BBC website in an article dated 11 April 2006.

125 The UK Sport website explains how its World Class Programme works, and details the funds distributed to individual sports and the number of athletes in each sport who receive APAs.

125 My refusal to be hanged on medal targets was referenced on the BBC website on 20 February 2007.

126   Charles van Commenee's resignation was reported by Simon Hart on the *Telegraph* website on 10 September 2012.

126   The removal of British Basketball's funding was described by Ben Rumsby on the *Telegraph* website on 4 February 2014. The funding decisions for all Olympic sports for the Rio cycle, including the cut for British Swimming, were outlined in a BBC Sport article posted on 18 December 2012.

133   The employment status and taxation of Lottery-funded athletes is explained in an article on the LawInSport website by Andrew Smith, Paul J. Greene, Christian Keidel and Alexander Engelhard dated 6 May 2016.

133   UK Athletics' team selection policies for the Games and for major championships are published on its website.

136   The number of people playing badminton, as well as data for all sports, can be found on the Sport England website.

138   Details of the Mission:East event are from my own records of the day.

139   The YouGov survey about Olympic inspiration and sports participation was commissioned by Pro Bono Economics, and is discussed on the latter's website. It was reported by Paul MacInnes on the *Guardian* website on 24 February 2017.

139   Katherine Grainger was interviewed by Dan Roan of the BBC on 29 June 2017; the video is available on its website.

Chapter 9. Olympian opportunity cost

140   The debate surrounding Caster Semenya's gender has been extensively documented since her win in Berlin. One contemporary report of the issue was an article by Christopher Clarey in the *New York Times* posted on 19 August 2009.

147   The Russian doping scandal, including the role of Yuliya Stepanova and her husband, has similarly been extensively reported. Hajo Seppelt's documentaries on doping in athletics can be viewed on his website.

Chapter 10. Lights out in London

150 The floodlight betting plot is described in two articles on the BBC News website dated 20 August 1999.

151 The totalSPORTEK.com website lists the value of Premier League shirt sponsorship deals.

152 Matthew Le Tissier's autobiography, *Taking Le Tiss*, was published in 2009.

152 The Gambling Commission publishes data from its Sports Betting Integrity Unit every quarter on its website. The Commission also publishes data on the size of the gambling industry and within that of the sports betting market.

153 Joey Barton's statement is available on the footballer's own website.

154 The Statista website contains various estimates of the size of the global gambling industry.

161 The Tennis Integrity Unit publishes an annual review of its activities on its website, as well as quarterly updates. These contain statistics about suspicious matches.

162 Information about betting on the London 2012 Olympics is contained in Interpol's *Handbook on Protecting Sport from Competition Manipulation*, published in 2016.

165 The American Gaming Association's website contains Super Bowl betting data.

165 The regulatory structure and scale of the US sports betting industry is described in an article by Jeff Desjardins on the Visual Capitalist website dated 18 July 2016.

Chapter 11. Just a little prick

167 Dwain Chambers' book *Race Against Me* was published in 2009.

168 The National Anti-Doping Panel's verdict in UKAD's case against Dr George Skafidas is published on UKAD's website, dated 22 February 2016.

169 Bernice Wilson clocked 13.0 seconds in her comeback 100 metres. Her performances can be viewed on UKA's thepower of10.info website.

172 Andy Murray's change of heart about the drugs testing regime can be seen by contrasting two articles. On the *Guardian* website on 6 February 2009 he was reported as describing it as 'draconian'. On the *Independent*'s website on 29 October 2012 he called for a tougher system including more whereabouts testing.

172 Aaron Hermann and Maciej Henneberg's study of doping is publicised on the University of Adelaide website in an article dated 26 July 2013.

173 ASADA's drugs testing charges are set out on its website. UKAD's charges are based on my own understanding of the services it provides. Both anti-doping agencies' annual reports of their activities and financial statements are available on their sites. USADA similarly publishes data on tests it undertakes across American sports, including for the UFC.

173 Cuts to ASADA's funding were reported by Mary Gearin on the ABC website on 27 May 2016.

175 MLB drug test data was referenced in an article by Jayson Stark on the ESPN website on 6 May 2016.

178 *Game of Shadows* by Mark Fainaru-Wada and Lance Williams, about the BALCO affair, was published in 2006. They reference Trevor Graham as the source of the syringe that was posted to USADA.

179 WADA's website details its finances, including sources of funds, and global drugs testing data.

179 The $3.7 million estimate for the cost of the investigations into Russian doping comes from an article by Alan Abrahamson of 3 Wire Sports, posted on 9 February 2017 and based on WADA's own statements.

181 The IOC's claim of $300 million global spending on anti-doping was reported by Nick Butler on the insidethegames.biz website on 16 March 2017.

182   The assertion that a high profit margin was priced into UKAD's work in Russia is based on my own conversations with the organisation.

Chapter 12. London's Coliseum

185   The BBC's report of the launch of the Olympic Stadium design is on its website, dated 7 November 2007.

188   David Gold's early views of athletics and the Olympic Stadium were reported on the BBC Sport website on 22 February 2010.

189   The cost and financing of the Emirates Stadium were set out on the Arsenal FC website in a section that has since been removed. However, the sums quoted are widely reported elsewhere online.

191   The BBC Sport website reported Lamine Diack's 'big lie' comment on 20 January 2011.

193   A detailed breakdown of West Ham's tenancy agreement was reported on the *Telegraph* website on 14 April 2016 in an article by Ben Rumsby.

194   Arsenal's gate and matchday revenues are contained in its financial statements, published on its website.

194   West Ham United Football Club Limited accounts are on the Companies House website.

196   Paul Kelso's story about the £8 million cost of moving the retractable seats in the Olympic Stadium was published by Sky News on 1 November 2016. Within a day the mayor's office had announced an inquiry and published the total bill for the Stadium of £752 million. Sky News reported this on 2 November 2016.

197   Wembley Stadium costs were detailed by Matt Scott in an article on the *Guardian* website on 24 February 2006.

197   The Moore Stephens Olympic Stadium Review was commissioned by the Mayor of London and published by the GLA on 1 December 2017.

198 AEG's 'bust in ten years' opinion about the Olympic Stadium is reported in a *Telegraph* article, also by Paul Kelso, published online on 9 February 2011.

Chapter 13. Possession of the law

200 The IAAF issued its press release about its new offices on 11 May 2015. Reuters reported Seb Coe handing back Villa Miraflores to the Principality and cancelling the Fairmont apartment on 26 November 2015.

201 The IAAF's constitutional structure and list of member federations are published on its website.

202 Athletics' $47 million receipt from the IOC after London 2012 is referenced in an online article from the *Queensland Times* dated 31 May 2013.

202 The IAAF's annual financial accounts are made available to member federations but, at the time of writing, are not currently published on its website. As at mid-2017, there was nothing in the IAAF's accounts or its future budgets to indicate that major cost-cutting was in train.

202 The IAAF Ethics Board decision in the case concerning Nick Davies and others was published on 31 January 2017.

203 Gianni Infantino's $5 million election promise was reported online by CBC Sports on 22 February 2016.

205 The IOC's finances are available in its annual report and financial statements, published on its website. These include sources of its revenue, as well as details of its expenditure, including disbursements to the organising committees in London and Rio and to the individual sports' international federations.

206 The IOC's new ranking of sports for the sharing of broadcast revenues for Rio 2016 was reported by Reuters on 29 May 2013, including the sums distributed to each sport after London 2012.

207 The birth of the ATP Tour and its car park press conference are described in an article dated 30 August 2013 on the Tour's own website.

207 The PGA European Tour accounts are available on the Companies House website, as are those of the R&A's holding company, R&A Trust Company (No 1) Limited.

208 Andy Murray's comments about the LTA were reported on the BBC Sport website on 1 December 2015.

209 The LTA's changed plans for Roehampton were reported by Simon Briggs on the *Telegraph*'s website on 23 August 2014.

209 The accounts for both the LTA and The All England Lawn Tennis & Croquet Club Limited can be found on the Companies House website. The Wimbledon Championships are operated by The All England Lawn Tennis Club (Championships) Limited.

210 FIFA's annual financial review is published on its website. This contains its forecasts for the 2015–18 cycle culminating in the World Cup in Russia.

211 The ICC's move to Dubai was reported on the BBC Sport website on 7 March 2005.

211 The ICC website contains its annual financial statements, which detail the profits generated by its events as well as dividends paid to member countries.

214 Shashank Manohar's resignation for personal reasons was reported by Nick Hoult on the *Telegraph* website on 15 March 2017.

214 The final agreed distribution model for ICC dividends was reported on the BBC Sport website on 22 June 2017.

Chapter 14. Ten million pounds a vote, or flexing Putin's pecs

217 The Grand Départ impact report *Three Inspirational Days* was published in December 2014. It is available on the event-IMPACTS website along with a number of similar case studies. The report cites Richie Porte's tweet.

218 A. T. Kearney's estimate of major events accounting for 8 per cent of global sports industry revenues in busy years is con-

tained in its 2011 paper *The Sports Market: major trends and challenges in an industry full of passion.*

218 Nick Clegg's lobbying for additional funding for the Grand Départ was reported by Matt Slater on the BBC Sport website on 21 March 2013.

219 The studyyorkshire.com website includes the £88 billion estimate of the county's economy, and the £7 billion tourism number.

222 The budget and funding numbers cited for the two London 2017 championships are based on my own understanding of the events.

224 Richard Caborn's defence of the England World Cup bid's handbag gifts was reported by James Pearce on the BBC Sport website on 23 October 2009. The *Guardian* reported Jack Warner's return of a handbag in an article written by Matt Scott on 4 November 2009.

224 The *Telegraph*'s Paul Kelso reported the £21 million cost of England's failed bid on 10 October 2011.

228 Doha's offer to pay the IAAF prize money if it won the right to host the 2017 World Championships was reported on the BBC Sport website on 10 November 2011.

229 The conclusion of the IAAF Ethics Board investigation into my 'brown envelopes' claim was published on 24 October 2016.

230 Isaiah Kiplagat's suspension was reported on the *Guardian* website by Owen Gibson on 30 November 2015. Gibson and the *Guardian* also outlined the allegations made about Papa Massata Diack in an article on 11 May 2016.

232 Mayor Walsh's comments on withdrawing Boston's Olympics bid were quoted by David Sheinin for the *Washington Post*, 27 July 2015.

233 The Welsh decision not to bid for the Commonwealth Games, and the possible costs involved, were reported by Sion Barry for WalesOnline on 26 July 2016.

233 The Rio Games $3.5 billion cost overrun was reported by Daniel Etchells for insidethegames.biz on 15 June 2017.

Chapter 15. E-dreams and broken dreams

234   Recollections of post-war speedway, and of the Catford Tigers, are provided by my father, John Warner.

235   The crowd in Cardiff for the British Grand Prix is referenced in an article in WalesOnline by Tom Houghton on 9 July 2016.

235   The closure of Wimbledon's greyhound stadium was reported in the *Evening Standard* by Megan Carnegie on 24 March 2017. She refers to twenty-eight London tracks; an article by Jon Henley in the *Guardian* on 9 August 2008 mentions thirty-three.

238   The demise of London Welsh's professional team was reported for WalesOnline by Anthony Woolford on 7 December 2016.

238   The legal action taken by former Bradford Bulls players and staff was reported by Aaron Bower on the *Guardian* website on 10 May 2017.

239   Durham's financial penalties and relegation were reported on the BBC Sport website on 3 October 2016.

240   Information on the World Championship of League of Legends, including viewing figures and the prize pool, is taken from the game's own website.

240   The Newzoo *Global Esports Market Report* is available on the company's website.

240   PwC's *The burgeoning evolution of esports* was published in April 2016 and is available on its website.

244   The European Court of Justice's ruling about bridge was reported by Liam Stack online for the *New York Times* on 26 October 2017. The High Court's earlier ruling against bridge was reported by the BBC News website on 15 October 2015.

244   The list of sports recognised as such by Sport England is on its website.

245   Esports featuring in the Asian Games were reported by Sean Morrison for ESPN on 20 April 2017. Thomas Bach's scepticism was relayed by Nick Butler on insidethegames.biz on 25 April 2017. Paris 2024's willingness to consider esports can be

seen in a report on the isportconnect.com website dated 9 August 2017.

246 Information about the World Esports Association can be found on the WESA website.

246 The doping allegation involving Cloud9 was reported by Richard Lewis on the Dot Esports website in an article dated 24 July 2015.

248 The formation of e-Ligue 1 was reported by Adam Barnes for Sky Sports on 16 October 2016. Paris Saint-Germain's purchase of the Huma League of Legends team appeared on the ESPN website in an article by Jacob Wolf, 20 October 2016.

248 The LPL's move to a franchise system is examined by Austen Goslin on the Rift Herald website, 10 May 2017.

MEDAL TABLE

Ashwin Rattan persuaded me onto the start line, Carrie Kania of Conville and Walsh prepared me for the race, and Frances Jessop of Yellow Jersey saw me over the finish. My heartfelt gratitude to each of them for helping me around the course. It was more a marathon than a sprint. I'm very grateful to all who provided their personal insights for publication, including those who preferred to remain anonymous. Thanks also to everyone at UK Athletics, in particular those who lasted the distance; to the Team of the Eighties and all Glaziers and Eagles who went before and followed after; to the Fittleworth Flyers; and to everyone – family, friend and foe alike – who has shared the exhilaration of a sporting event with me.

INDEX

EST.1998

Yellow Jersey Press celebrates 20 years of quality sports writing

Yellow Jersey Press launched in 1998, with *Rough Ride*, Paul Kimmage's William Hill Sports Book of the Year. In those early days, the Yellow Jersey list sought to give a platform to brilliant stories, which happened to be framed within a sporting environment. Over the past two decades, its name has become synonymous with quality sports writing, covering all sports from the perspective of player, professional observer and passionate fan.

Sport is about more than simple entertainment. It represents a determination to challenge and compete. It binds individuals with a common goal, and often reflects our experiences in the wider world. Yellow Jersey understands this as much as its readers.

This edition was first published in the Yellow Jersey Press 20th Anniversary Year.

YELLOW JERSEY PRESS
LONDON